LEGENDS
AND LIES

Forge Books by Dale L. Walker

Legends and Lies
The Boys of '98

LEGENDS AND LIES

GREAT MYSTERIES OF THE
AMERICAN WEST

DALE L. WALKER

FOREWORD BY JOHN JAKES

A TOM DOHERTY ASSOCIATES BOOK   NEW YORK

LEGENDS AND LIES.

Copyright © 1997 by Dale L. Walker.

Foreword copyright © 1997 by John Jakes.

This book is printed on acid-free paper.

A Forge Book
Published by Tom Doherty Associates, Inc.
175 Fifth Avenue
New York, NY 10010

Forge® is a registered trademark of Tom Doherty Associates, Inc.

Design by Lynn Newmark

Library of Congress Cataloging-in-Publication Data

Walker, Dale L.
  Legends and lies: great mysteries of the American West / Dale L. Walker.
    p.   cm.
  "A Tom Doherty Associates book."
  Includes bibliographical references and index.
  ISBN 0-312-86848-0 (acid-free paper)
  1. West (U.S.)—History—Miscellanea.
  I. Title.
F591.W25   1997
978—dc21

                                                    97-20792
                                                    CIP

0 9 8 7 6 5 4 3 2

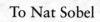
To Nat Sobel

Men's memories are uncertain and the past that was differs little from the past that was not.

—Cormac McCarthy, *Blood Meridian*

CONTENTS

CALAMITIES

THE BURIED TREASURE

A LEGEND

FOREWORD

John Jakes

Dale Walker is a friend and professional colleague, so let there be
no misunderstanding. What follows is the testimony of a friendly
witness.

When Dale asked me to read this book in advance of publication, I was intrigued, because the American frontier, its lore
and legendary characters, have been interests of mine for more
than five decades. I dove into a few chapters at random and curiosity soon became rapt attention.

I went first to the Custer section, because the general's story
has gripped my imagination for a long time, and refuses to let go.
You may be pulled to other chapters—on a disputed death, or a
disappearance, or someone who claimed to be the "real" Jesse
James or Billy the Kid. The point is, Dale's tapestry—his saga, his
collection of mysteries major and, as he calls them, "miniature"—contains a sufficient quantity of drama and dark doings
to satisfy virtually anyone drawn to the story of our country's expansion in the 1800s.

I won't go further and redundantly explain the book's plan
and purpose, or the way certain stories interweave and touch via
coincidences that would never be allowed in fiction. Dale has
done this well in his Introduction and brief afterword. Instead, let

me say a little about the man himself, and how I perceive him as a writer and student of history.

Dale Walker is a Westerner by adoption. Originally from Illinois, he arrived in far west Texas in 1959 following four years in the Navy. His purpose was to visit his father, a career Army sergeant. Dale liked what he saw in Texas, and stayed.

A college journalism graduate with a newspaper background, he's had a long love affair with nineteenth-century American and English history, particularly military history. His newspaper training and experience no doubt account for a secondary theme of his work expressed in books about John Reed, Jack London, Januarius MacGahan of the *New York World,* and others who practiced a freewheeling brand of journalism, that of foreign correspondent. (Dale considers MacGahan the greatest foreign correspondent America ever produced.) Jack London is a favorite study of Dale's, dealt with in no less than five books.

But the West is his major creative venue. To quote him—"I live in the West, travel in it, research and write about it. The nineteenth century is still alive out here." For many years, as director of the Texas Western Press of the University of Texas at El Paso (UTEP), he prodded and inspired dozens of other Western scholars to do the same kind of traveling, researching, and writing.

Dale is a member of the Texas Institute of Letters, twice a winner of the Spur Award given by the professionals of Western Writers of America for especially fine writing, and a contributor to so many magazines and reference works on the West that to list them would wear out your patience and mine too. During the last seven or eight years since I first got acquainted with Dale, I've particularly liked his newspaper columns, now in their ninth year, in the *Rocky Mountain News.* The columns feature opinion and commentary on matters Western, and reviews of worthy fiction in the field that might otherwise be missed by a public currently drowned in a Niagara of pop novels about trial lawyers and missile terrorists.

So it's clear—Dale was fully qualified to write this book. No one, in fact, more so. Let me assure you, Dale is no armchair researcher. For this book he walked the Custer battlefield, followed Ambrose Bierce's last trail, visited the Alamo, Sacajawea's grave, and the places where Meriwether Lewis, Billy the Kid, Jesse James, and Crazy Horse died. He explored the site of the Fancher wagon train massacre in Utah, the Illinois farm of "Black Bart" Boles, and the fancied location of the Lost Dutchman mine in the Superstition Mountains of Arizona.

Dale is a smooth and expert stylist, and you will find his prose friendly and engaging. But what I like best about his work is its backbone; the author's underlying approach to his material.

Call it balanced. I find Dale Walker neither a wild revisionist, bent on burning and pillaging traditional Western history, nor a dogmatic guardian of rosy "facts" that have turned out to be myths, often shameful ones. He rejects the faddishness of the first along with the narrow-mindedness of the second. To him the story of America's westward expansion is not a wholly inglorious coast-to-coast rape of lands and cultures, but neither is it a triumphant march of pure white Anglo-Saxon heroes—noble John Waynes and high-minded Gene Autrys walloping outlaws and always villainous Indians—with a few pliant women, African-Americans, Chinese, and Latinos tagging along for variety and, too often, comedy. Dale, I believe, sees all aspects of the story, in fair and balanced fashion, and reflects it in his writing, including this latest book.

Which is why I promise you an entertaining read but, in addition, a provocative one. *Legends and Lies* will open doors you may never have seen before, and tickle your mind with possibilities whose existence you may never have imagined.

Hilton Head Island
January 3, 1997

INTRODUCTION

The important part of history is the
last five letters of the word.
—Stephen E. Ambrose, 1996

Since all history is mystery—and "a huge Mississippi of false-hood," as Matthew Arnold said—all historical writers routinely encounter mysteries in their researches. I have been stumbling over them for all the thirty-five years I have been writing biography and other nonfiction works.

By "mysteries" I do not mean those of the magnitude of the Sphinx, the Man in the Iron Mask, the *Mary Celeste*, or the Shroud of Turin—or even Sasquatch, crop circles, or Elvis sightings. Most of my mysteries are small, nagging things created by gaps in the historical record, conflicting testimony, or by the failure of somebody to stop and figure something out.

Many of the miniature mysteries I have encountered remained mysteries despite a lot of time and effort trying to solve them. Some I was able to solve, at least to my satisfaction.

In 1972, I became captivated by the great equestrian statue of Captain William Owen "Buckey" O'Neill in front of the Yavapai County Courthouse in Prescott, Arizona. This noble work depicts the territorial lawman, Populist politician, and mayor of Prescott as the spirit and hero of Roosevelt's Rough Riders in Cuba in 1898. It is the work of Solon Borglum, younger brother

of Mount Rushmore's Gutzon Borglum, and was inspirational—
at least to me. I wanted to know more about O'Neill and
when I learned that no real biography of him existed, I set out to
write one.

Very little of substance had been written on O'Neill then and
I had a lot of blanks to fill. Even such an elementary thing as his
birthplace was in dispute. Buckey himself claimed both Ireland
and St. Louis; others said Washington, D.C., where he grew up
and where his father John, a wounded veteran of Meagher's Irish
Brigade at Fredericksburg, worked as a minor government func-
tionary.

I worked hard on this question but had no luck. Buckey
was born on February 2, 1860, but *where* remains unknown to
this day.

Then there was the matter of his death.

I thought I knew all about that. Buckey died just before the
attack on Kettle Hill on July 1, 1898, and old War Department
records and historians of the Cuban Campaign of the Spanish-
American War were pretty precise on the timing of that little
skirmish.

I even found an *eyewitness* to Buckey's death.

Jesse Langdon of Red Hook, New York, a private in the First
U.S. Volunteer Cavalry Regiment (the "Rough Riders"), was
eighty-nine, animated and alert, when he gave me his story. He
was located only a short distance from Captain O'Neill when it
happened, he said. Buckey, true to his fatal custom, was pacing
in front of his hunkered-down troopers, smoking his perpetual
cigarette, and at 10:00 A.M., give or take a minute, on that July
1, a Mauser bullet, fired by a Cuban sniper on the slope of Kettle Hill, struck the captain "square in the mouth." Langdon said
Buckey crumpled to the ground without a sound, stone dead,
and was hastily buried near where he fell.

The old trooper's account tallied precisely with the historical
records and with the testimony of others.

But in the Sharlot Hall Museum in Prescott, where I spent
many hours in the archival vault poring over the O'Neill papers

there, I discovered *another* version of his death, one that had been used unquestioningly by several writers.

Among the O'Neill memorabilia in the museum, carefully protected in a glass case, lay Buckey's American Waltham pocketwatch, retrieved when his body had been exhumed at Kettle Hill in the spring of 1899 for reburial at Arlington. The watch's authenticity was not in question: it had been donated to the museum by Buckey's heirs, its provenance supported by good paperwork.

The problem with the watch lay in the typewritten card accompanying it in the Sharlot Hall display: "Buckey O'Neill's watch, showing the time of his death on San Juan Hill."

The watch's hands were frozen at 4:12.

I could understand the "San Juan Hill" error: Kettle Hill, where he died, lay just east of the San Juan Hill ridges and Kettle served as the curtain-raiser for the San Juan battle that day. But the *time?*

The romantic soul who made the watch display and typed the card must have been unconsciously humming that old song about Grandfather's Clock—"it stopped—short—never to go again, when the old man died."

But clocks do not stop when people die, nor do watches on a battlefield unless hit by a bullet.

Buckey was struck in the head by a single bullet. His big Waltham was undamaged, glass, case, and works intact.

He was killed at 10:00 A.M. and buried quickly, his big stemwinder in his tunic pocket.

Six hours and twelve minutes later, the watch ran down.*

I have been preoccupied by the nineteenth-century American West for the past twenty years and its mysteries, most of them infinitely larger and more perplexing than that of Buckey O'Neill's watch, loom over all its history. It is the perfect place and time to

---

*The watch is still there. The archivist at the new Sharlot Hall Museum tells me the card now reads, "Worn by him on his death on July 1, 1898, below Kettle Hill."

discover the keenness of Edward Gibbon's remark that "History is little more than the register of the crimes, follies and misfortunes of mankind," and it is a fertile breeding ground for all the great constants of historical mystery. In the Old West, nobody ever died when history said they died; conspiracies lurk everywhere; there are a minimum of two, most often several, versions of every historical event; and more often than not, legendry, lies, and lingering doubts supersede fact.

Of the dozen "cases" here, half are about disputed deaths, a commonplace in historical mysteries. There are countless examples of these, published in everything from supermarket tabloids to hardcover books: theories that President Zachary Taylor died in 1850 not from cholera morbus but as a result of arsenic poisoning; that James Dean survived the collision that wrecked his Porsche 550 Spyder near Salinas, California, in 1955, and died a paraplegic in a remote seacoast sanitarium; that Princess Anastasia escaped execution in 1917 and lived as Anna Anderson until 1984. There is a whole book that attempts to prove that Marshal Michel Ney, one of Napoleon I's greatest generals, did not die before a firing squad in 1815 but ended up teaching school in North Carolina, and there are two whole books devoted to the premise that Ney's chief died on the island of St. Helena in 1821 not of cancer of the colon but of poisoning—arsenic again—by a traitor in his entourage.

In my book, the stories of Meriwether Lewis, Sacajawea, David Crockett, and Crazy Horse are even more intriguing disputed deaths than these. As for the case of J. Frank Dalton as Jesse James, here is an example showing how DNA research, as became depressingly clear in the O. J. Simpson trial, can solve a mystery to everybody's satisfaction except certain members of the public "jury." And Ollie Roberts, who said he was Billy the Kid, simply had the best story of any "claimant" in Old West history.

Three chapters here deal with disappearances, the most exasperating of all historical mysteries since in the absence of the corpus delicti, the most preposterous-seeming theories have the same currency as the most reasoned ones. The vanishings of

Black Bart, Boston Corbett, and Ambrose Bierce are not as renowned as those of Judge Crater, Amelia Earhardt, and Jimmy Hoffa, but they are no less fascinating and bewildering.

The Mountain Meadows massacre of 1857 and the Custer battle of 1876 are immense, intricate mysteries in which countless smaller mysteries reside. Each remains among the most contentious of events in our Western past. For a century the Mountain Meadows episode of mass murder was considered "delicate" since it involved a great church and religious movement. But long ago Mormon leaders wisely decided that the sins of a handful of their real or spiritual fathers could not in common sense comprise a permanent blot on an established, respected modern church and its members. The 1857 massacre, beginning with the incomparable scholarly work of the late Juanita Brooks, a Mormon, is now an open book—a book still freighted with mysteries, but one that is open for all to see and study.

The Custer battle is so complex, and so much has been written on it, that it is a daunting subject for any writer, even those who have studied it for a lifetime. Nothing that happened in the nineteenth-century West is such a repository of mystery as that terrible summer Sunday afternoon along the Little Bighorn River.

And the Lost Dutchman Mine is a fine example of how a story of riches at the rainbow's end, no matter how thin the evidence, can captivate and mystify us forever. It is a choice illustration of how mystery (Napoleon said "history" but it works both ways) can be "fraud agreed upon."

Since history—that is, our interpretation of it—is always changing, new information may be unearthed that will shed light on these twelve episodes. But until that happens, these mysteries remain, by the very definition of the word, unsolved.

In "recorded" history terminology, the old trans-Mississippi West occupies about a hundred years, give or take a decade, of our national past. The beginning of it is most often flagged by the signing of the Louisiana Purchase of 1803, and the end any exit marker from the last land rush "boomers" in the Cherokee Strip of Oklahoma in 1893 to the admittance to statehood of the last Western territories, Arizona and New Mexico, in 1912.

This Old West is a century-long, half-continent-wide quilt of a saga, the patchwork made up of legends, myths, tales, and probable truths, stitched with mystery.

The twelve episodes in this book are adjoining patches in the quilt, related to one another, part of the bigger saga. The book is bracketed by the stories of David Crockett and Crazy Horse, two formidable legends of the Old West who may otherwise seem to have little in common. Davy, who died five years before the great Oglala warrior was born, is an exemplar of that magic white man's word "frontier," before it moved west of the Mississippi; Crazy Horse is a tragic but true representative of the people who occupied and settled the American frontier before there was an America or any notion of its frontiers.

And with a grand irony and within the space of just forty years, both David Crockett and Crazy Horse, almost mythic figures in their separate worlds, became victims of the white man's relentless passion to expand his frontiers.

Six of the subjects in this book—Jesse James, Black Bart, George Armstrong Custer, Boston Corbett, Jacob Waltz, and Ambrose Bierce—were connected by the Civil War; the fate of three of these subjects had a link to Mexico; four had California connections; two met during the Lewis and Clark Expedition, two others may have had an encounter during the Little Bighorn battle, the Last Stand for one and, for that matter, a year later for the other.

They are all patches in the quilt, all masks in the drama that is the Saga of the Old West, bound together by the mystery of it all.

A LEGEND

I

The Day Davy Died

A Rendezvous at the Alamo

One of the most indelible and enduring images of Western American history was portrayed on television on February 23, 1955, in the final episode of the Disney three-part miniseries "Davy Crockett, King of the Wild Frontier." Just before the final fade-out, Davy (Fess Parker) is seen swinging his long rifle in the midst of an attacking force of Mexican soldiers. The program, which was for kids, didn't show him dying, but kids knew, as their parents had long known, that Disney and Fess Parker got it right: that was how Davy died.

We may never have really believed he was born on a mountaintop in Tennessee or that he killed a bear when he was only three, but we knew he died at the Alamo, his dander up, in the heat of the battle, a pile of corpses at his feet, clubbing the enemy with the rifle he called "Old Betsy."

Did we buy into the myth of Davy Crockett and place a coonskin crown with a halo over it on the King of the Wild Frontier?

Well, of course *we did—and what's wrong with that? He died fighting at the Alamo, didn't he?*

Well, didn't he?

We begin with the battle and the part David Crockett played in it, and how, some say, he was trapped there by his own legend.

It is 161 years ago; 5:00 A.M., Sunday, March 6, 1836.

As the first glowing stripe of dawn rose on the eastern horizon there was a bugle call and shouts of *"Viva, Santa Anna!"* Then, 2,000 Mexican foot soldiers, cavalry, and artillerymen formed up in four columns and marched forward through the dewy grass, their breath visible in the sunrise chill, the soft morning light glinting off a hedgerow of bayonets. Each man was armed with a British-made musket, spare flints, and cartridge packs; some carried nine-foot lances, others had sabers, pistols, picks, pikes, prybars, axes, and scaling ladders.

For thirteen days General Antonio López de Santa Anna's artillery had belabored the Alamo and during the siege sharpshooters from the fortress had picked off thirty of his cannoneers. The night before he had silenced his guns, hoping to lull the weary enemy sentries into napping at their posts.

The president-dictator of Mexico, self-styled "Napoleon of the West," gambler, ruthless but charismatic politician, and egoistic general of some considerable skill, Santa Anna had come a long way to do battle. He had begun his march north from his capital on November 28, had strengthened his army in Saltillo, 200 miles south of the Rio Grande, and had crossed the river on February 16 with over 2,000 men, 21 cannon, 1,800 pack mules, 33 four-wheeled wagons, and 200 ammunition carts. On the twentieth he camped on the Rio Hondo, fifty miles south of San

Antonio de Béxar, and on the twenty-third arrived in the town and captured it without resistance.

His first act there was to order the raising of a bloodred flag from a church steeple, a warning to the Alamo defenders that there would be no prisoners, no quarter.

East of the town came a quick response—a cannon shot from the Alamo's biggest gun.

Now, after thirteen days, the siege had ended and the battle had begun.

Inside the battered walls that contained the old Spanish mission, the band of defenders, numbering on this day of reckoning probably 183 fighting men, took their places along the walls that formed the Alamo's perimeter. Some manned the eighteen serviceable cannon that were mounted on ramps and scaffolds along the ramparts and the church top and surveyed their scarce ammunition supply, including the chopped-up horseshoes, nails, and random iron pieces that would soon have to be used. Others checked their musket and pistol loads, shot pouches, and powder horns, and took their stations and waited.

On the north wall, his double-barreled shotgun propped beside him as he watched the advancing enemy through his glass, stood the commander of the Alamo's defenders, Lieutenant Colonel William Barret Travis of the Texian* cavalry, a fiery, red-haired, twenty-seven-year-old South Carolina gentleman-lawyer who doted on the works of Sir Walter Scott and who believed, correctly, that his destiny lay in military glory.

Defending a portion of the south wall with his dozen Tennessee Mounted Volunteers stood David Crockett, forty-nine, the graying legendary marksman, bear hunter, backwoods orator, humorist, and three-term congressman. He had come to San Antonio on February 8, dressed in old buckskins, his fiddle and long rifle among his sparse possessions, and leading the men he had collected on his long ride from Nacogdoches. "I have come

---

*At the time of the Alamo and in pre-statehood Texas, a "Texian" was a resident, usually an Anglo newcomer, of the Mexican province of Texas y Coahuila.

to aid you all that I can in your noble cause," he announced. After a grand fandango was held for him and his men on the tenth, just a week before Santa Anna crossed the Rio Grande, he reported to Travis for duty in the Alamo defenses.

On the roof of the Alamo chapel, helping serve the cannon there, stood Travis's South Carolina friend and fellow lawyer, Lieutenant James Butler Bonham, twenty-nine, who had journeyed to the town after Travis wrote him of the "stirring times" in Texas. As a courier, he had made a dangerous ride out of the besieged mission compound since arriving there with Bowie.

In his room in the low barracks on the southeast wall, near where Crockett and his Tennesseans were stationed, forty-year-old Colonel James Bowie lay sick on his cot. He had a persistent cold, fever, and painful cough—perhaps pneumonia or incipient tuberculosis. A Kentuckian, Bowie had a spotty history. He had sold contraband slaves in Louisiana (working, legend has it, for the pirate Jean Lafitte) and worthless land titles in Arkansas, and had drifted to Texas in 1828 where he married into the prominent Veramendi family in San Antonio de Béxar. In September, 1833, his wife died of cholera, a tragedy that lowered over him like an angry storm cloud.

He had ridden into town with thirty men on January 19 on orders from Sam Houston, commander of the Texas army, to assist in evacuating the place. Houston wanted to fight Santa Anna in a hit-and-run war of attrition in which his force would move rapidly and distantly over familiar terrain and force the Mexicans to follow, extending them from their supply bases. Houston had no interest in a standstill fight, wanted all the fortifications in Béxar destroyed and the town's occupants—including those in the Alamo—to march out and join him in the open.

Lieutenant Colonel James C. Neill, an artillerist and veteran Indian fighter from Alabama, commanded the Alamo garrison and persuaded Bowie that the Alamo had to be defended, not abandoned. When Travis arrived on February 2 with thirty cavalrymen, he, too, saw the need to shore up the mission's defenses rather than tear them down.

Travis's arrival presented a problem. Governor Henry Smith

had named him commander of the Alamo garrison without re-
lieving Neill. Moreover, Bowie, a colonel, outranked both Travis
and Neill. This awkward situation was reduced but not resolved
on February 13 when Neill departed on furlough to attend to illness in his family and to secure supplies, money, and reinforcements for the garrison. His departure left the Alamo in a sort of
joint command between the two remaining men: Bowie commanding the volunteers; Travis, the regulars.

The two men were instantly at odds. The day Neill left the
Alamo, Travis wrote to Governor Smith that Bowie "has been
roaring drunk all the time . . . & is proceeding in a most disor-
derly irregular manner . . . If I did not feel my honor & that of
my country compromitted I would leave here instantly for some
other point with the troops under my immediate command—as
I am unwilling to be responsible for the drunken irregularities of
any man."

On February 24, the first day of the siege, Bowie, whose
health had collapsed to the point he had to retire to his bed,
turned over full command of the Alamo to Travis.

The fortress had the rough configuration of two adjacent rec-
tangles, one large, one small, with the church at the southeast
corner, next to the small rectangle that contained a hospital,
horse and cattle pens, and the infantry barracks. The larger area
had walls twelve to twenty-two feet high and enclosed barrack
rooms, officers' quarters, a well, guardhouse, and artillery em-
placements, including the "lunette," a U-shaped gun position
that jutted out from the south wall. On a large barbette (plat-
form) on the southwest corner of the plaza stood the largest of
the defenders' cannon, an eighteen-pounder (for the weight of the
ball it fired).

The Alamo's guns, varying from four- to twelve-pounders
and with the single eighteen, were commanded by Captain
William R. Carey, a Virginian, assisted by a twenty-six-year-old
Tennessee blacksmith, Captain Almeron Dickinson.

Travis, even as he watched Santa Anna's army advance that

chill dawn of March 6, held out hope that reinforcements would come to assist him. Ten days earlier he had sent a courier to Colonel James Fannin in Goliad, about ninety miles to the southeast, hoping the Texas army regulars there would come as a relief force. But Fannin, who set out for San Antonio on February 26 with 320 men, suffered some minor mishaps on the trail—a supply wagon broke down, some oxen ran loose—and on the twenty-seventh marched his force back to Goliad.

On February 24, Travis scribbled a message to "The People of Texas and all Americans in the world," underlined one phrase, triple underlined the last three words, and sent thirty-year-old Captain Albert Martin, a good horseman who knew the roads around Béxar, to carry it through the enemy lines. Martin was to deliver the appeal to the town of Gonzales, seventy miles away, and to have couriers take copies of it to Goliad, San Felipe, Washington-on-the-Brazos (which, on March 1, became the first capital of the Texas Republic), Nacogdoches, south to the Gulf, on to New Orleans, and other places near and far.

Travis's message said:

> I am besieged, by a thousand or more of the Mexicans under Santa Anna—I have sustained a continual Bombardment & cannonade for 24 hours & have not lost a man—The enemy has demanded a surrender at discretion, otherwise, the garrison are to be put to the sword if the fort is taken—I have answered the demand with a cannon shot, & our flag still waves proudly from the walls—I shall never surrender or retreat. Then, I call on you in the name of Liberty, of patriotism & everything dear to the American character, to come to our aid, with all dispatch—The enemy is receiving reinforcements daily & will no doubt increase to three or four thousand in four or five days. If this call is neglected, I am determined to sustain myself as long as possible & die like a soldier who never forgets what is due to his own honor & that of his country—Victory or Death.

On March 5, Travis called the garrison together and announced that he believed there would be no reinforcements, no relief. He told his stalwarts that their options were limited: they could surrender, attempt to escape, or stay and fight. Legend has it that he drew a line in the dirt with his sword and invited all who would stay to cross the line. Only one man held back—a Frenchman named Louis "Moses" Rose who had fought with Napoleon's army and who had come to the Alamo with Bowie's men. He alone elected to escape and did so that night.

Crockett told Susanna Dickinson, wife of the artillery captain, "I think we had better march out and die in the open air. I don't like to be hemmed up."

But hemmed up they were that frosty morning of March 6, 1836, at the Alamo in San Antonio de Béxar in the Mexican province of Texas y Coahuila—about 183 fighting men facing ten times that number of advancing enemy.

The storming of the Alamo was not so much a battle as a melee and a slaughter. The Mexican columns struck the four walls more or less simultaneously. The greatest concentration of men, led by Colonel Francisco Duque (accompanied by an aide named José Enrique de la Peña, a name to remember), advanced on the north side of the fortress where Travis stood on the rampart shouting, "Hurrah, m'boys! Give 'em hell!" and, directing his words to Captain Juan Seguín's company of Mexican defenders, *"No rendirse, muchachos!"* ("Don't give up, boys!") All that followed was chaos. The Texan cannon cut a bloody swath through the enemy columns until the guns could not be depressed enough to have effect. The attackers managed to prop their scaling ladders against the walls but were repelled time and again in hand-to-hand combat with sword, shotgun, pistol, and close-range musket fire that created a dense clot of dead and wounded at the foot of the wall, the bodies trampled over by the oncoming waves of Santa Anna's troops.

As the first column—Colonel Duque's First Brigade in the

vanguard—hit the north wall, Travis grabbed his shotgun and fired both barrels point-blank at the jostling enemy soldiers below. Almost instantly a sniper's bullet struck him in the head and he fell dead, rolling down the earthen cannon ramp to the ground.

Meantime, despite the withering fire from the muskets of the Texans and the devastating effect of cannon fire directed by Captain Dickinson, the Mexicans regrouped at the north and west walls and made some progress. Those attacking on the east and south, where Crockett and his men defended, were stalled momentarily by the brutal fire from the six-pounders in the lunette and the cannon on the Alamo church roof where Dickinson, Bonham, and their men furiously worked their guns.

For a brief time, the Mexican columns on the east and west side of the Alamo surged toward those still struggling for a foothold on the north, the result being the formation of a frenzied and disorganized mob being decimated by the fish-in-a-barrel musketry from above.

Santa Anna, observing the battle from an earthwork to the northeast of the fortress, now called up his reserves, including the elite grenadiers and *zapadores* ("sappers"—engineers), and these 400 men rushed forward as Mexican bandsmen struck up the eerie Spanish march known as the "Degüello," signifying there would be no quarter.

The Alamo's Achilles' heel—an ill-repaired weakness in the eastern sector of the north wall—was now found and exploited and the Mexicans made their way into the Alamo's central compound. At about the same time, on the west side, the thinning ranks of the Texans could not fend off the enemy pouring over the parapets and massing inside the wall. On the southwest corner, the great eighteen-pounder emplacement was captured and turned against the cannon on the church roof, killing Dickinson, Bonham, and their gunners.

Crockett and his Tennesseans were caught in the open in front of the church and hospital and all, or nearly all, killed.

As the Mexicans captured the church, Robert Evans, the Alamo's big, good-humored, Irish-born master of ordnance, though wounded, grabbed a torch and made his way to blow up the powder magazine on the north side of the building. He fell from musket fire within feet of his objective.

Santa Anna's troops, by now overrunning the entire fortress, broke into the hospital and killed forty men there, entered each room of the barracks and shot all inside, and, in the low barracks on the south wall, found the pale, fevered Jim Bowie in his cot. As he rose to defend himself with a brace of pistols—said to have been given him by Crockett—he was bayoneted to death. His sister-in-law, who was among the Alamo survivors, said the Mexican soldiers "tossed his body on their bayonets until their uniforms were dyed with his blood."

By 6:30 the fighting was over and Santa Anna hewed to his red-flag warning and to the "Degüello": all who bore arms were killed, including the two young sons of gunner Antony Wolfe. Jacob Walker of Nacogdoches, who sought protection in the church sacristy where Susanna Dickinson, widow of the slain artillery officer, awaited the end, was found, shot, and carried from the room on bayonets.

Five or six prisoners were brought before the commanding general. He was infuriated that these men had been spared even momentarily and ordered them executed on the spot. Among the captives, so said Colonel Duque's aide, José Enrique de la Peña, was David Crockett.

Upward of twenty noncombatants survived including several Mexican women (two of them Bowie's sisters-in-law), children, Mrs. Dickinson and her fifteen-month-old daughter Angelina, and Travis's slave, Joe.

The Mexican dead and wounded numbered about 600.

Santa Anna ordered the bodies of all the Texans burned. The Mexican dead were either placed in trenches and covered over or thrown into the San Antonio River.

For Santa Anna, the victory would be short-lived and bitter. On March 27 he ordered the massacre of over 340 Texan prisoners at Goliad (known as La Bahía to the Mexicans), including

Colonel James Fannin, who had failed in his efforts to lead a relief force to the Alamo. But under the rallying cries "Remember
the Alamo!" and "Remember Goliad!" Sam Houston's force of
800 men met the Alamo victor and his 3,000-man army at San
Jacinto on April 21, forty-six days after the fall of the Alamo. In
an eighteen-minute battle, Houston, who lost two men killed
and twenty-three wounded, routed the Mexicans, killing 630
and taking 730 prisoner. Included among the captives was Santa
Anna who, fearing execution, signed an order for all Mexican
troops to retreat south of the Rio Grande. He was released from
custody in November, and after a year's absence he returned to
Mexico where he retired, temporarily, to his hacienda in Vera
Cruz.

It was but a small affair," Santa Anna reportedly said of the
Alamo, but Texans tend to think of it as a bit larger affair, con-
trasting it to the Persians and Spartans at Thermopylae, seeing
the old fortified church and its grounds as a sort of Valhalla of
Texas heroes and placing those ninety deadly minutes in 1836 as
the cornerstone of Texas independence and, ultimately, of statehood.

    In 1936, when the state of Texas unveiled at the Alamo a
monument depicting Travis, Crockett, Bowie, and Bonham and
listing all the Texans who fell there, the inscription on the great
sculpture summed up the meaning of the place and the battle:

    They chose never to surrender or retreat; these brave
    hearts, with flag still proudly waving, perished in the
    flames of immortality, that their high sacrifice might lead
    to the founding of this Texas.

    Of all who died at the Alamo, David Crockett dominates the
mind and heart. He was a beloved national personality long before he ventured to Texas with his gathering of Tennesseeans. His
engaging, openhanded, good-humored, guilelessly honest character had preceded him from the southern canebrakes when he

first earned a seat in Congress. There can be little wonder that revisionist historians, forever discomfited by bigger-than-life, heroic figures, would eventually focus on him and find him a maker of self-myths, a man who made his way into history largely out of tall tales and fancy.

Clearly, there was more to him than that.

David Crockett was born in a wilderness cabin on the Nolachucky River in eastern Tennessee on August 17, 1786, the fifth of six sons of an Irish immigrant farmer who had soldiered in the American Revolution.

He grew up in Creek Indian country (two of his grandparents were killed by Indians in 1777), and left home at age twelve to work as a teamster driving cattle into Virginia. At twenty he married and with his bride, Mary "Polly" Finley, built a farm in the Duck River country, later moving to Lincoln County near the Alabama border. But he worked at the soil only intermittently, preferring wilderness roaming, hunting bear and deer. "I found I was better at increasing my family than my fortune," he admitted.

After the massacre of thirty-six white settlers at Fort Mims, Alabama, in August 1813, Crockett left his wife and his farmer's life, joined the militia, and served as a scout in the Creek War of 1813–1814, the overall campaign commanded by General Andrew Jackson.

His wife died of malaria in 1815 and soon after, Crockett, with three children to care for, married Elizabeth Patton, a widow with two children of her own plus an attractive dowry. The family removed to Shoal Creek, in Lawrence County, Tennessee. There he began his rise in politics, beginning as a local magistrate, justice of the peace, town commissioner, and colonel of the local militia. In 1821 he won election for the first of two terms to the Tennessee legislature and in 1827 ran successfully for a seat in Congress, having to borrow the train fare to Washington.

At first, he was identified with "Old Hickory," Andrew Jackson, who was elected the seventh U.S. president in 1828. Crockett seemed to be the perfect Jacksonian legislator. The two men had much in common. The president, the first one born west of the Alleghenies, came from a similar humble background—born in a log cabin in South Carolina—and became known as a "man of the people" in contrast to the New England patricians who had preceded him. Also, Jackson had been a Tennessean since after the Revolutionary War.

But Crockett soon became disillusioned with his "old chief." In particular the backwoodsman opposed Jackson's and the Democratic Party's Indian Removal Bill that proposed moving southeastern Indians from their ancestral lands into reservations in Indian Territory (Oklahoma today). The idea behind the bill was nothing new—it had first been proposed by Thomas Jefferson—but Crockett, despite the support of it in his own district, somehow found it odious and bolted the president and the party.

He served three undistinguished terms in Congress, 1827–1831 and 1833–1835, bored by tedious legislative procedures from start to end. He earned a reputation as a close friend of what he called "arden spirits," and as a storyteller, gambler, layabout, and canebrake "character." The French writer-politician Alexis de Tocqueville saw Crockett in Washington in 1831 and was horrified that such a primitive could have risen to such high station. "Two years ago," the Frenchman wrote, "the inhabitants of the district of which Memphis is the capital sent to the House of Representatives in Congress an individual named David Crockett, who has no education, can read with difficulty, has no property, no fixed residence, but passes his life hunting, selling his game to live, and dwelling continuously in the woods."

But Crockett's buckskin persona was irresistible to many. In the year of de Tocqueville's observations, a stageplay titled *The Lion of the West* premiered in New York City, its lead character, Colonel Nimrod Wildfire, a swaggering coonskin-cap-wearing Kentucky congressman, patently patterned after that "individual named David Crockett." The play, written by James Kirke Paulding, became an instant hit and when Paulding moved the production to Washington in December 1833, Crockett had a reserved seat at the opening performance. At the end of the play, Nimrod actor James Hackett bowed toward the congressman, paying his respects to the distinguished guest in the audience who served as the inspiration for his character. When Crockett rose from his seat to return the bow, he brought the house down.

In the spring of 1834, Crockett toured the northeast, now a lionized national personality, leaving in his wake an image of a buckskinned frontiersman carrying an old flintlock rifle he called "Betsy," wearing a fox- or coonskin cap with the tail on, living by the homespun motto: "Be always sure you are right, then go ahead!"—Nimrod Wildfire in the flesh. His autobiography, *A Narrative of the Life of David Crockett of the State of Tennessee*, was ghostwritten and published in Philadelphia in 1834 and the next year *Davy Crockett's Almanack of Wild Sports of the West, and Life in the Backwoods* appeared, the first of fifty editions. The books, innocent fun in their day, have been labeled by one modern historian "mouthpieces of jingoistic expansionism."

Crockett's political career and vague presidential aspirations ended in 1835 when he was defeated for reelection to Congress. "He had two basic character flaws that doomed his political career from the start," historian Paul Hutton has written. "He was just too independent and too honest to be a congressman, much less president."

He had told his Tennessee constituents that if they did not reelect him they could "go to hell and I would go to Texas," and he kept his end of the promise. He felt pulled to Texas by the opportunities other Tennesseans had seen in the huge, raw, land-rich territory fighting for its independence from Mexico.

And so he traveled there, via Little Rock, Arkansas, and Natchitoches, Louisiana, and with his twelve Tennessee Mounted Volunteers came to Washington-on-the-Brazos in January, and rode into San Antonio in early February 1836.

"I have come to aid you all that I can in your noble cause," legend says he told William Barret Travis, and Travis assigned him and his volunteers to the log palisade between the church and the south wall of the Alamo.

Perhaps the most familiar and beloved visual image of the Alamo battle is the 1903 painting by Robert Jenkins Onderdonk. In it, Crockett is depicted dressed in fringed buckskins and wearing his coonskin cap and a big hunting knife at his belt. His flintlock rifle is held over his head like a club as the Mexicans advance through a hanging cloud of gunsmoke, through a field of dead and wounded, toward him and the half dozen of his Tennesseans left alive.

This, we knew for 119 years, is how Davy died and there exists a sizable body of evidence that seems to prove it.

Sergeant Felix Nuñez, a soldier with Santa Anna at the Alamo, was interviewed in 1889 by a Professor George W. Noel and gave his eyewitness story. Nuñez never mentioned Crockett by name—and may never have known the name—when he remembered:

> He was a tall American of rather dark complexion and had on a long buckskin coat and a round cap without any bill, made out of fox skin with the long tail hanging down the back. This man apparently had a charmed life. Of the many soldiers who took deliberate aim at him and fired, not one ever hit him. On the contrary, he never missed a shot. He killed at least eight of our men, besides wounding several others. This being observed by a lieutenant who had come in over the wall, he sprang at him and dealt him a deadly blow with his sword, just above the right eye, which felled him to the ground, and in an instant he was pierced by not less than twenty bayonets.

Another statement, one of the most often quoted, came from Susanna Dickinson, widow of the Alamo's artillery commander, Almeron Dickinson. J. M. Morphis, in his *History of Texas* (1875), says Mrs. Dickinson gave an account of the battle years after the event in which she said, "I recognized Col. Crockett lying dead and mutilated between the church and the two story barrack building, and even remember seeing his peculiar cap by his side."

Another account was that attributed to Travis's slave Joe who stated that "Crockett and a few of his friends were found together with twenty-four of the enemy dead around them."

One of the most detailed stories of Crockett's death came from Andrea Castañon Villanueva, eighty-eight years old and known in San Antonio as "Madam Candelaria" (she was the wife of Candelario Villanueva), who was often interviewed as an Alamo survivor. In a *San Antonio Express* story published on March 6, 1892, she told of being in the room next to the Alamo chapel where she had been called upon to nurse Colonel Jim Bowie who lay on a cot sick with typhoid (others said pneumonia or consumption). She said Bowie died with his head in her lap minutes before Santa Anna's troops burst through the door, and added a grim detail: a soldier thrust his bayonet into Bowie's head and lifted him off her lap.

In February 1899, not long after Madam Candelaria's death, another San Antonio newspaper reprinted a longer and more detailed account of her Alamo memories, this one including her recounting of Crockett's death.

She said of "Colonel Crockett," who "frequently came into the room and said a few encouraging words to Bowie":

> He was one of the strangest looking men I ever saw. He had the face of a woman and his manner was that of a young girl. I could not regard him as a hero until I saw him die. He looked grand and terrible standing in the door and fighting a whole column of Mexican infantry. He had fired his last shot and had no time to reload. The cannon balls had knocked away the sand bags and the infantry was pouring through the breech. Crockett stood there swinging something bright over his head. The place was full of smoke and I could not tell whether he was using a gun or a sword. A heap of dead was piled at his feet and the Mexicans were lunging at him with bayo-

nets, but he would not retreat an inch. . . . Crockett fell
and the Mexicans poured into the Alamo.

Another professed eyewitness was Enrique Esparza, twelve-
year-old son of Gregorio Esparza, an Alamo defender who died
in the battle. In 1907 Esparza, then about eighty-two and
thought to be the last of the Alamo survivors, told of seeking
refuge in the church with his mother, sister, and brothers. Crockett, who Esparza said was called "Don Benito" by the Mexican
defenders,

> . . . was everywhere during the siege and personally slew
> many of the enemy with his rifle, his pistol and his knife.
> He fought hand to hand. He clubbed his rifle when they
> closed in on him and knocked them down with its stock
> until he was overwhelmed by numbers and slain. He
> fought to his last breath. He fell immediately in front of
> the large double doors which he defended with the force
> that was by his side. . . . When he died there was a heap
> of slain in front and on each side of him.

But from the beginning there had been other versions of
Davy's death; there was even momentary speculation that he
didn't die at the Alamo at all. (Newspaper reports exist that state
that he was not even at the Alamo, that he was hunting in the
Rocky Mountains and would be returning home in the spring.)

In 1840 Crockett's son John, then a Tennessee congressman,
was reported to be investigating information that his father was
alive and enslaved, working in the Salinas mine near Guadala-
jara.

Nothing came of this.

And there were reports, soon after the battle, appearing in the
New Orleans Post-Union, that Crockett and five other Alamo
defenders had been taken prisoner and executed. The *Louisiana
Advertiser* said that the entire Alamo garrison was executed after
surrendering, and the *New Orleans True American* reported that
Crockett and others had cried for quarter and when it was de-

nied, they continued fighting "until the whole were butchered."

In July 1836, a Detroit newspaper ran a story in the form of a letter by a Sergeant George M. Dolson. This man claimed to have been an interpreter for an unnamed Mexican officer taken prisoner after the battle of San Jacinto on April 21, 1836, in which Sam Houston and his force of volunteers defeated Santa Anna's army. Dolson wrote that the captive officer gave an account of Crockett's surrender and execution that he had heard from another officer who was present during the incident. According to this thirdhand account, several prisoners, Crockett among them, were taken by General Manuel Fernández Castrillón to the Mexican commander after the Alamo battle. Castrillón then is supposed to have announced to his chief, "Santa Anna, the august, I deliver up to you six brave prisoners of war." In Dolson's story, Santa Anna replied, "Who has given you orders to take prisoners? I do not want to see those men living— shoot them." Then, Dolson said the Mexican officer said his informant said, "As the monster uttered these words each officer turned his face the other way, and the hell-hounds of the tyrant despatched the six in his presence and within six feet of his person."

Dolson's letter to the Detroit paper was unearthed and reprinted in 1960, five years after a much more significant development had occurred in the mystery of how David Crockett died.

In 1955, the same year Fess Parker, portraying *Davy Crockett, King of the Wild Frontier,* faded out in the television version of the Onderdonk painting, an obscure antiques dealer in Mexico City named Jesús Sánchez Garza self-published a "diary," allegedly written in 1836 by a man who said he witnessed Davy's execution.

The diary, written by José Enrique de la Peña the aide to Colonel Francisco Duque, who led Santa Anna's First Brigade assault on the Alamo, was published by Sánchez Garza under the title *La Rebelión de Téxas—Manuscrito Inedito de 1836 por un*

Oficial de Santa Anna ("The Texas Rebellion—Unpublished Manuscript of 1836 by one of Santa Anna's Officers") and buried in its pages lay a ticking bomb. This was a passage in which de la Peña described how, after the fall of the Alamo, seven prisoners were brought before Santa Anna by his aide-de-camp, Brigadier General Castrillón.

> Among them, De la Peña wrote, . . . was one of great stature, well proportioned, with regular features, in whose face was the imprint of adversity, but in whom one also noticed a degree of resignation and nobility that did him honor. He was the naturalist David Crockett, well known in North America for his unusual adventures, who had undertaken to explore the country and who, finding himself in Béjar at the very moment of surprise, had taken refuge in the Alamo, fearing that his status as a foreigner might not be respected. Santa Anna answered Castrillón's intervention in Crockett's behalf with a gesture of indignation and, addressing himself to the sappers, the troops closest to him, ordered his execution. The commander and officers were outraged at this action and did not support the order, hoping that once the fury of the moment had blown over these men would be spared; but several officers who were around the president and who, perhaps, had not been present during the moment of danger, became noteworthy by an infamous deed, surpassing the soldiers in cruelty. They thrust themselves forward, in order to flatter their commander, and with swords in hand, fell upon these unfortunate, defenseless men just as a tiger leaps upon his prey. Though tortured before they were killed, these unfortunates died moaning and without humiliating themselves before their torturers.

Here, in just over 200 words, was the first and only seemingly credible eyewitness story of Crockett's death—from an educated Mexican officer no less, and one who was clearly no admirer of President-General Santa Anna.

As subsequent research revealed, de la Peña was a sort of maverick in the Mexican army. Born in Jalisco in 1807 and educated as a mining engineer, he had entered the naval service in 1825 and later was assigned to the *zapadores*. He accompanied Santa Anna's army to San Antonio in 1836, served under Colonel Duque in the Alamo battle, then returned to Mexico City where he was imprisoned for taking part in a revolt against the government. He devoted much of the next five or six years (it is believed he died between 1841–1842) as a sort of armchair critic and strategist of Santa Anna's failed Texas campaign.

Sánchez Garza's privately printed Spanish language version of the de la Peña memoir remained obscure for twenty years although its existence was known to a handful of Texas history scholars and writers. Lon Tinkle, in his *13 Days to Glory* (1958), listed the book in his sources but made no use of it; Walter Lord had a portion of it translated, and in his *A Time to Stand* (1961) still regarded as the best Alamo book, judged de la Peña's story "possible."

Then, at some unspecified date, the original manuscript of the controversial memoir was purchased from Sánchez Garza by John Peace, a collector of Texana and chairman of the University of Texas Board of Regents, who loaned it to the research library of the University of Texas at San Antonio. In 1975 Carmen Perry, archivist and director of the Daughters of the Republic of Texas Library at the Alamo, translated the work and in 1975 published it as *With Santa Anna in Texas—A Personal Narrative of the Revolution by José Enrique de la Peña*.

Since 1975 virtually all writers of the Texas War of Independence in general and of the Alamo in particular have taken the de la Peña diary as the only reliable eyewitness account of Crockett's death.

Stephen Hardin, in his *Texian Iliad* (1994), subscribes to and uses the Mexican officer's account as does Crockett's most recent biographer, Mark Derr, in his *The Frontiersman: The Real Life and the Many Legends of Davy Crockett* (1993). Some writer-historians have hedged a bit in their use of the de la Peña book—Albert Nofi, in his *The Alamo and the Texas War for*

Independence (1994), calls it "pretty convincing"—while others have delighted in it, seeing it as the final opportunity to bring a legend to earth. Paul Hutton, a New Mexico-based historian who has written extensively on Crockett and the Alamo, says of the various accounts of Davy's death, "none is more reliable than that of Lieutenant Colonel Enrique de la Peña," and elaborates: "There is no doubt . . . that he [Crockett] was taken prisoner, for numerous witnesses reported it. There is no eyewitness account of his death in battle, despite the wishful thinking of generations of writers and readers."

And Jeff Long, in his *Duel of Eagles* (1990), making use of the Dolson letter as well as de la Peña's diary, even seems to know what was in Crockett's and Santa Anna's mind, what Crockett said to his captors and what they said to him. He portrays the Tennessean cringing and wriggling on the hook, trying to convince his captors that he was merely a traveler accidentally swept into the whirlwind of the revolution. Long says Crockett, at the moment of truth, "straightened up, perhaps already formulating a speech. He folded his arms across his chest" and that Santa Anna saw before him "an arrogant mercenary with gunsmoke staining his creased face. He saw a wetback. A slave trader and smuggler. A pirate. A heretic." Santa Anna, who Long says "did not look into David Crockett's eyes," said to his officers and men gathered at the place of execution, "I do not want to see those men living," then, turning his back on the prisoners, said, "Shoot them."

Long's colorful story caused but a momentary stir among Alamo buffs and authorities, but de la Peña's book had staying power. Even the most Texan of Texas historians eventually abandoned the beloved, century-old image of Davy clubbing the enemy with Old Betsy until overwhelmed and killed in the heat of battle.

But not all who read de la Peña fell in line.

In fact, one long-time student of the Alamo battle says de la Peña's memoir is "is very likely a forgery, a fake, a lie."

❦

Bill Groneman may seem an unlikely candidate to do battle with the Peñaphiles—many of them academic historians with Ph.D. degrees. He is a captain and former arson investigator with the New York City Fire Department and lives on Long Island, a long way from the Alamo.

But Groneman is no lightweight: he has a history degree from Manhattan College, has a variety of intellectual interests, has made a subcareer as a student of Texas independence, in particular the Alamo battle and its participants, is a member of the Texas State Historical Association and the Alamo Society. And he is the author of *Roll Call at the Alamo* (1985), *Alamo Defenders* (1990), *Eyewitness to the Alamo* (1996), and other works and spends a lot of time poring over the sources of Alamo history—including the original, handwritten de la Peña manuscript.

Groneman states that Crockett "went from a hero to a coward in the public's mind, based primarily on the translation and publication of the de la Peña 'diary,' " a book, he says, that contains many "anomalies, errors and misinformation," and which "may very well be a complete hoax."

In 1991 and 1992 Groneman spent time examining the original manuscript at the University of Texas at San Antonio and came away from the experience more puzzled than illuminated. Among other things, he discovered:

- the holograph document contained more than one handwriting;
- the document was written loose-leaf, on at least fifteen makes, kinds, and sizes of pieces of paper;
- the manuscript contained many errors of fact and questionable material such as the anachronistic use of the phrase "crimes against humanity," which first came into use in 1915 to describe war atrocities;
- the "diary" was dated 1836, as if written before, during and shortly after the Alamo battle, yet contained material from other sources that the author could not have known until later.

Groneman wondered how de la Peña could know that David Crockett was among the prisoners brought before Santa Anna, when the lieutenant had never been in the U.S. before, had arrived in San Antonio only two days before the battle, and would not have known Crockett on sight or been able to identify him. And he wondered about the lack of "provenance" (origin) of the diary. In the original publication of it in Mexico City in 1955, its owner and publisher, Sánchez Garza, provided forty pages of introductory material yet not a clue as to how he obtained the manuscript.

And there was yet another critical matter: the curious similarity between certain phrases in the de la Peña memoir to those in *The Journal of Jean Lafitte*, a book published by a vanity press in 1958 and a proven forgery by a retired railroad engineer named John Andrechyne Laflin. This man, who claimed to be the great-grandson of the notorious New Orleans pirate, traveled around the U.S. in the 1940–1970 period peddling alleged Lafitte documents (most of them ending up in Texas), and was the subject of a chapter in the book *Great Forgers and Famous Fakes* by the renowned handwriting expert Charles Hamilton of New York. Laflin was also believed to have forged a letter purportedly by an Alamo defender and thus had, Groneman believed, an Alamo "connection." Could Laflin have been the origin, author, forger of the de la Peña memoir?

Charles Hamilton, the handwriting authority who knew Laflin's "work" better than anyone, examined photocopies of pages of the de la Peña diary and in 1991 expressed the opinion that the pages were the work of John Andrechyne Laflin.

Groneman published his exposé of the diary in his *Defense of a Legend* and the book stirred a lively debate (which continues to this day) among students of the Alamo battle and its participants. But academicians viewed Groneman's findings as speculative, unscientific, and unproven, an attempt to defend the Crockett legend and what North Carolina professor James Crisp, a Penãphile, calls "the heroic and filiopietistic versions of Crockett's last stand."

Groneman says he is not trying to prove that Davy died as

Onderdonk, Fess Parker, John Wayne, or any other legendary version of the Alamo story has it. "I don't believe that anyone knows how Crockett died," he says, but "Since he was an active participant in a battle in which everyone on his side was killed, it is not outrageous to conclude he died fighting." As to the execution theory, Groneman states that since there were about 250 defenders of the Alamo and only five were executed, the odds are fifty to one against Crockett being among them. "Investigation has shown that there is no credible evidence that he was one of those executed," he concludes.

Groneman and most others with an interest in the unvarnished truth agree that we do not need a Betsy-swinging balm for our national psyche, and that even if the de la Peña account is the true one, there is nothing dishonorable in the way Davy died (nor did de la Peña suggest such a thing). The defenders of the Alamo died heroically and David Crockett died as he lived—with courage.

OTHER DEATHS
IN DISPUTE

Incident at Grinder's Stand

The Last Night of Meriwether Lewis

There is an eerie monument over the remains of Meriwether Lewis in the Natchez Trace National Park near Hohenberg, Tennessee, seventy-two miles southwest of Nashville. The memorial, which lies 400 feet north of the site of an old inn, is in the form of a limestone column resting on a massive plinth, the whole about twenty feet high. The topmost foot or so of the column is "broken," as if snapped off—just as the explorer's life ended suddenly at its apex.

Meriwether Lewis, who, as Robert Penn Warren observed, was as close to a son as Thomas Jefferson ever had, commanded the most consequential and "perfect" exploration in the history of the United States. He was, in brief, the Lewis of Lewis and Clark and when he died at age thirty-five, tragically and bloodily and under inexplicable circumstances in the wilderness of

Tennessee, he left behind a splendid legacy of achievement. He also left us one of the greatest mysteries of our history.

He came from the west, forded the Tennessee River and the smaller Buffalo River, and rode north a few miles through dense forests and canebrakes, ridge-back hills and deep glens gloomy in the failing light. Now, amid a profusion of old oaks, persimmons, dogwoods, and azalea shrubs along Little Swan Creek, he intersected the wilderness road known as the Natchez Trace, an old path that ran north out of Natchez 550 miles through the valley of Tennessee to Nashville. The route had been in use by Indians and hunters since 1733, and by Ohio River valley settlers who floated their crops down the Mississippi to Natchez or New Orleans, sold their boats, and returned home by horseback or on foot along the Trace.

He dismounted at the stand, a clearing in the wilderness, where, separated by a narrow breezeway, stood two rough-hewn, mud-chinked cabins, smoke pluming from the chimney of one and a faint orange glow of light within it. Behind him rode his servant, a man named John Pernier, who led a packhorse laden with two bulky trunks, and behind Pernier followed a black man, the slave of John Neelly, the Indian agent of the Chickasaw Nation.

The sun was disappearing behind him as he spoke a few courtly words of greeting to Priscilla Grinder, wife of the proprietor of the stand, who stood nervously in the path between the cabins. He asked for lodging, explained that he had been eleven days on the trail out of Fort Pickering and was en route to Nashville and to Washington. He said his companion, Mr. Neelly, had stayed behind, recovering some strayed horses, but would be along soon.

Mrs. Grinder listened anxiously. Her husband Robert was away, working on their farm at Duck River, ten miles north, leaving her to mind the cabins with two of their youngest children and a black servant girl named Malinda, about twelve years old. The Natchez Trace was notorious for the land pirates, thieves, and murderers hiding in its forests and Mrs. Grinder had learned to be cautious of strangers. But the man standing before her, while odd in his measured, lawyerlike speech and the fevered look in his eyes, seemed a person of substance and so she offered him the vacant cabin and a warm meal.

After Pernier and Neelly's slave took his trunks into the cabin, the man instructed them to take the animals to the nearby barn and remain with them for the night. The servant girl Malinda brought food to the barn for the two men while their master ate sparingly of the meal Mrs. Grinder prepared for him.

All this occurred at twilight on October 10, 1809, and the man who threw a bearskin on the rude puncheon floor of the cabin at Grinder's Stand and, wrapped in a buffalo robe, retired for the last night of his life, was more a person of substance than Mrs. Grinder then knew.

He was Meriwether Lewis, governor of Upper Louisiana Territory, a soldier and scientist, once President Thomas Jefferson's private secretary, and, only six years past, leader of the first expedition to cross the North American continent from the Mississippi to the Pacific Coast.

The circumstances of Meriwether Lewis's death in the Natchez Trace of Tennessee in the late night or early morning hours of October 10–11, 1809 (the time, like almost everything else in the story, is uncertain), is perhaps the most unsettling of all the mysteries of American history.

Virtually everything we know of Lewis's final hours derives from the testimony of Priscilla Grinder (who was probably illiterate), her words filtered through others. She told her story several times over a thirty-year period, on each occasion adding new information in a conversational embroidery that, while perhaps innocent and natural for a frontier woman thrust into the role of accidental bystander at a momentous event, further muddied an already confusing event.

A rough distillation of her various accounts of the tragedy is this:

Before he retired, she heard Lewis (whose history she did not know, nor even that he was governor of Louisiana Territory) striding back and forth in the path between the cabins, talking to himself "like a lawyer."

A bit later, or perhaps a bit before this, three men rode into the stand to ask for lodging but rode on after being threatened by Lewis, who stood by his cabin brandishing a brace of pistols.

At about three o'clock in the morning of October 11, she heard two (or perhaps three) gunshots and a few minutes later heard Lewis at her door saying, "O madam! Give me some water and heal my wounds!"

She was terrified, alone in the pitch-black night, and would not open her door.

She later heard the scraping of a gourd dipper in a water bucket.

She waited about two hours and at dawn sent her two children to the barn to fetch the two men who slept there.

They found Lewis, still conscious, lying on his blood-soaked bearskin, a piece of his forehead blown away and his brain exposed, another gaping wound in his chest.

He died about two hours later.

(In another account, Mrs. Grinder said that Lewis, after pleading for water, had crawled away to a point north of her cabin and out of her vision. She said he was discovered there after dawn by Pernier, who took his master back to the cabin where Lewis died soon after. Yet another version of the story was told by John Neelly from Priscilla Grinder's testimony. Lewis, after begging for water, returned to his cabin, and when the servants arrived there at dawn, he was found to have not only the gunshot wounds but to have cut himself repeatedly with a razor, telling Neelly's slave that he had killed himself to deprive his enemies of the pleasure of murdering him.)

Whatever the precise circumstances, Meriwether Lewis died violently at Grinder's Stand that night of October 10 or morning of the eleventh, and after Neelly arrived on the scene in the forenoon of the eleventh, the explorer was hastily buried north of the cabins, his coffin made from a felled oak split into four sections and joined with wooden pegs.

Although there exists no written evidence of it, oral tradition has it that a coroner's inquest was held at Grinder's Stand, or nearby, and that the verdict was suicide with two jurors favoring a finding of murder. And, while the grave remained unmarked for thirty-nine years, when the Tennessee Legislature got around to erecting a monument on the supposed site of his grave in 1848, state commissioners asserted that Lewis "probably died at the hands of an assassin."

Thomas Jefferson, Lewis's mentor and the man responsible for his achievements as explorer and territorial governor, seems to have had no moment's doubt that his admirable friend had killed himself. Nor did William Clark, Lewis's partner in the great Corps of Discovery expedition. But Lucy Meriwether, Lewis's mother, is said to have stoutly maintained to her death that her son was murdered and she had no hesitation in pointing her finger at the culprit.

While it is unlikely, over 187 years after the fact, that new evidence will surface to solve the puzzle of the manner of the death of Meriwether Lewis, and the reason for it, a recounting of who he was and the circumstances that led him to the Tennessee backwoods sheds some light on what happened to him there.

The Meriwether Lewis who rode into the Natchez Trace that fall in 1809 was a far different person than the one who had grown up, like his mentor and sponsor, Thomas Jefferson, in the Blue Ridge foothills of Albemarle County, Virginia. He was born near Charlottesville in 1774 and received a good education from private tutors. He joined the state militia during the Whiskey Rebellion in 1794, then served with William Clark, a soldier with whom he would share his destiny twelve years later, in the Indian operations in the Ohio River Valley that culminated in the Battle of Fallen Timbers near Toledo. (In overall command of the campaign was General "Mad Anthony" Wayne, and Wayne's aide was another man who some say would figure in Lewis's later history, Colonel [later Brigadier General] James Wilkinson.)

Lewis was posted to the infantry in 1796, rose to a captaincy, and commanded the post at Fort Pickering, Tennessee, on the Mississippi (to which he would return under far different circumstances thirteen years later) and Detroit. When his Virginia neighbor and family friend Thomas Jefferson won election as president in March 1801, Lewis was invited to Washington to serve as Jefferson's private secretary. The president, a widower for nearly twenty years, later wrote of he and Lewis baching in the White House "like two mice in church."

For many years, Jefferson had been interested in sending a scientific expedition up the Missouri River and to the Pacific and in 1803, on the eve of the Louisiana Purchase treaty with France, received congressional backing for the transcontinental exploration.

Jefferson selected Lewis to lead the expedition and Lewis chose his army comrade and friend William Clark, then managing his family's Kentucky plantation, as co-captain of what became known as the Corps of Discovery.

Clark, a courageous and coolheaded soldier, served ostensibly as his co-equal in command of the expedition but the heart and soul of it was the indefatigable Meriwether Lewis.

They led their party of thirty young soldiers and French boatmen from near St. Louis up the uncharted Missouri in the spring of 1804, worried and labored it over the Rockies, crossed the Continental Divide, journeyed by foot and horseback, by portage, keelboat, pirogue, and canoe to the Columbia River and to the Pacific. The expedition returned to St. Louis on September 23, 1806, two years and four months after its departure.

It took a strict, decisive, self-assured leader to take that path-making mission over 4,000 miles of savagely pristine wilderness inhabited by tribes of Indians who had never seen a white man, and then back again. But Lewis had changed radically, so say dependable accounts, after the great event ended. He became governed by a mercurial temper, on the one hand impulsive, on the other given to self-doubt and melancholia. He worried about his health and dosed himself with pills and powders and various nostrums, many containing addictive opiates. Always introspective, he became sentimental and solitary and appears to have been plagued by a sort of mental paralysis or at least inertia. After Jefferson named him governor of Louisiana Territory in March 1807, Lewis dawdled for a full year in Washington, Philadelphia, and his home in Virginia before taking up the post. He came down ill with a fever, scouted for a publisher for his massive exploration journals, hired from dwindling personal resources naturalists and artists to illustrate the work, sat for portraits, fell in and out of love, and even managed to take offense at something Jefferson said or wrote—more than likely a scolding for not using his time to write the text for the great book. (He died without submitting a publishable line of it.)

He turned more and more to alcohol, fretted more and more about what lay before him—possible bankruptcy, ill health, loneliness, loss of his patronage—and in March 1808, probably still ill from a malarial fever, he finally reached St. Louis to take up his post as governor.

In an unremarkable year in the office, Lewis's personal affairs and mental state continued to plummet. He earned, almost instantly, it appears, the enmity of the territorial secretary, a peculiarly vindictive man named Frederick Bates, a crony of Lewis's predecessor, General James Wilkinson. Bates would soon be telling others that the new governor was "insane." In that first year, Lewis lost money in land speculations in St. Louis while spending more of his funds commissioning artists for maps, paintings, and drawings for his journals; and he fell afoul of the War and Treasury Departments in Washington. This latter grievance was based on the refusal of the federal government to honor the vouchers (one for a paltry $19) he submitted for payments made out of his $2,000 salary for official territorial business. This became the ostensible purpose of his return to Washington.

Another purpose was to move publication of his journals off dead center. Lewis's inertia in this matter had been a source of contention between Lewis and Jefferson for at least two years. Less than a month before he departed from St. Louis for Washington, the explorer received a letter in which the former president repeated his anxiety over the journals. "I have so long promised copies to my literary correspondents in France, that I am almost bankrupt in their eyes. I shall be very happy to receive from yourself information of your expectations on this subject. Every body is impatient for it."

(Another theory, as will be seen, is that Lewis needed to visit the capital to turn over to President James Madison's government evidence of the traitorous conduct of General Wilkinson, who had illegal dealings with the Spanish government for decades. Five months after Lewis's death, Wilkinson was summoned to Washington to answer charges of collusion with Spanish officials but was cleared and permitted to return to his duties as military commander in New Orleans.)

On September 4, Governor Lewis, intending to travel to the capital via New Orleans and a sailing vessel around the Floridas, left St. Louis by flatboat, accompanied by his servant John Pernier (or Pernia; he had been one of Jefferson's servants in Washington and was variously described as a Creole, Frenchman, Spaniard, and a "free mulatto") and four large trunks. These contained saddles and tack, weapons, clothing, personal belongings, and papers, including his disputed expense accounts and the sixteen notebooks comprising the journals of the Corps of Discovery.

At New Madrid, 200 miles below St. Louis, he had to be taken ashore to see a doctor, probably because of his intermittent fever. During his time ashore he wrote his last will and testament, bequeathing his estate to his mother, and after three days in the frontier town he was placed on a litter and returned to the riverboat.

Crewmen carried him ashore again at Chickasaw Bluffs (on the site of present-day Memphis) on a muggy September 15, still quite ill and dosing himself with opiates and "tartar" (tartar emetic, a poisonous compound of the day used to induce sweating and vomiting). At Fort Pickering, the town's military post, to which Lewis had been assigned in 1797, he fell under the care of the commander of the fort, Captain Gilbert Russell. This man, who owed his appointment to General Wilkinson, wrote to ex-President Jefferson and William Clark three months after Lewis's death that he found the governor "in a state of mental derangement" and that the riverboatmen said Lewis had twice tried to kill himself during the voyage. Later Russell would write Jefferson again, detailing Lewis's "free use of liquor," flatly calling Lewis's death a murder, and accusing Pernier as having "aided in it." Russell said that during the governor's stay at Fort Pickering he had to be kept under close watch since he "had made several attempts to put an end to his existence." (Russell is the only recorded source for this critical information.) Jefferson, in turn, wrote Russell that Lewis's death "was an act of desperation." The former president, now sixty-six and retired to Monticello, his hilltop villa overlooking Charlottesville, went on to say that Lewis "was much afflicted & habitually so with hypochondria."

During his eight days of recuperation at Fort Pickering, Lewis's purported mental derangement did not prevent him from writing a lucid, clearly worded letter to President Madison explaining why he had decided to travel overland to Washington and not via New Orleans: he said he felt the overland route would be less taxing on his "indisposition" and that he feared the possibility of his "original papers relative to my voyage to the Pacific falling into the hands of the British." (The British were not in or even close to New Orleans at this time, but Lewis may have acted on erroneous intelligence. Some theorists have it that he used the excuse to cover the real reason for avoiding New Orleans: the presence there of James Wilkinson.)

Captain Russell apparently offered to accompany Lewis to Nashville, perhaps even to Washington, but for some reason was deterred from doing so. He ended up loaning Lewis $100 in gold, two horses and saddles, the total loan of $379.58 secured by a promissory note signed by both men on September 27, 1809.

On September 29, Lewis left Chickasaw Bluffs for the Tennessee River and the only evidence we have of his conduct on the trail for the next eleven days is the testimony of the mysterious John Neelly, agent for the Chickasaws.

Little is known of the elusive Neelly except that he was a former militiaman commissioned as Indian agent less than three months before he met Lewis at Fort Pickering, that he was intensely disliked by Captain Russell, and that he would be dismissed as agent by the Secretary of War in July 1812, for "hostility to the Indians."

The extraordinary and unexplainable fact about Neelly is that he came into Fort Pickering from the Chickasaw Agency in Mississippi, 150 miles to the southeast, only three days before Lewis arrived and that he apparently volunteered to accompany Lewis back toward Nashville. His reason for this rather extravagant offer, unless it was to ingratiate himself to the governor, is unknown, but it was Neelly alone who attested, in a letter to Jefferson, that Lewis appeared "deranged of mind" on the trail and it is Neelly who first reported Priscilla Grinder's account of Lewis's death by suicide.

And Neelly, too, owed his appointment to General Wilkinson.

Lewis left two of his four trunks at the fort and together with his servant Pernier, Neelly, the agent's slave (whose name is not recorded), a remuda of packhorses, and perhaps a few Chickasaw Indians, departed the fort on September 29. They crossed the Tennessee River on October 8 and made camp. On the morning of the tenth Neelly discovered that two packhorses had slipped their hobbles during the night and had strayed. He stayed behind to locate them while the restless and anxious Lewis, Pernier, and the black man accompanying him proceeded toward the Natchez Trace, about a day's ride to the north.

In the evening of October 10, the governor and the two servants arrived at Grinder's Stand.

A few hours later Meriwether Lewis was dead.

Neelly rode into the stand during the forenoon of the eleventh, leading one of the two strayed horses. He left no record of what he found as he entered the clearing and rode up to the cabins. In the letter he wrote to Jefferson on October 18, he said that he had possession of Lewis's trunks, rifles, silver watch, brace of flint-lock pistols, dirk and tomahawk, all of which he subsequently forwarded to the former president. (The currency Lewis had with him, about $100 in gold, was never found.) And he related to Jefferson the story Mrs. Grinder had told him, saying that Lewis appeared "deranged of mind" on the trail and that "He had shot himself in the head with one pistol & a little below the Breast with the other."

He made no mention of razor wounds.

John Pernier, taking Lewis's packhorse with him, traveled on to Virginia and talked to Jefferson, his old employer, on November 26. Thereafter the servant paid a visit to Lewis's family near Charlottesville where he attempted to collect $240 in back wages he said was owed him. The result of this visit was to convince Lewis's mother that Pernier had murdered her son.

Six months after his return to Washington, John Pernier apparently killed himself. When Priscilla Grinder gave her story to an anonymous schoolteacher in 1838 she said she had heard that Pernier, after being rebuffed by Lewis's mother, "finally cut his own throat, and thus put an end to his existence."

But what really happened to him was contained in a letter to Jefferson from John Christopher Sueverman, also a former servant. The May 5, 1810, letter reported that "Mr. Pirny" (Pernier), who Sueverman described as "wretchedly destitute," had died of an overdose of laudanum and was "buried neat and decent the next day."

The news of Lewis's death first appeared in the Nashville *Clarion* ten days after the event, the story containing the essentials of what Priscilla Grinder told John Neelly. A similar account appeared in the Washington *National Intelligencer* on November 15.

The first person after Neelly to interview Mrs. Grinder about the incident was the Scottish-born ornithologist Alexander Wilson who was traveling from Nashville to Natchez in the spring of 1811 and decided to visit the site of the great man's untimely death. The account Wilson wrote in his diary on May 6, 1811, added significant details to the story.

Mrs. Grinder told him that Lewis rode into the stand at about sunset, that he was wearing a large white-and-blue-striped linen duster and that he did not identify himself. After making arrangements with her, he took his saddle into the cabin. When his servant (Pernier) came up with the black man, Lewis made an inquiry about his "powder"—signifying that the pistols he carried were unloaded and that he did not carry his own powder horn.

He paced nervously and spoke "violently" (meaning loudly), his face flushed, and ate but little of the food she prepared for him, Mrs. Grinder said. He lit his pipe, drew up a chair, apparently in the breezeway between the cabins, and said in a kindly way to his hostess, "Madam, this is a very pleasant evening." Later, after refilling his pipe, he looked out toward the dying light in the west and said, "What a sweet evening it is."

Deep into the night she heard a gunshot, heard something fall heavily to the floor of the cabin, heard the words "Oh, Lord!" Then she heard a second shot and in a few minutes the man was at her door.

She peered through the cracks between the logs of her kitchen and saw the man stagger back and fall against a stump, crawl some distance away and raise himself against a tree. Then he returned to her door but said nothing.

Mrs. Grinder, terrified at all this commotion, did not unbar her door. (Years later, the Grinders' slave girl Malinda confirmed this.) She waited until daybreak, perhaps two hours after she heard the first gunshot, and sent two of her children to the barn to waken the servants.

Lewis died about two hours later, at sunrise, and was buried (on October 12) in a hastily dug grave—dug by whom, Mrs. Grinder did not say, but apparently by Pernier and the black man.

Alexander Wilson was shown the grave and said he asked Robert Grinder, apparently present when Wilson interviewed Mrs. Grinder, to fence the area to keep hogs and wolves from foraging in it. Wilson said he obtained a written promise from Grinder that the fence would be erected.

In 1893 the army surgeon and naturalist Elliott Coues, a New Hampshire man who retraced much of the Corps of Discovery route and visited the site of Lewis's death, published in four volumes his vastly annotated *A History of the Expedition Under the Command of Captains Lewis and Clark.* In this work Coues stated that Alexander Wilson was a precise and dependable man of science. "There is no more reason to doubt Wilson's painstaking correctness than there is reason to doubt his veracity," he wrote. But, he added, Mrs. Grinder's testimony "is not to be believed under oath" and said of her account of Lewis's death, "there is every sign that it is a concoction on the part of an accomplice in crime, either before or after the event."

Coues was the first writer of eminence to call into question Mrs. Grinder's entire story, in particular her odd behavior after hearing the pistol shots, seeing her guest staggering about the yard begging for water, and waiting until sunrise to notify the servants in the barn of what she heard and saw. "Governor Lewis may have committed the deed . . . in a fit of suicidal mania," Coues wrote, "and the woman's incoherent story may not have been intended to deceive, but may have arisen from confused memories of an exciting night. That is conceivable; but my contention is that the testimony, as we have it, does not suffice to prove suicide, and does raise a strong suspicion that Governor Lewis was foully dealt with by some person or persons unknown—presumably [Robert] Grinder, or him and some accomplices."

He stated unequivocally his belief that "Mrs. Grinder was

privy to a plot to murder Governor Lewis, and therefore had her own part to play in the tragedy, even if that part was a passive one."

☙

In 1838, after her husband's death, Priscilla Grinder, now in her sixties, spoke again of the incident, this time to a schoolteacher who came to visit the Lewis gravesite. Her story contained some weighty, if inexplicable new details.

She told the teacher she heard *three* pistol shots and that when she saw Lewis at sunrise, the dying man had *exchanged clothes with his servant Pernier.* She said that Pernier had Lewis's gold watch, and that Lewis said, "O, how hard it is to die. I am so strong."

☙

Murder or suicide?

The murder advocates ask if a veteran soldier and frontiersman would fail twice (or was it three times?) to kill himself with his weapons? That he could have held the long-barreled flintlock pistol in such a manner that the ball penetrated his breast and exited low in his back? That he could have blown off part of his skull, exposing his brain, then shoot himself through the chest, or vice versa, and manage to stagger to Mrs. Grinder's door begging for water? That a man bent on suicide would have botched the job with guns and razor, then begged his hostess not only for water but for help to "heal my wounds"?

And why would a frontier woman, toughened by her life in the wilderness, in a place inhabited by outlaws and thugs, be so terrified by a gentleman guest's pacing and talking to himself that she could not sleep? And why would she not unbar her door to the dying man begging for water and succor? Why would she wait for hours before seeking help?

And what of such a suspicious character as Frederick Bates, whose sudden, insubordinate conduct toward Lewis, his superior, seems inexplicable but who was a close associate of Wilkinson's? And what of those other potential culprits John Neelly and John

Pernier? And Robert Grinder, a man some said had a violent history, who sold liquor to the Indians, who was feared by all in the vicinity—where was *he* on that deadly night and morning of October 10–11?

And what of the three men who rode into the stand? Who were they and what did they say or do that caused Lewis to threaten them with his pistols?

And what happened to the $100 in gold Lewis had with him? Might his death have been a simple matter of a violent robbery, a commonplace occurrence in the dark and bloody history of the "Devil's Backbone"—the Natchez Trace?

And why, when Lewis's body was exhumed in 1849 for burial under the monument erected at Grinder's Stand, did the Tennessee commission that arranged for the memorial state in its report that "The impression has long prevailed that under the disease of body and mind . . . Gov. Lewis perished by his own hand. It seems to be more probable that he died by the hands of an assassin"?

The most gloriously intricate of the conjectures on Lewis's death-as-murder is the massive conspiratorial web constructed by the late Pulitzer Prize historian David Leon Chandler. In his 1994 book, *The Jefferson Conspiracies: A President's Role in the Assassination of Meriwether Lewis,* Chandler's theme is that Lewis's death was the result of intrigues that involved Thomas Jefferson, Aaron Burr, and, as the controlling spider in the web, the infamous commanding general of the U.S. Army, James Wilkinson, a man described by another Pulitzer historian, Samuel Eliot Morison, as "a traitor to every cause he embraced."

Chandler's plot, in its way as byzantine as any concocted by Kennedy assassination conspiratorialists, is worth recounting.

A recurring name in accounts of Lewis's final days, James Wilkinson was a Marylander and medical school graduate who rose from the rank of private in the revolutionary army to command of it. He fought at Montreal (and was promoted to major by General Benedict Arnold) and Ticonderoga, then at Saratoga as an aide to General Horatio Gates. He married a wealthy woman, made a fortune in land and mercantile trading in Kentucky, and in 1791 returned to the army when President Washington offered him a commission as a lieutenant colonel. He took an active role in the Indian campaigns in the Ohio Valley, fought bravely at the Battle of Fallen Timbers on August 20, 1794 (as did two young soldiers named Meriwether Lewis and William Clark), and was promoted to brigadier general. In 1797, with the death of General Anthony Wayne, he assumed the position of General of the Army and would serve, and have the confidence, in varying degrees, of four presidents.

From his days as a merchant and land speculator in the Kentucky frontier, Wilkinson had established a dangerous rapport with Spanish authorities, who then controlled the Mississippi River trade routes, by promising to assist their government in defending their North American possessions. While a civilian, such an alliance was not illegal, but Wilkinson continued to maintain his contacts with the Spanish after he returned to the army and engaged in outright traitorous conduct by trading information with them for gold. Even in 1804, after assignment to New Orleans to establish U.S. authority over Louisiana Purchase territories, he accepted $12,000 in gold from the Spanish government in exchange for his "opinions" and assistance.

David L. Chandler's theory also involves Wilkinson's association with another of the period's greatest scoundrels, Jefferson's vice president, Aaron Burr. He writes that the two men were special partisans by 1804, meeting in Washington and subsequently passing coded letters back and forth that discussed Burr's ambition to establish a colony in Louisiana and to eventually separate the Mississippi Valley from the Union. Burr even proposed his plan to a British minister, offering to detach Louisiana from the the Union in exchange for a half million dollars and the loan of a naval force. The British were not interested.

Toward the end of 1806, Wilkinson got very cold feet and betrayed Burr by writing a lurid and self-serving letter to Jefferson about Burr's "deep, dark, and wicked widespread conspiracy" to annex Louisiana.

Burr was brought to trial in Richmond for treason but escaped conviction. While Wilkinson's own traitorous conduct was eventually revealed, after Lewis's death, he, too, escaped punishment and, with Jefferson's support, returned to duty as governor of Louisiana Territory.

(Wilkinson's military career ended in 1815. He went to Mexico in 1822 to obtain colonization grants for Texas lands and died there in December 1825.)

Chandler's *Jefferson Conspiracies* suggests—rather states baldly—that Meriwether Lewis's journey from St. Louis to Washington had as its objectives the commonly held motives of straightening out his expense accounts, rejected vouchers, and other problems with federal agencies, and of delivering his nearly completed exploration journals to his publisher. But the author adds an all-important purpose for the mission: that Lewis had critical information to deliver to President Madison and to former President Jefferson—information on James Wilkinson, his predecessor as governor. Lewis, Chandler says, stood ready to report on Wilkinson's dual treachery of spying for Spanish authorities and his involvement with Aaron Burr's plot to invade Louisiana and create a new state and perhaps to invade Mexico and conquer that country as well.

Wilkinson, Chandler writes of the critical period when Lewis was heading out on his last journey, "is the unseen force here, the conductor hidden in the pit." The author states that the two most important figures in Lewis's last days, Russell, the commander at Fort Pickering, and Neelly, the Indian agent, were both Wilkinson appointees. And he speculates that Lewis's abrupt change in his plans to travel to Washington via New Orleans had nothing to do with fears of the British but did perhaps have to do with a fear of Wilkinson. The general was not only in New Orleans but in trouble over the public revelations of his Spanish connections.

"There were scandals in the making," Chandler says.

"Wilkinson may well have feared that Lewis was about to spring another."

Chandler also points out the seemingly strange fate of three of the principals in the case: two years after Lewis's death, Gilbert Russell was arrested and discharged from the army under unknown circumstances; John Neelly, a year after Russell's arrest, was removed as Indian agent and disappears from history; and John Pernier, seven months after his visit with Jefferson and Lewis's mother, died of an overdose of laudanum in Washington.

"Wilkinson seems to be our man, a general covering up his crimes," Chandler concludes, saying Wilkinson was "a man who did not hesitate to use whatever men or measures were required to protect his interests."

If Wilkinson had Lewis murdered—by whom, precisely, the author does not say—what role in the conspiracy did Lewis's spiritual "father" play?

"Thomas Jefferson's complicity is a substantial one," Chandler states, "and includes his endorsement of the suicide theory, his suppression of an investigation, and his years-long protection of Wilkinson." Jefferson, the author says, knew an investigation would invariably have led to Wilkinson and if Wilkinson sank, Jefferson would have sunk with him.

This intricate thesis, constructed by a historian with a vast knowledge of the Jeffersonian era, is by far the most elaborate of all the Lewis death theories. It is not, however, any more compelling than Lewis's mother's suspicion that John Pernier killed her son, or Gilbert Russell's conviction that John Neelly was the culprit, or the idea that Robert Grinder or some unnamed Natchez Trace outlaw may have murdered Lewis for the $100 in gold he carried with him.

Neither Chandler's conspiracy theory nor any of the other, simpler ones have any real documentary evidence to support them.

For that matter, neither do the theories that Lewis committed suicide.

It seems incontrovertible that in the final month or so of his life Meriwether Lewis was despondent over the government's rejection of his expense account as governor of Upper Louisiana Territory. It also seems clear that he was harried by personal debts, perhaps on the verge of bankruptcy, that he experienced recurring bouts of "ague," "bilious fever," and other ailments, and that he had an addiction to alcohol if not to opiates. Sources as varied as Frederick Bates, Gilbert Russell, John Neelly, and Priscilla Grinder attested to his "deranged" behavior, and his greatest friends, Thomas Jefferson and William Clark, had no difficulty in believing he killed himself.

(Bernard DeVoto called Lewis "mercurial," and said he was introspective, temperamental, sentimental, withdrawn, and solitary.)

These factors, however classic a pattern of a potential suicide, are too circumstantial for many who have looked into the Lewis tragedy.

In recent times a Seattle epidemiologist, writing in a medical journal, put forth the theory that Lewis may have killed himself because he was dying of paresis, the terminal phase of syphilis (which affects the brain), contracted from a Shoshoni Indian woman in 1805 during the continental crossing.

(The expedition did encounter venereal disease among the Indian tribes of the Upper Missouri and indeed, Clark, using the mercury compounds that were the specific of the era, treated a number of the Corps members who contracted it.)

If Lewis ever received or self-administered a mercuric treatment, traces of it might be found with his remains. James E. Starrs, the celebrated forensic scientist at Georgetown University, would like to open Lewis's grave at the Natchez Trace monument and examine the remains. But the eminent historian Stephen E. Ambrose, whose biography of Lewis, *Undaunted Courage,* was published in 1996, is opposed to any exhumation plans. Ambrose's conviction is that Lewis was a suicide and that the most convincing evidence of it is that "Neither Jefferson nor Clark ever doubted that Lewis killed himself." The biographer states that if Clark had any suspicion of murder he would have gone to Tennessee to personally investigate the matter and that if Jefferson had any such suspicion he would have insisted the government launch an investigation.

"There is simply no question whatsoever about how he died," the biographer told *USA Today* in October 1995. "Let him rest."

But in fact there *is* a question about how Meriwether Lewis died—a question no one, 187 years after the fact, can answer with certainty.

3

The Life and Deaths of Sacajawea

The Bird Woman in 1812 and 1884

When Meriwether Lewis and William Clark first saw her that winter of 1804 she was a pregnant sixteen-year-old Shoshoni girl living among the Mandans of the Upper Missouri River with her French-Canadian husband Toussaint Charbonneau. From that moment, and for sixteen months thereafter, we have fleeting glimpses of her, recorded in the explorers' journals: an indomitable figure, her baby securely lashed to a cradleboard on her back, moving through the forests gathering herbs and wild vegetables; in camp dressing game, making moccasins, mending clothes, nursing the sick and injured; in the villages serving as interpreter and intermediary for the white men among tribes as varied and unpredictable as the Lakota, Arikara, Hidatsa, Shoshone, Nez Perce, Cayuse, Flathead, Wishram, Skilloot, Clatsop, Cathlamet, Walla Walla, and Blackfoot.

But for all her inestimable contributions to the greatest over-land exploration in our history, her status as the "Madonna of the Lewis and Clark Expedition," she is a shadowy figure in our history and all the images we have of her are blurred.

Even in death, perhaps at age twenty-four, perhaps at age ninety-six, she eludes us.

The twenty-eight-month epic journey of exploration known as the Lewis and Clark Expedition may be said to have begun in Paris on April 30, 1803, when President Thomas Jefferson's minister to France, Robert Livingston, signed a document, shook hands with his French counterparts, and announced, "We have lived long, but this is the noblest work of our lives."

The paper, perhaps the most consequential in American history excepting only the Declaration of Independence and the U.S. Constitution, called for the payment of $15 million in exchange for France's Louisiana Territory. This tract, over half a billion acres of wilderness, doubled the size of the United States with the stroke of a pen. It comprised the lands between the Mississippi and the Rocky Mountains as far north as present-day Montana and North Dakota, and including the states-to-be of Louisiana, Arkansas, Oklahoma, Missouri, Kansas, Iowa, Nebraska, and South Dakota, plus most of Wyoming and Montana and portions of Minnesota, North Dakota, New Mexico, and Colorado.

Three months before the treaty signing in Paris, Jefferson, supremely confident of gaining these great and largely unexplored lands and electrified by their potential, sent a secret message to Congress in which he shared his plans to explore the lands west of the Mississippi "even to the Western Ocean." He asked for and received an appropriation of $2,500 to finance a military expedition to assert U.S. claims to the Territory and to explore a route "across the continent, for the purpose of commerce."

And just over a year from the Paris signing, Jefferson named his private secretary to lead the expedition. Meriwether Lewis, a Virginia neighbor of Jefferson's, was an intense twenty-nine-year-old captain of infantry who had served in the Whiskey Rebellion in 1794 and in General "Mad Anthony" Wayne's Ohio Indian campaign. He in turn sought out as his expedition co-leader his comrade-in-arms at the Battle of Fallen Timbers, William Clark. This burly, redheaded, six-foot-tall brother of that hero of the American Revolution in the Ohio Valley, George Rogers Clark, was a veteran artillery officer and Indian fighter.

The "Corps of Discovery," Lewis's name for the expedition, headed into the unknown from St. Louis on May 14, 1804, traveling up the Missouri River in a fifty-five-foot keelboat carrying a small cannon and two large blunderbusses, and two flat-bottomed canoes called pirogues. In addition to the co-leaders, Clark's slave York, and Lewis's Newfoundland dog "Seaman," the party consisted of forty-odd men—largely young unmarried soldiers (equipped with the latest in weapons, the Model 1803 .54 caliber flintlock musket)—plus boatmen and hunter-interpreters.

In the summer, crawling up the river in the cloying heat and humidity at the rate of fifteen miles a day, the explorers reached modern-day Nebraska in the lands of the greatest of the Plains tribes, the Lakota (Sioux). The expedition encountered no Indian problems until reaching the vicinity of what is today Pierre, South Dakota. There, in late September, a band of Teton Sioux led by their chief Tortohonga threatened Clark and attempted to seize one of the pirogues. Clark drew his sword and signaled his men to prepare for action. The swivel cannon was aimed at the Indians and for a moment time stood still—then, Tortohonga ordered his warriors away from the boat and the crisis passed.

Now, with the first bite of cold in the air, the captains made plans to winter among the Mandan villages of the Upper Missouri. In October they reached the mouth of the Knife River (near modern-day Washburn, N.D.) and there constructed a triangular-shaped log stockade, each side fifty-six feet long and seven feet tall, which they named Fort Mandan.

That winter, temperatures fell to forty-five degrees below zero but the commanders still managed to make good use of their time. Hunting and wood-cutting parties were sent out, boats, equipment, and clothing were mended, drawings and journal entries were made. Clark found a Mandan chief named Big White who claimed to know the lands to the west and with the expedition interpreter worked with the chief making tentative maps. Both Lewis and Clark met with delegations of Mandans, Minatarees (Hidatsas), and Arikaras who came in gaping curiosity to the strange log fort on the Missouri to see the white chiefs and to marvel over the black skin of Clark's trusted slave, York.

It was a Minataree visitor who told Clark a significant story: that the Shoshoni people (called "Snakes" by early white trappers) of the Rocky Mountains had a great many horses and might be persuaded to trade for some that could be used as pack animals for the portages through the mountain passes.

And Clark, on November 3, made a brief but momentous entry in his journal: "A Mr Chaubonie interpreter for the Gros Ventre nation Came to See Us." "Mr. Chaubonie" was a forty-six-year-old French-Canadian trapper named Toussaint Charbonneau who indeed lived among the Gros Ventre ("Big Belly," another name for the Minatarees or Hidatsas) and although he would prove to be accident-prone, a magnet for disaster, and a source of exasperation for the co-captain, he was hired on as intrepreter that winter. And into the bargain came a person who must have seemed to all who saw her an unlikely candidate to be a prized crew member. This was one of Charbonneau's wives, a slim, raven-haired, copper-skinned Shoshoni girl named Sacajawea ("Bird Woman" in her native tongue), who had been captured by the Minatarees at the age of eleven and who later had been sold to Charbonneau or won by him in a gambling game. She was about fiteen or sixteen years old, heavily pregnant, and anxious to travel upriver with the expedition to near the headquarters of the Missouri where she might rejoin her people. The co-captains recognized that she could prove invaluable in dealing with the Shoshoni for packhorses.

(Charbonneau had at least one other Indian wife at this time, Otter Woman, also a Shoshoni, and a son by her named Toussaint, about two years old. In years to come the two wives and their offspring would be fatefully confused.)

On February 11, 1805, at Ford Mandan, Sacajawea had a long and agonizing labor. Lewis, whose medical skills were improving out of the necessary rigors of the trail, talked with another of his interpreters, René Jusseaume. This man advised that a dose of crushed rattlesnake rattles would ease the girl's delivery. Lewis apparently had a rattler among his collected specimens (any snake would have been difficult to find in the winter) for he reported in his journal, "Having the rattle of a snake by me, I gave it to him [Jusseaume] and he administered two rings of it to the woman broken in small pieces. I was informed that she had not taken it more than ten minutes before she brought forth."

Sacajawea gave birth to a boy named Jean Baptiste but who Clark quickly nicknamed "Pomp" or "Pompey"—said to be a Shoshoni word meaning "first-born." Clark fell in love with "my boy Pomp" and spoiled the child all the way to the Pacific and back, as did other members of the crew who loved to bounce Pomp on their knees and sing and dance with him. Clark also had a high regard for Sacajawea, whose name he could not pronounce or spell. He called her "the Indian woman" and eventually "Janey" and was protective of her, on at least one occasion upbraiding Charbonneau for mistreating her.

With the ice on the Missouri thawed in the warming spring temperatures, the expedition departed Fort Mandan on April 7 to continue its journey up the Missouri. The thirty-three expedition members were distributed among six small canoes and two large pirogues, the lead "White Pirogue" carrying Sacajawea and her baby.

From the start, she not only earned her way but proved to be inspiring in her cheerful willingness to work. She gathered wild artichokes, berries, fruits, roots, and goose eggs, provided invaluable information on the country of her people, and demonstrated a great presence of mind in such incidents as that occurring on May 14 when one of the pirogues, with her husband at the helm, foundered in the river. Lewis was infuriated at

Charbonneau's handling of the boat, calling him "the worst steersman in the party" and "perhaps the most timid waterman in the world," while Clark recorded that "The Indian woman to whom I ascribe equal fortitude and resolution . . . caught and preserved most of the light articles which were washed overboard." Among the articles she managed to retrieve from the river were priceless navigational instruments and books.

On about June 10, near the Great Falls of the Missouri, Sacajawea fell gravely ill and Lewis administered his special brand of trail medicine: he bled her, applied "cataplasms"—poultices—of medicinal barks (which probably contained quinine) and fed her laudanum, then water from a sulphur spring. Lewis, who was himself unwell at this time, suffering from some unnamed illness that he treated with a strong tea made from chokeberry twigs, noted in his journal that his treatment of the "Indian woman" had good effect: "When I first came down I found that her pulse was scarcely perceptible, very quick, frequently irregular, and attended with strong nervous symptoms. . . . now the pulse has become regular, much fuller, and a gentle perspiration had taken place; the nervous system has also in great measure abated, and she feels herself much freer of pain."

She recovered, sleeping in her "bier"—a framework of twigs and branches draped with gauze to keep out mosquitoes and other insects—and resumed her work, carrying Jean Baptiste on her ever-present cradleboard.

The grueling month-long portage around the Great Falls led the expedition into the high country. As the Corps of Discovery neared the headwaters of the Missouri, Sacajawea was so familiar with the landmarks of her Shoshoni people—the "Lords of the Rocky Mountains"—that on July 28 she found the exact spot where, five years ago, she had been taken captive by the Minatarees of the Knife River country.

Lewis noted, "She does not . . . show any distress at these recollections, or any joy at the prospect of being restored to her country. For she seems to possess the folly or the philosophy of not suffering her feelings to extend beyond the anxiety of having plenty to eat and a few trinkets to wear."

In this, the explorer misread her entirely. He did not understand the natural reticence of the Indian, especially the Indian woman, to wear their emotions for all to see. As events were to demonstrate, Sacajawea, while perhaps apprehensive at the coming reunion with her people—were any of her relatives alive? would anybody remember her?—was, in fact, very happy to be home.

They pushed on toward a pass in the Bitterroot Mountains, crossed the Continental Divide by way of Lemhi Pass into present-day Idaho, and on August 11, 1805, sighted their first Shoshoni warrior, armed with a bow and quiver of arrows and handsomely mounted on a saddleless horse.

In a Shoshoni village a few days later, Lewis and his advance party were greeted in a friendly, if at first a somewhat cool and dubious, manner by the village elders. But the explorers distributed trinkets, had their cheeks painted with vermilion—emblematic of peace—and soon received the embraces of the villagers and shared the peacepipe in their lodges. Lewis later cynically noted, "We were all caressed and besmeared with their greasepaint until I was heartily tired of the national hug."

There were some tense moments at first. Chief Cameahwait told Lewis he had heard that the explorers were in league with a hostile tribe and had come to draw his people into an ambush. Apparently Lewis was able to fend off these concerns until Sacajawea arrived, on August 17 with Clark's rear guard, to translate.

Upon seeing her village for the first time in five years she could no longer contain her emotions, and she danced about and in sign language said, "This is my tribe!" Pennsylvania-born Patrick Gass, a Corps member who kept a journal, recorded that the Indians upon seeing her "were transported with joy."

Now the white chiefs sat with Cameahwait on a buffalo robe in a specially prepared bower smoking the ritualistic pipe and preparing for serious talks. Sacajawea was sent for to interpret and when she saw the chief, she ran to him and embraced him, weeping. Cameahwait was her brother.

In their talks with the chief, the captains explained that they came in peace but that the Shoshoni were now subject to Amer-

ican sovereignty. Cameahwait seems to have taken this odd declaration unquestioningly and in good spirits and pledged his help,
especially after learning that his lost sister had decided to continue on westward with her husband and baby.

Corps members formed hunting parties and killed deer and
antelope for the meat-starved Shoshonis and traded shirts, tobacco, and other goods for horses—twenty-nine of them in all.
On August 18, Lewis's thirty-first birthday, Clark rode out to
look at the Lemhi and Salmon rivers to determine if they were
navigable. Both waterways looked dangerous and he advised that
the journey must continue overland until tamer water could be
found.

On the twenty-ninth, the expedition, its gear loaded on
Shoshoni horses, set out again along the Lemhi. As they lum-
bered on at a snail's pace down the Clearwater, Snake, and Columbia rivers—the latter of which they reached on October
16—they encountered Nez Perce, Flathead, Skiloot, and other
potentially hostile tribes. But Sacajawea's presence, as Clark
wrote, "reconsiles all the Indians as to our friendly intentions."

The Corps of Discovery reached the Pacific Coast on November 8, 1805, after a journey of more than 4,000 miles. Seven
miles inland from the "Great Western Ocian" (as Clark, who
had only a nodding knowledge of spelling, called it), they built a
fifty-foot-square stockade, named it Fort Clatsop after a friendly
Indian tribe of the area, and settled down for the winter

The return journey began on March 23, 1806, and until July the
days passed relatively uneventfully. Sacajawea, always resourceful, gathered roots of the yampa plant and the yellow-flowered
fennel and found other edibles—berries, onions, and artichokes—to supplement the scurvy-inducing diet of venison and
bear meat.

In May, in Nez Perce country on the Clearwater, the baby
Pomp, now fifteen months old, fell ill with a swollen neck and
throat. Clark, who shared medical duties with Lewis, treated the
child with wild onions and a salve of resin, beeswax, and bear

grease that, amazingly, caused an improvement in the boy's condition.

In a little over three months from the Pacific the expedition reached the mouth of the Flathead (Bitterroot today) River at a point called Traveler's Rest. Here the commanders decided to split up, Lewis and nine men to explore north to the Marias to determine if that river provided a route into the Canadian fur country, Clark south to the Yellowstone. The two parties made plans to rendezvous at the juncture of the Yellowstone and Missouri, about 200 miles west of their 1805 winter quarters at Fort Mandan.

On July 3, Lewis headed north and Clark's party, consisting of York, Charbonneau, Sacajawea and her son, twenty men and fifty horses, marched up the north bank of the Gallatin River toward the Yellowstone. They traveled along the easternmost north-south ridges of the Rockies and along what became known as the Bozeman Pass, following Sacajawea's description of a trail her Shoshoni people had used. (Clark acknowledged her assistance in this leg of the journey by writing, "The Indian woman . . . has been of great service to me as a pilot through this country.")

Along the Jefferson River, Clark split his party, with some of the men driving the horse herd along the riverbank, the others descending the Yellowstone Valley on foot in search of timber to build boats. The foot-sore travelers reached the Yellowstone River (at a point near present-day Livingston, Montana) on July 15.

On the twentieth, some days before half of their horse herd was run off by a band of Crow Indians and at a point just below the future city of Billings, Clark's men located the trees they needed. They built two crude dugouts, eighteen feet long and sixteen inches deep, and lashed the two boats together. Clark, York, the Charbonneaus, Pomp, and all but three of the men boarded the raftlike vessel on the morning of the twenty-fourth while the others began driving the remaining horses along the river toward the rendezvous point.

The Yellowstone, or the Roche Jaune as French trappers

called the river, ran languidly under the blistering July sun. Clark was anxious to make his rendezvous at the headwaters of the Missouri but after a day of enervating work keeping the clumsy craft on course, he found the opportunity for his party to paddle to the shore and stretch their legs. Just past a slight northward bend in the river, the captain spotted a curious landmark jutting up from the shimmering bottomlands in the near distance, a "remarkable rock," he would record in his journal.

They all pushed ashore and set up a quick camp while Clark took a few men—and perhaps the ever-curious Sacajawea and her son—to see the remarkable rock. He measured its circumference at 400 paces and estimated the height at 200 feet. The grayish, gritty sandstone seemed to afford no opportunity for climbing, but on the northeast face of the bulwark, where a gully broke the uniform steepness, he found a way to the summit. With some of the others following, he climbed to the top and saw the Rocky Mountains to the southwest, the mountains later to be named the Little Wolf and the Bull, and, just below the rim of the rock on which he stood, the petroglyphs carved there by Indians in the unknown past.

On the way down, Clark saw more animal figures carved on the rock face and found a clear space for his own inscription. He carved into the soft sandstone:

Wm. Clark
July 25, 1806

Later, no doubt with a grin on his face and perhaps with a glance in the Indian woman's direction, he commemorated his beloved "son" as he wrote in his journal. "This rock . . . I shall call Pompy's Tower."

Nine days later, on August 3, Clark and his party reached the juncture of the Yellowstone and Missouri and set up camp. On August 12 Lewis's party arrived from their adventures in the Marias River country, where, in a fracas with Piegans of the Blackfoot confederacy, two Indians were killed—Lewis shooting one of them.

At Fort Mandan, where they had first met, the explorers departed from Charbonneau, Sacajawea, and little Pomp.

Clark paid Charbonneau a bit over $500 for his services to the expedition, presented to him and Sacajawea a medal bearing a likeness of Thomas Jefferson, and offered to take the interpreter and his family with him to St. Louis. Charbonneau declined the offer and Clark countered by proposing to take Pomp to the city and provide him a home and education. The tough Virginia frontiersman later wrote in his journal that Charbonneau and his Indian woman were "willing" to let the "butifull and promising child" go "provided the child had been weened." Charbonneau told Clark that in one year the child "would be sufficiently old to leave his mother."

Three days after their departure from Fort Mandan, Clark, at camp in an Arikara village downriver, wrote a letter to Charbonneau that contained an oblique apology for not providing a better reward to Sacajawea:

> You have been a long time with me and have conducted Your Self in Such a manner as to gain my friendship, your woman, who accompanied you that long dangerous and fatigueing rout to the Pacific Ocean and back, diserved a greater award for her attention and Services on that rout than we had in our power to give her at the Mandans.

He then repeated his offer to care for "my boy Pomp," saying, "you well know my fondness for him and my anxiety to take and raise him as my own child" and making Charbonneau a generous offer:

> if you wish to live with white people and will come to me I will give you a piece of land and will furnish you with horses, cows & hogs . . . if you wish to return as Interpreter for the Mennetarras . . . I will procure you the place—or if you wish to return to, trade with the Indians and will leave your little son Pomp with you, I will assist

you with merchandise for that purpose and become my-self concerned with you in trade on a Small scale.

Clark ended his plea to Charbonneau by saying, "If you are disposed to accept either of my offers, and will bring down your son, your famn [wife] Janey had best come along with you to take care of the boy until I get him."

He ended the letter, "Wishing you and your family great suck-cess & with anxious expectations of seeing my little dancing boy Baptiest I shall remain your friend, William Clark."

On September 23, 1806, the Corps of Discovery completed one of the most momentous explorations in world history. Clark wrote of the last of the 7,689 miles of their journey: "Descended to the Mississippi and down that river to St. Louis at which place we arrived at 12 o'clock. We suffered the party to fire off their pieces as a salute to the town."

In the city, now capital of Louisiana Territory, the explorers caught up on the news—Alexander Hamilton's death in a duel with Vice President Aaron Burr, Napoleon crowning himself Em-peror of France, the Battle of Trafalgar—and Meriwether Lewis hurried off a letter to his benefactor, President Jefferson: "In obe-dience to your orders we have penetrated the Continent of North America to the Pacific Ocean . . ."

Both Lewis and Clark received $1,228 and a 1,600-acre tract of Missouri land as a reward from the federal government for the successful conclusion of their expedition; other Corps of Dis-covery members received $166 in cash and 320 acres of land.

In February 1806, Meriwether Lewis was appointed governor of Upper Louisiana Territory. He died, under quite sinister cir-cumstances, in the Natchez Trace of Tennessee on the night of October 10–11, 1809.

William Clark also settled in St. Louis, as a brigadier general of the Louisiana Militia and superintendent of Indian Affairs for the Territory. He married Julia Hancock of Virginia in 1808 and the couple named their first child Meriwether Lewis Clark. In 1813 the general was named governor of Missouri Territory. He died in St. Louis on September 1, 1838.

Although the exact dates and details are either confused or not recorded, it appears that in the fall of 1806 William Clark realized his dream of caring for Jean Baptiste, the "butifull promising child" he called "Pomp," when Toussaint Charbonneau, Sacajawea, and their son came to St. Louis to visit the explorer.

(There is evidence that Charbonneau brought at least one other wife and perhaps one or two other of his children with him. At one time Clark noted in his diary that he paid school tuition for two of Charbonneau's boys. One of these was Jean Baptiste, the other may have been Toussaint, son of the lusty Charbonneau and another Shoshoni wife named Otter Woman. Further confusing the issue is the fact that Rene Jusseaume had a thirteen-year-old son, also named Toussaint, who was indentured to Clark in St. Louis in 1809. Charbonneau's other mates—he married Shoshoni, Minataree, Ute, and Assiniboine women and probably others—and the offspring of these "marriages," confuse the historical record to this day.)

Charbonneau took up one of Clark's offers and tried his hand at farming on a tract of Missouri land, but sold it back to his sponsor within a few months. After that he probably returned to the Hidatsa country along the Knife River, which was to serve as his pied-à-terre to the end of his life.

Jean Baptiste was apparently left in Clark's care when Charbonneau and Sacajawea returned home in 1807. Clark later provided another reason for their departure when he wrote, "The woman, a good creature, of mild and gentle disposition, was greatly attached to the whites, whose manners and airs she tries to imitate; but she had become sickly and longed to revisit her native country; her husband also, who had spent many years amongst the Indians, was become weary of civilized life."

Toussaint Charbonneau's life after 1807, and the place and time of his death, is shrouded in mystery. We catch a fleeting glimpse of him in March 1811, when he joined the jurist-traveler Henry

M. Brackenridge and fur trader Manuel Lisa on a Missouri River expedition. He took part in a trading expedition into New Mexico in 1816, and in June 1823, he cropped up when Paul William, Prince of Württemberg, made the first of his several expeditions in the American West and met Charbonneau, his wife (possibly Sacajawea), and son Jean Baptiste, then eighteen, at the mouth of the Kaw River in Kansas. Prince William, like William Clark, apparently became much devoted to Charbonneau and his family and shared with Clark an interest in seeing Sacajawea's son have a good education.

Charbonneau was seen often around the Knife River villages and survived the terrible smallpox epidemics that later decimated the tribes in the area. And he continued to serve as interpreter for the Indian Bureau at the Upper Missouri Agency until 1838, the year he is said to have married a fourteen-year-old Assiniboine girl. In 1839 Charbonneau, described by Superintendent of Indian Affairs Joshua Pilcher as "tottering under the infirmities" of his age (about eighty years by then), appeared in St. Louis to ask the Indian Bureau for salaries he claimed were owed him for services rendered to the U.S. government. He was paid and the transaction is the last we know of him.

Jean Baptiste continued his education under William Clark's care, probably at first with private tutors and later in fine private schools in St. Louis, into the early 1820s, and is said to have learned French and English, classic literature, history, mathematics, and science.

He returned periodically to the Upper Missouri to live with his parents and was there in the summer of 1823 when Prince Paul of Württemberg came wandering up the Missouri and persuaded Charbonneau and Sacajawea to let him take the young man to Europe. There Jean Baptiste stayed six years as a member of a royal household, receiving a classical education and becoming a capable linguist.

He returned to the Missouri in 1829, worked as a trapper in Idaho and Utah, traveled with such mountain legends as Jim

Bridger, Jim Beckwourth, and Joe Meek, and worked as a guide from Santa Fe to San Diego during the war with Mexico in 1846. He served briefly as *alcalde* (mayor) of Mission San Luís Rey in California and spent many years in the goldfields of the American River country around Sacramento. He was remembered as an intrepid mountain man, dependable guide, and a charming "man of two worlds," comfortable among Indians and whites alike.

Like his father and mother, the place, time, and manner of his death is a historical mystery. He may have died of pneumonia in Oregon in 1866, or may have spent his last years on the Wind River Shoshoni reservation with his mother, dying there in 1885, his body buried in the mountains in an unmarked grave.

The Bird Woman died on two occasions, seventy-two years apart.

Her first death occurred at Fort Manuel (named for the eminent fur trader Manuel Lisa) at the confluence of the Bighorn and Yellowstone rivers. There, a former Baltimore and St. Louis businessman named John C. Luttig, a clerk in the fur-trading fort, kept a daily journal. In it he mentioned Charbonneau, an interpreter at the fort, several times, mostly in vaguely derogatory terms. Luttig made his most important entry on December 20, 1812, when he wrote, "This evening the wife of Charbonneau, a Snake squaw, died of a putrid fever. She was a good and the best woman in the fort, aged about twenty-five years. She left a fine infant girl."

Charbonneau had apparently been away from the fort several weeks before his wife's death and had not returned when, in March 1813, Fort Manuel was burned to the ground by a raiding party of British soldiers and their Indian allies. Now, it was left to John Luttig to take the infant, named Lizette, to St. Louis. In the city he applied to the Orphan's Court to be named her guardian. Luttig, in addition to reporting the death of the baby's mother, must also have speculated that Lizette's father, Charbonneau, was also dead, for the clerk was granted guardianship of the child as well as for another of Charbonneau's children, "a boy about the age of ten years," named Toussaint.

The historical record is inadequate to explain it, but in August 1813, John Luttig's name was crossed out in the records of the Orphan's Court and William Clark's substituted. It may be that Luttig fell ill (he died in 1815) and sought out Clark to take over responsibilities for the children.

In any event, it appears that Clark did not at first believe Sacajawea was the "Snake squaw" Luttig reported to have died at Fort Manuel. He believed the woman who was buried in an unmarked grave near the fort to be another of Charbonneau's Shoshoni wives (Otter Woman) and that Lizette and little Toussaint had been born of that union.

Many years later, Clark seems to have readjusted his ideas. At some point between 1825 and 1828 he annotated a list of thirty-four Corps of Discovery members and beside the name "Se car ja we uh" he wrote the single word "Dead."

But did the Bird Woman die at Fort Manuel in 1812?

In the 1920s, Dr. Charles A. Eastman, an eminent authority on the Western Plains tribes, set out to answer the question.

His father a Santee Sioux and his mother half Sioux, Eastman was a Dartmouth graduate, an 1891 medical school graduate of Boston University, and author of nine books on the Indian tribes of the West when he began his investigation into Sacajawea's life and death for the Bureau of Indian Affairs.

He spent a year, much of it on the Wind River reservation and in North Dakota where he interviewed Mandans, Hidatsas, and others who had known Sacajawea. Although neither these tribes nor the Shoshonis had a written language, all had strong oral history traditions and Dr. Eastman was able to piece together a remarkable story of the Bird Woman's life after the Lewis and Clark Expedition.

The testimony related that Sacajawea left Charbonneau at some unknown time after suffering his beatings and that she spent many years wandering from tribe to tribe—as far as the

Assiniboines in Canada, the Kiowas, Wichitas, and Comanches in Kansas and Oklahoma, and at other times among the Nez Perce, Bannocks, Hidatsas, and Blackfeet. She spent many years with the Comanches (a tribe related to the Shoshoni), Eastman concluded, married a man of that tribe, and bore him five children. When her husband was killed in battle, the Comanches, who called her Porivo, gave her a new name: Lost Woman.

Eastman reported the Shoshoni tradition that Sacajawea eventually returned to her own people at Fort Washakie on the Wind River reservation and there became a beloved elder of her people, a woman who would proudly show the Jefferson medal given her by the white chiefs and speak of the time when she accompanied them west to the great ocean.

Shoshoni history, Eastman said, had Sacajawea reunited at Fort Washakie with her son Baptiste—Clark's "Pomp"—and that she lived out her long life with Baptiste and with Bazil, who Eastman believed was the son, originally named Toussaint, of Charbonneau and Otter Woman, who others believed was either Sacajawea's own child or the orphan son of her sister.

To the Commissioner of Indian Affairs in 1925 Eastman wrote "I report that Sacajawea, after sixty years of wandering from her own tribe, returned to her people at Fort Bridger and lived the remainder of her life with her sons in peace until she died April 9, 1884, at Fort Washakie, Wyoming. That is her final resting place."

In the 1930s, Grace Raymond Hebard, a teacher at the University of Wyoming, extended Eastman's research, interviewing many Shoshoni relatives of Sacajawea's, plus non-Indian agents and missionaries such as Reverend John Roberts who served the Shoshonis for fifty years. Roberts knew Sacajawea in the last year of her life and presided over the Christian services at her burial in 1884. The missionary said of her, "The old lady was wonderfully active and intelligent, considering her age. . . . She walked alone and was bright to the last."

She was buried, Roberts said, in the "white man's cematary" at Fort Washakie.

Baptiste, Shoshoni tradition has it, died the year after his

mother and was buried between two crags in the Wind River
Mountains.

Bazil died in 1886 and was buried beside Sacajawea.

Traces remain.

Pompey's Pillar lies twenty-eight miles northeast of Billings,
Montana, off Interstate 94. William Clark named it "Pompy's
Tower" but for some unrecorded reason the landmark was re-
named "Pompey's Pillar," perhaps in some vague association
with the Pompey's Pillar in ancient Egypt.

A railed wooden walkway leads the visitor to a landing,
about halfway to the top, near which is located Clark's inscription on the rock, protected by a thick screen of lucite but clearly
readable: "Wm. Clark, June 25, 1806."

There is a grave marker for Sacajawea at the Fort Washakie
cemetery near the Wind River valley town of Lander, Wyoming.

And, in Portland, Oregon, a magnificent statue of her was un-
veiled in 1905, the centennial of the year she joined the great expedition.

The sculpture depicts a beautiful girl in buckskins, her outstretched arm pointing the way, her baby—Jean Baptiste, baby
Pomp—serene in his cradleboard on her back.

4

The Man Who Would Be
Jesse James

J. Frank Dalton vs. DNA

On July 18, 1995, a backhoe punched through the grass on Jesse James's grave at Mount Olivet Cemetery in Kearney, Missouri. For three days a team of forensic experts spaded, troweled, and brushed their way to the disintegrated wooden coffin and picked among pieces of skull, miscellaneous other bones, teeth, cloth, and bullet fragments.

The bones and teeth were especially important: they contained deoxyribonucleic acid—DNA—that unique genetic material scientists use as a biological "fingerprint," and the forensics people wanted to learn if that was really Jesse buried in Jesse's grave these past 113 years.

Fifteen high-powered scientists puttering around in a famous outlaw's grave in a small Missouri town cemetery to learn something everybody already knew?

Actually, there are people who say Jesse lived sixty-nine years after he was supposedly killed by that "dirty little coward" Bob Ford; a lot of people who believe the real Jesse is buried in a graveyard in Texas under a stone marker reading "Jesse Woodson James, Sept. 5, 1847–August 15, 1951."

In a 1949 speech in Missouri, President Harry Truman gave a nod to another of his state's favorite sons in remarking, "Jesse James was a modern-day Robin Hood. He stole from the rich and gave to the poor, which, in general, is not a bad policy."

The offhand statement from "Give 'Em Hell" Harry, not bad politics but poor history, was a reflection of a genuine and long-standing myth about Jesse James: that he was the American rendition of that twelfth-century English folk hero. The Robin Hood legend is the tale of a man driven to outlawry by the persecution of a corrupt government; a fun-loving, noble man on horseback who steals from the rich and gives to the poor, the oppressed and the exploited, and who is betrayed by a traitor in his midst.

Robin Hood probably never really existed except in Middle English folklore and aside from an occasional flash of humor and the traitor-in-his-midst part, Jesse James's role as Robin Hood is a similar fabrication. From their first bank robbery, in Liberty, Missouri, in February, 1866, and for fifteen years thereafter, Jesse and his "merry men" took part in perhaps a dozen bank jobs (many in Jesse's own stamping grounds, banks where his neighbors kept their money), about seven train robberies, four stagecoach holdups, and miscellaneous other crimes. At least a dozen citizens were killed in these exploits and another ten innocents wounded.

There is no evidence that any of the loot was distributed anywhere except among his gang members.

Jesse James stole from the rich and the poor and kept the proceeds.

His father, Robert Sallee James, a farmer and Baptist preacher, graduated from Georgetown College, Kentucky, in 1843, two years after he met Zerelda Elizabeth Cole at a revival meeting and married her. The couple settled on a 275-acre farm near Kearney, Clay County, Missouri, and there Zerelda gave birth to four children: Alexander Franklin ("Frank") on January 10, 1843; Robert (who lived only thirty-three days) on July 19, 1845; Jesse Woodson on September 5, 1847; and Susan Lavinia on November 25, 1849.

Reverend James earned prominence in the Kearney community as an industrious and respected man. He preached the Gospel, founded two churches and a college, organized revival meetings and baptismal services, and ran a good farm with the slaves he brought with him from Kentucky. In 1850, perhaps asked to serve as a sort of chaplain to the Missouri argonauts and no doubt hoping to improve his family's fortunes, the reverend joined a Clay County wagon train headed for the gold diggings in California. Little is known of this adventure except that he died in a Placerville gold camp on August 18, 1850, and was buried in an unmarked grave.

Zerelda James, faced with raising three small children alone, married a neighboring farmer in 1852. Then, after this man was killed in a horse accident, wed again in 1855, this time to a kindly country physician and farmer, Dr. Reuben Samuel. He was to sire four children of his own with Zerelda and he became the only father little Susan and the James brothers ever knew.

Clay County, where the James children grew up, lay in the turbulent Missouri-Kansas frontier. It was in this region, in 1855, that abolitionists such as John Brown were leading raids into Missouri, burning crops and barns, stealing slaves and returning them to Kansas and freedom.

Zerelda James Samuel, by any standard a formidable, enduring rock of a frontier woman, was a Kentuckian and a slave owner and with the coming of the Civil War, her sympathies were solidly with the Southern cause. It came as no surprise then, that in May 1861, when he was eighteen, Frank James enlisted as a Confederate volunteer. He fought under General Sterling Price, the pre-war governor of the state, in the battle of Wilson's Creek in southwest Missouri on August 10, 1861, and after a brief period home, left again to fight the war on a different front: he joined forces with William Clark Quantrill, the Ohio-born former schoolteacher and now a hate-filled psychopath who was leading a band of Missouri farm boys and turning them into the bloodiest guerrilla force of the Confederacy. Frank and a newfound friend, seventeen-year-old Thomas Coleman "Cole" Younger, from Lee's Summit, Missouri, were with Quantrill in August 1863, during the most heinous act of the war, the raid on Lawrence, Kansas, during which the town was sacked and more than 150 of its citizens, most of them noncombatants, murdered.

Just three months before the Lawrence raid, a party of Union troops invaded the Samuel farm in Clay County looking for information on the location of Quantrill's camp. Fifteen-year-old Jesse was questioned, then horsewhipped when he refused to answer questions. Dr. Samuel, who also denied any knowledge of the guerrilla leader, was dragged from his home and repeatedly hanged from a tree in his yard as the Federals tried to extract a confession from him. He survived but his mind was so affected by the ordeal that he eventually had to be placed in an asylum in St. Joseph. (He remained there until his death in 1908.)

Jesse, a skinny sixteen-year-old with a festering hatred of the Union, early in 1864 joined a bushwhacker band under the notorious Quantrill lieutenant William "Bloody Bill" Anderson, a seasoned outlaw even before the war began. Jesse took part in the battle at Centralia, Missouri, on September 27, 1864, when twenty-five unarmed Union soldiers, many of them prisoners, were shot down, and was credited with killing Major A.V.E. Johnson, a Federal officer who led 100 men in pursuit of Anderson's band.

Jesse's Civil War service with Quantrill included fighting in support of Colonel Jo Shelby's brigade in northwest Arkansas, at Cane Hill near the Indian Territory border, and at Big Cabin Creek in Indian Territory. His service ended in the spring of 1865 when he rode into Lexington, Missouri, carrying a white flag, and was shot in the chest as he attempted to surrender.

With the war's end he went to Rulo, Nebraska, where his family had resettled, to recuperate from his wound, then returned to Missouri. There, near Kansas City, where his aunt operated a boardinghouse, he fell in love with his cousin, Zerelda (named for Jesse's mother) Mimms, who nursed the young guerrilla fighter back to health.

In 1866, a war-weary, wounded veteran at age nineteen, Jesse had reached adulthood early and the physical and character traits that won Zerelda Mimms's heart were not to change overmuch in the sixteen years he had left to live. He stood five feet nine in height and weighed 135 pounds. He had notably small hands and feet, sandy-red hair, and crystallike blue eyes. He dressed immaculately. He was likable, extroverted, enjoyed a good practical joke, and retained a moderate amount of Baptist piousness. He sang in church choirs, his Bible was said to be well thumbed, and he did not use the Lord's name in vain. (When in rage or pain he shouted his own made-up cuss word, "Dingus!" and it became his brother Frank's and close friends' favorite nickname for him. Frank was called "Buck" by family and friends.)

But while he observed at least some of the Commandments, Jesse did not always keep the Sabbath; he used it on at least one occasion for an armed robbery.

There is some question whether or not Jesse was actually involved in the nation's first peacetime bank robbery, that which occurred at the Clay County Savings Association Bank in Liberty, Missouri, on February 13, 1866, but if he was not present physically, he was there in spirit with his brother Frank, and Cole and Jim Younger. This first James-Younger robbery was a huge success—the take was $60,000, a considerable fortune in 1866— even though it resulted in the death of the first of several innocents caught in the gang's gunplay. A college boy named George C. Wymore died in the crossfire in the street as the outlaws made their escape.

With the gang now hunted by lawmen and with Jesse needing a drier climate to recuperate from his weakened lung, the hiatus after the Liberty robbery provided the James brothers an opportunity to distance themselves from their reward posters. Using the bank loot for funds, Jesse traveled to New York that spring of 1866 and took passage to Panama, crossing the Isthmus by train and on to California by sailing vessel. Frank journeyed overland and the two rendezvoused in San Francisco. The brothers tried to locate their father's grave around the Placerville area, failed to find it but used their time to visit their uncle, who ranched near Paso Robles, near where Jesse took mineral baths to improve his health.

By the time the Jameses returned east, avoiding Missouri and rejoining the Youngers in the Kentucky-Tennessee border area, they were being blamed for a spate of bank robberies that occurred during their absence. So, as if to live up to their press clippings, on March 20, 1868, they robbed a bank in Russellville, Kentucky, of $14,000. In the heat of the heist, Cole Younger shot and wounded the bank president in the head.

The brothers spent most of 1868–1869 in the Nashville area, Jesse using the name John Davis Howard and Frank identifying himself as Ben Woodson, the two posing as grain dealers and horse buyers. In fact, their involvement with horses consisted of indulging their passion for playing the ponies at racetracks in Tennessee, Kentucky, Kansas, Iowa, and Illinois, and quickly running through their shares of bank job booty.

The two managed to return to Missouri and Kansas long enough to resume their courtships—Jesse with Zee Mimms, Frank with a Missouri farm girl named Annie Ralston. But for the twelve years between 1869 and 1881, they stayed on the move, often in partnership with the Youngers, sometimes leading an independent band of bank, train, and stagecoach bandits.

While most of the robberies attributed to the Jameses run to a tedious pattern, some were remarkable:

On December 7, 1869, Frank and Jesse robbed a bank in Gallatin, Missouri, a job that netted only $700 in cash but that resulted in the killing of a teller named John Sheets. It appears that Jesse had a grudge against Sheets, a former Union officer who may have been involved in the killing of Bill Anderson, and shot the clerk in the head and heart while pretending to conduct a bank transaction with him. The Gallatin robbery resulted in a $3,000 reward being posted for the brothers, now wanted for murder as well as armed robbery.

(It was after Gallatin that Jesse wrote the first of his several letters to newspapers, delivered by his mother, proclaiming his innocence. The Jameses, Zerelda prominent among them, waged a sort of public relations campaign throughout their outlaw careers, an effort that contributed immeasurably to their Robin Hood folk-hero image.)

In June 1871, the brothers robbed a bank in Corydon, Iowa, taking $6,000 in cash and negotiable bonds. An Iowa politician named Henry Clay Dean was making a speech to a large crowd outside the Methodist church as the outlaws rode out and Jesse is said to have stopped and told the candidate and crowd, "The fact is, Mr. Dean, some fellows have been over to the bank and tied up the cashier, and if you-all ain't too busy you might ride over and untie him. We've got to be going."

At the Kansas City Fairgrounds in September 1872, the gang seized a cash box amid a crowd of 10,000 fairgoers. A little girl was accidently shot in the leg in the melee but this did not prevent a local James apologist from writing in the newspaper that the robbery was "a feat of stupendous nerve and fearlessness that makes one's hair rise to think of it." The writer also used such words as "chivalric," "poetic," and "superb" and the newspaper likened the outlaws to the Knights of the Round Table. Later, one of the James-Younger gang, caught up in the Robin Hood fable promulgated by newspapers and dime-novel sensationalists, wrote a letter to a Kansas City newspaper saying, "We rob from the rich and give to the poor." Many believed it.

On July 21, 1873, the gang boarded an Iowa, Chicago, Rock Island and Pacific Railroad train near Adair, Iowa, killed the engineer, and took $26,000 from the passengers and express car.

At Gad's Hill, Missouri, in January 1874, five members of the gang barged into a train depot, held everybody at gunpoint, waited for the train, and robbed its passengers and express car. One of the Jameses left a note for police detailing the robbery and stating, "We prefer this to be published in the newspapers rather than the grossly exaggerated accounts that usually appear after one of our jobs."

On January 15, 1874, near Hot Springs, Arkansas, the band of brothers committed their first stagecoach robbery. The loot from passengers and strongbox has been variously estimated at from $1,000 to $8,000.

Jesse, perhaps hoping to retire from the owlhoot trail, married Zee Mimms on April 24, 1874, at Zee's sister's home in Kearney and took his wife on a honeymoon in Texas. Frank, who married Annie Ralston in Omaha in June that year, joined his brother there. Texas was also the home base of the Younger boys—Cole, Bob, and Jim—and their gang member Jim Reed (who in 1866 had married Myra Belle Shirley, later the celebrated "bandit queen" Belle Starr).

Bankers and railroad owners had hired Alan Pinkerton's famous national detective agency as early as 1871 to pursue and arrest the James gang and it infuriated the Scotsman (whose byword was "I do not know the meaning of the word 'fail' ") that his agents had failed to locate, let alone arrest, a single James, Younger, or cohort. Nor did his temper improve when he learned that during the Gad's Hill train holdup, one of the gang had asked the conductor, "Where is Mr. Pinkerton?"

Now occurred the incident that destroyed any notions the James boys may have had of retiring from their outlaw trade. Pinkerton had an agent posing as a field hand posted on a farm across the road from the Samuel place near Kearney and in January 1875, the agent thought he spotted Jesse and Frank at the farmhouse, visiting their mother. The boys were, in fact, many miles from Kearney at the time but on January 26 a force of Pinkerton detectives, brought in by special train, surrounded the

Samuel farmhouse and tossed an incendiary device through the window. The bomb exploded and shrapnel from it struck and killed eight-year-old Archie Peyton Samuel, Zerelda and Reuben's son and Jesse's half brother. The blast also mangled Zerelda's right forearm so badly it had to be amputated at the elbow.

The Pinkertons later said the device was a flare, intended to light up the darkened house but others were not so sure and many newspaper accounts plainly labeled the device a bomb. (Modern researchers have found papers in the Library of Congress that seem to prove the Pinkerton "device" was in fact a grenade-type bomb, obtained from the Rock Island, Illinois, arsenal.)

Newspaper coverage of the incident elevated the James boys beyond mere knight- or Robin Hood-dom—to martyrdom.

Since it was unsafe to be near Kearney and their injured mother, Jesse took his wife to Tennessee and leased a farm near the town of Waverly. There, on August 31, 1875, their son Jesse Edward was born. Later, after the Northfield raid, Zee James gave birth to twin boys but they lived only a few weeks and were buried on the Waverly farm.

In August 1876, with the Waverly farm used as a staging area, Frank and Jesse, the three Younger brothers, and three other outlaws—Quantrill veterans Clell Miller and Charlie Pitts and a Minnesotan named Bill Chadwell—took a train tour of Minnesota, lured there by Chadwell's tales of easy takings at his home state's banks. Posing as cattlemen they gambled and visited a whorehouse in St. Paul, bought horses and saddles, and then split up, rendezvousing in the southern Minnesota town of Mankato, about fifty miles north of the Iowa line, whose main bank Chadwell considered an easy mark.

But somebody recognized Jesse in Mankato and the job was called off. The eight outlaws then rode in pairs fifty miles northeast toward Northfield. They met on the outskirts of the town on September 6, rode in, and after a cursory "casing" of the First National Bank, made plans to rob it the next morning.

They trotted into Northfield wearing long linen dusters over their clothes and side arms. Jesse, Bob Younger, and Charlie Pitts crossed the iron bridge over the Cannon River, split off from the others, and without drawing attention, they studied the town square, particularly the bank and its neighboring buildings—a drugstore, a mercantile building, a hotel. The three men ate a leisurely breakfast at a nearby restaurant, then rode to the bank and tied their horses on the rail in front of it. With perfect timing, as they tended the horses, the other five gang members came riding up, firing their six-guns in the air, shouting and hollering and scattering bystanders on the street and sidewalks. During this commotion, Jesse and his two companions charged into the bank, guns drawn. Jesse clubbed a cashier on the head with his pistol while Bob Younger kept other bank employees on their knees and under guard while he cleaned out the tills of coins and bills. One clerk ran out the back door and was shot and wounded by Charlie Pitts.

Meantime, in front of the bank, the five outlaws serving as lookouts found themselves under fire from citizens drawing arms from hardware stores along the street. Clell Miller was struck by shotgun pellets and a rifle bullet and fell dead from his horse. A passerby was shot dead by one of the now-panicky lookouts. Inside the bank, Jesse killed the cashier he had knocked to the floor as the three inside men made their way to the door.

In the street the seven desperadoes were caught in a lethal crossfire. Bill Chadwell was shot off his horse and died as he hit the ground. Cole Younger took a bullet in the shoulder. Frank James was hit in the leg. A bullet struck Jim Younger in the face and Bob Younger's horse was shot from under him, another bullet striking him in the thigh and a shotgun blast disabling his right arm as his brother Cole pulled him onto his horse.

The Northfield "raid" was over in under twenty minutes and the six surviving outlaws—four of them wounded—clattered across the iron bridge and fanned out into the woods. With a posse on their trail, they managed to rendezvous at a point between Northfield and Mankato. Jesse and Frank rode off together at night, stole fresh horses along the way, and headed for Dakota Territory. The Youngers were captured east of Mankato a week after the raid. In the shootout with the posse, Charlie Pitts was killed and the Youngers, all wounded, surrendered and were subsequently sentenced to life terms in prison.

Jesse and Frank managed a few more jobs with a Younger-less gang, over the next five years—a $40,000 take from a train robbery at Glendale, Missouri; a stagecoach holdup near Mammoth Cave, Kentucky; a government payroll taken at Muscle Shoals, Alabama—but the Northfield fiasco had marked the beginning of the end for the James boys.

In 1879 Jesse, Zee, and their son moved from the Waverly farm to Nashville and stayed for a time with Frank and Annie. That year Zee gave birth to a daughter, Mary Susan, and Jesse took his family to the Mimms home in Kansas City. On Christmas Eve 1881, he moved to St. Joseph where he rented a house under the name Thomas Howard. The return to Missouri was accomplished quietly despite a $10,000 reward offered for his capture by Missouri governor Thomas T. Crittenden.

Jesse, now thirty-four, had a fifteen-year career as an outlaw behind him and little to show for it. So, he planned one final robbery to obtain enough money to purchase land in Nebraska and retire with Zee and the children to the life of a gentleman farmer.

With the Youngers in prison and Frank dodging the law in Tennessee, Jesse took two new gang members, Bob and Charley Ford, sons of a Ray County, Missouri, farmer, into his confidence in the planning to rob the Platte City Bank in Kansas City.

On April 3, 1882, Jesse and the Fords discussed the bank job at the James house at 1318 Lafayette Street in St. Joseph. Jesse then relaxed in his parlor reading the morning paper that contained a story that Dick Liddil, a James-Younger gang member and friend of the Ford brothers, had surrendered. There was some discussion of that while Zee worked in the kitchen. After breakfast, Jesse returned to the parlor, removed his gunbelt, and resumed reading the paper. Soon after, Charley Ford walked out into the backyard while Bob remained in the parlor nervously making small talk with Jesse.

At about 8:30 A.M., Jesse glanced up from his newspaper and

noticed that a needlepoint picture, sewn by his mother, was hanging crookedly on the wall. He picked up a feather duster and moved a cane chair to the wall and stood on it to straighten and dust the picture, his back to the room.

Bob Ford's moment had arrived. He pulled his .38 Smith & Wesson revolver (it may have been a Colt .44 or .45, the stories vary) and shot Jesse just below the right ear.

The gunshot echoed through the house and two James children were first to reach their father. Zee followed and knelt beside Jesse, trying to stanch the flow of blood from his head. Bob Ford meantime had fled to the backyard and vaulted the fence as Zee shouted after him, "Bob Ford, what have you done!" Charley lamely tried to explain the shooting as an accident, then ran off to join his brother.

In a few minutes, law authorities arrived at the Lafayette Street home—Sheriff Timberlake, St. Joseph marshal Enos Craig, and others—and Zee at first tried valiantly to keep up the pretense that her dead husband was the businessman Tom Howard. The Ford brothers soon returned, however, and Zee, from that moment on, believed that the assassination of her husband had been part of a plot, perhaps staged by Governor Crittenden, with the Fords the key conspirators. This belief was validated for Zee James when the Ford brothers were quickly pardoned by Crittenden and, so it was believed, awarded the $10,000 bounty on Jesse's head.

A coroner's inquest opened on April 4. Zerelda Samuel arrived in St. Joseph by train and, along with Zee and others, formally identified the body. An autopsy was then performed by Dr. Jacob Geiger, a professor of surgery at the Missouri College of Physicians, and the fatal bullet removed from Jesse's skull (the surgeon had to remove the brain to find it). The coroner's verdict surprised no one: "he came by his death by a wound in the back of his head caused by a pistol shot fired intentionally by the hand of Robert Ford."

Jesse's body was packed in ice and taken by train to Kearney where it was placed on display and where hundreds of friends and admirers—including many old Quantrill veterans—filed by for a last farewell. Services were then held at the First Baptist Church, the ceremony including the singing of Jesse's favorite hymn, "What a Friend We Have in Jesus."

He was buried on the Samuel farm with only close family members present. The seven-foot-deep grave lay near Zerelda's front door so that she could keep an eye out for intruders and souvenir hunters. She had a stone made for the grave, the inscription on which read:

In Loving Remembrance of My Beloved Son
JESSE JAMES
Died April 3, 1882
Aged 34 Years, 6 Months, 28 Days
Murdered by a Traitor and Coward Whose
Name is Not Worthy to Appear Here

Later, when Zerelda could no longer manage living alone and moved into Kearney, her son's body was reburied, on July 29, 1902, at Mount Olivet Cemetery in the town. Zee had died in November 1900, and Jesse was placed next to her grave. Jesse Edwards James, Jesse and Zee's only son, supervised the 1902 exhumation and after four hours of digging, a rainstorm turning the ground into a muddy gumbo, the wooden coffin was uncovered. When it was opened and the remains removed, Jesse's skull rolled back into the grave. Before the skull was placed in a metal box, Jesse Edwards studied it, noting a bullet hole and gold fillings in some of the teeth.

The *Kansas City Times* reported on June 30, 1902, that Jesse's remains were placed into a new coffin and "As it fell, [the corpse] collapsed utterly. The ribs sank in, the hands fell apart, the trousers flattened out, the stocking-shod feet shrank to nothing." The *Times* writer said the new coffin was too short for the remains and that "the bones of the feet were doubled back" to make them fit.

Frank James was present at the reburial of his brother. He had surrendered to Governor Crittenden in Jefferson City, the Missouri capital, on October 5, 1882. Despite the efforts of the state's attorneys, all cases against Frank collapsed for lack of evidence and were dismissed. He worked at various honest jobs, including brief stints on the stage and in circuses, and in 1903 joined in partnership with Cole Younger (who had been paroled in July 1901) in the James-Younger Wild West Show. Frank James died at age seventy-two on the James farm in Kearney on February 18, 1915.

Bob Ford, "the dirty little coward who shot Mr. Howard" of the celebrated rhyme and song, was forced to leave Missouri after being pardoned by Governor Crittenden. He wandered throughout the West, part of the time performing in a stage show about the James boys. In a saloon in Creede, Colorado, on June 8, 1892, he was shot and killed by an ex-policeman named Ed O. Kelly.

Ten years earlier Charley Ford killed himself in Richmond, Missouri.

Eleven days after Jesse was buried the first time, the Liberty, Missouri, *Tribune* reported: "Certain parties still aver that Jesse James is not dead, and intimate that the man killed and buried was not Jesse, but someone inveigled into Jesse's house and killed, to get the reward." The story pointed out that such a plot would have had to involve Zee James and her children, Zerelda James Samuel, Sheriff Timberlake, Marshal Craig, Dr. Geiger, and many others who saw the corpse and heard the testimony about its identity. The newspaper disavowed such a fantasy and announced, "We believe nothing of the kind and have no doubt of Jesse's death."

Others continued to have doubt, however, and the patent impossibility of such a conspiracy as it would have taken to fake the death and burial of Jesse James did not stop the rumors. Nor, as time passed, did such a realization prevent a host of strange men from emerging from the shadows of obscurity to announce that indeed, they had buried the wrong man back in '82.

Jesse Edward James kept track of these imposters and had knowledge of twenty-six of them. Robert James, son of Frank and Annie James, often laughed about having "eleven Uncle Jesses since 1882."

One of the most notorious of the Jesse James claimants was a man who gave his name as John James. As a horse trader in Illinois in 1926, he had killed a man from whom he had borrowed fifty cents and spent time in Menard Penitentiary. In prison, it appears, John James read deeply into Jesse's life and constructed a marvelous story, one that contained an important element that would outlast even his own twenty years of claiming to be Jesse James.

John James told of a Missouri outlaw named Charley Bigelow, a man about Jesse's size and general apearance, who had pulled off several robberies and left evidence that they were the work of Jesse James and his gang. Somehow Bigelow was lured to St. Joseph and on April 3, 1882. Jesse killed him, took the body to his home, and laid it out on the parlor floor. Zee James, the story went, spattered chicken blood on her dress and arranged for Bob Ford to shoot a hole in the wall and for Charley Ford to run for the law.

Zee, Zerelda, and all the family were in on the plot, and Jesse fled town, ending up in Argentina where he spent several years before returning to the U.S. where he took the name John James.

In the 1930s, apparently certain that crimes committed fifty or sixty years ago had fallen to a statute of limitations, John James began making "Jesse James Alive!" appearances, telling his tales on the road to crowds of rubes and Jesse-as-Robin-Hood true believers. Occasionally, he met his match, as in the case of a lecture he gave in Exelsior Springs, Missouri, too close to Jesse's home grounds. There, a lady in the audience stood up and announced, "If you truly are Jesse James, I have a pair of Jesse's boots here for you to try on." The boots were size seven and a half, Jesse's diminutive foot size; John James's feet didn't fit and he was laughed out of town.

The lady in the audience was Annie James, Frank's widow.

John James died in an Arkansas mental hospital on December 24, 1947.

Six months later, Jesse showed up again.

❧

The most acclaimed of the Missouri outlaw's claimants was a man named J. Frank Dalton who cropped up in Lawton, Oklahoma, in May, 1948, sixty-six years after they laid Jesse James in his grave.

Apparently unrelated to the Frank Dalton who served as a U.S. deputy marshal in the Cherokee Nation nor to any of the other Daltons who terrorized Kansas and Indian Territory in the 1890s, J. Frank was reported to be 101 years old when he made his debut in Lawton. Whatever his real age, his promoters managed to cram a lot of activity into the three years he had yet to live.

Dalton went public under the tutelage of a man named Orvus Lee Howk (it gets confusing here) who had his own claim: that he was the grandson of Jesse James, his real name Jesse Lee James III, and that therefore he had unique qualifications to be able to say with certainty that Dalton was his, Howk's, grandfather, Jesse James.

The old man, it turned out, did have a considerable knowledge of the Quantrill era and of the James and Younger boys and so Oklahoma newspapers gave him plenty of ink. Soon the story found its way into the national press and was given a rare boost by one of the most widely read and respected of syndicated columnists of the day, Robert Ruark (later author of the best-selling novels about Africa, *Something of Value* and *Uhuru*).

After interviewing Dalton in Stanton, Missouri, Ruark wrote three lengthy columns in the New York *World Telegram* in July 1949, in the course of which he made it clear that he bought Dalton-as-Jesse part and parcel. Ruark, who in his columns called Dalton "Uncle Jesse," recounted the centenarian's story—a story borrowed liberally from that of the late Jesse claimant John James. Dalton also told of the unfortunate Charley Bigelow who, the old man said, "looked enough like me to be my own twin" and who was "using" Dalton's house in St. Joseph on that April day in 1882. Dalton's story contained a significant variation on John James's tale—it was Bob Ford who killed Bigelow. Dalton told Ruark:

One day I was out in my barn waterin' my horses when I
heard a gunshot in the house. When I heard the gun go
off, I knowed it wasn't no play-party because we argued
with guns in them days. I run into the house and there was
Bob Ford standing over Charlie Bigelow with a gun in his
hand and blood on the floor. I said to Ford, "Looks like
you killed him, Bob" and Bob says, "Looks like I did,
Jesse." Then I says, "Looks like my chance, Bob. You tell
'em it was me you killed. You call on my mother and say
so, and you take care of that Bigelow woman. I'm long
gone."

Dalton said he lit out on horseback to Kansas City, made his
way to Memphis, then to New Orleans, shipped out to Brazil,
kicked around South America for several years, came home via
Mexico, and settled first in Oklahoma, later in Texas, where he
taught school for a time and eventually adopted the name J.
Frank Dalton.

Ruark's columns caught the fancy of a wide audience and the
story took on new dimensions as the months passed.

The *Police Gazette,* an old "true crime" publication that in
the 1950s had become a counterpart to today's sensationalist
tabloids, interviewed Dalton and ran a list of Jesse James's scars,
wounds, and other identifying marks and reported that Dalton
had them all—and others.

Dalton and a Stanton, Missouri, promoter named Rudy
Turilli appeared on NBC's popular "We the People" radio program in January 1950.

And, on September 5, 1950, the 103rd birthday of Jesse
James, Turilli organized a huge promotion at Meramec Caverns
near Stanton, a place used as a hideout by the James-Younger
gang in its heyday. Present and on display in the caverns that
day were at least three self-proclaimed centenarians, two of them
supposed-dead outlaws: J. Frank Dalton, who, if Jesse James,
was 103; a 106-year-old man from Nashville named James R.
Davis who claimed to be Cole Younger (who had apparently
not died in 1916 at his home in Lee's Summit, Missouri, as his

family—and the history books—tells us); and a black man named John Trammell from Oklahoma, age 110, who said he had cooked for the James-Younger boys in the pre-Northfield days, knew them all, and could positively identify Dalton and Davis as the real articles.

Also present was Al Jennings, once a bona-fide Oklahoma bank robber, now in his nineties, who had his picture taken with Dalton and who also identified the old man as Jesse.

But despite the promotions and the "legitimacy" it was given by Ruark and others, Dalton's story began to crumble. The James family heirs, among others, would have no part of it. Stella James, wife of Jesse, Jr., traveled from her home in California to Missouri to challenge Dalton and the old man did not do well under her questioning. He could not, for example, remember Frank James's nickname ("Buck") and when Stella asked Dalton to try on Jesse's boots—the same fatal request made by Frank James's widow to claimant John James some years earlier—Dalton proved to wear size nines.

Another blow was struck by Homer Croy, author of *Jesse James Was My Neighbor* and an authority on the James family. Croy had interviewed Dalton in Lawton and said the old man had failed miserably to answer basic questions about Jesse and his kin.

Even Al Jennings, who had gone on record saying Dalton was Jesse, later told Jesse James biographer Carl Breihan that yes, he had said that. Then he added, "Why not? They paid me a hundred dollars!"

The costliest, if not the final, blow to the Dalton claim was visited upon promoter Rudy Turilli, the Meramec Cavern formerly-believed-dead outlaw reunion organizer. Turilli, in 1967, long after Dalton's death, wrote a crude book, *The Truth About Jesse James*, self-published it, and offered a $10,000 reward to anybody who could prove that J. Frank Dalton was not Jesse James. Stella James, Dalton's number one nemesis, and two of Jesse's grandchildren, challenged Turilli in a Franklin, Missouri, circuit court in May 1970. The verdict instructed Turilli to pay the $10,000 to the James family.

An appeals court refused to overturn the verdict but Turilli died in 1972 without ever paying the judgment.

J. Frank Dalton, the man who would be Jesse James, died on August 15, 1951, in a shack in Granbury, Texas. Orvus Lee Howk, aka Jesse Lee James III, the man who introduced Dalton to the world in May 1948, financed a tombstone for the old man's grave. The legend—and that is the proper word—read, "Jesse Woodson James, Sept. 5, 1847–August 15, 1951. Supposedly killed in 1882."

Forty-four years passed, during which time a sizable library on Jesse James and his era accumulated, few of the historians and biographers giving more than an amused sentence or two to that "other" Jesse James buried down in Granbury.

But the Dalton story, indeed the general view that somebody other than Jesse James was buried in that Mount Olivet plot, did not completely die (such things never do, completely) and so, in the summer of 1995, scientists, in keeping with a growing number of "historical exhumations" performed to prove or disprove some nagging theory or other, got into the act and dug Jesse up.

They had plenty of precedent:

- Lee Harvey Oswald's body was exhumed in 1981 to prove that a Soviet double agent hadn't been substituted for President Kennedy's assassin.
- In 1984, in Lima, Peru, a mummy said to be the body of Francisco Pizarro was removed from a cathedral and proven to be a fake; the real conquistador, stabbed to death in 1541, actually had been hidden away in a nearby crypt.
- The bones of Josef Mengele, the Nazi death camp doctor, said to have drowned in 1979, were exhumed in São Paulo, Brazil, and identified through medical records and photographic superimposition of the skull on photographs of Mengele.

• In 1991 the remains of President Zachary Taylor, who died in office in 1850, were dug up in Springfield, Kentucky, to test a theory that he had died of arsenic poisoning. (Toxicologists found no arsenic in the Taylor fragments.)

Jesse's remains were to undergo the high-tech perusal of that relatively new science of forensic anthropology that employs DNA experts, botanists, biologists, physicians, dentists, radiologists, biochemists, toxicologists, computer wizards, and other specialists. These scientists can examine human bones and determine age, sex, stature, handedness, diseases, and healed fractures, and make identifications based on matching postmortem findings with known antemortem data.

Of all the forensic investigator's tools, deoxyribonucleic acid (DNA)—that genetic "fingerprint" inherited from our parents—has been proven the most useful and irrefutable. DNA is unique in each human but the DNA of biological relatives has similarities and the DNA from human remains—bones and teeth in the case of the long-dead—can be compared to the DNA in the blood of known living descendants of the deceased to prove a biological relationship.

James E. Starrs, professor of law and forensic science at Georgetown University, is an authority on historical exhumations and a passionate proponent of answering historical mysteries through the use of DNA and the other forensic tools. With the permission of the James family and Clay County, Missouri, authorities and with a grant from his university, Starrs and a team of fifteen other scientists supervised the exhumation of Jesse James's remains in July 1995.

The dig at Mount Olivet Cemetery took three days, from a backhoe to break the ground to dry paint brushes and small trowels to uncover the coffin. Under the crushed glass faceplate and splinters of collapsed wood, Starrs and his assistants found over twenty skull fragments, portions of arm, leg, collar, and other bones, fourteen teeth (gold fillings in some), a .36 caliber slug, perhaps from an 1851 Navy Colt revolver, which may have been the bullet causing Jesse's Civil War chest wound, and a .38 caliber lead chunk showing damage consistent with having struck a bone. (Whether it is the bullet that killed Jesse is not known. Some historians insist Bob Ford used a Colt .45 to shoot Jesse in the back of the head.)

The coffin and remains were taken to a crime lab in Kansas City, then to Kansas State University for X-raying, cleaning, and cataloguing.

Bone samples, to be pulverized for DNA extraction, were sent to laboratories at Pennsylvania State University and to Cellmark Laboratories in Maryland, a company that became prominent during the O.J. Simpson murder trial in Los Angeles.

The testing involved mitochondrial DNA, found in a cell's cytoplasm and passed on generation to generation only through the maternal side of a family. Since Jesse's mitochondrial DNA, inherited from his mother, would not have been passed on by him to his own children, it was compared to descendants of his sister Susan, namely her great-grandsons, Robert Jackson, an Oklahoma City attorney, and Steven C. Benson of Maysville, Arkansas, both of whom agreed to provide blood samples for comparison.

On February 24, 1996, Professor Starrs brought his findings to the convention of the Academy of Forensic Sciences at the Opryland Hotel in Nashville, Tennessee. In a three-hour presentation, Starrs patiently placed the evidence before his fellow scientists and told how the mitochondrial DNA in the bones and two of the teeth from the exhumed remains in the grave at Mount Olivet Cemetery compared to blood samples from the two descendants of Jesse James.

"The eerie and unnatural elusiveness of Jesse James plainly qualifies him to be termed the Houdini of American outlaws," Starrs said. "The question this morning is whether Jesse James has carried his elusiveness beyond the grave."

The long-awaited answer came at last: the DNA testing

showed "better than a ninety-nine percent certainty" that the bones in Jesse James's grave were those of Jesse James.

In the audience during Starrs's presentation was Jesse James IV, an Austin, Texas, carpenter and great-grandson of J. Frank Dalton. "We're going back down to Texas to exhume that body," Jesse IV told reporters. "I'm going to get a different group of scientists and get a second opinion."

On October 27, 1995, while the DNA testing was still being conducted elsewhere in the country, Kelly Garbus, a reporter for the *Kansas City Star,* wrote, "Jesse Woodson James, 34, of St. Joseph, died April 3, 1882, of a gunshot to the head. He will be buried Saturday—for the third time—in Mount Olivet Cemetery in Kearney."

Even the reburial was controversial and laden with ironies.

- During the uncovering of the grave, around-the-clock security and crowd control became necessary. The company that volunteered its services? The Pinkerton Detective Agency, the organization that, over a century previously, had relentlessly pursued Jesse, Frank, and the Younger boys, and whose agents had killed Jesse's half brother in a raid on the Kearney farm.
- The Kearney First Baptist Church of which Jesse had been a member, rejected making the funeral arrangements for the third burial on the basis that they wanted no part of a "media circus."
- William Jewell College in Kearney, cofounded by Jesse's father, also rejected the funeral arrangements when the college's politically correct authorities learned that a Confederate flag ("a racially inflammatory symbol") would drape the casket and that Jesse's service in the Confederacy would be mentioned in the services.

And so, on Saturday, October 28, 1995, there were standing-room-only services for Jesse James at the Knights of Columbus

Community Center in Kearney, following which a horse-drawn hearse carried the casket, draped with the Stars and Bars, to the windswept slope of Mount Olivet. There, sermons were heard, prayers said, hymns sung—including Jesse's standby, "What a Friend We Have in Jesus."

Six hundred people—including reporters from several states and from France, Germany, England, Belgium, South Africa, Australia, and Canada—witnessed the final burial of Jesse James.

☙

What mystery remains?

None for those who believe DNA evidence irrefragable.

Some for those clinging to the one percent possibility remaining from Dr. James E. Starrs's "ninety-nine percent certainty" on the teeth (the bones were too degraded by ground water to yield a DNA result) at Mount Olivet.

And there are always these nagging scraps of contrary "evidence" cropping up, mysteries within mysteries.

For example, there is the letter Martha Jane Cannary wrote from Deadwood, South Dakota, to her daughter Jean, then living in England, in November 1889. In part, the letter said:

> I met up with Jesse James not long ago. He is quite a character—you know he was killed in '82. . . . He is passing under the name of Dalton but he couldn't fool me. I knew all the Daltons and he sure ain't one of them. He told me he promised his gang and his mother that if he lived to be a hundred he would confess. . . . To make it stranger Jesse sang at his own funeral. Poor devil he can't cod me—not even with his long hair and a billy goat's wad of hair on his chin.

Cannary, a Missourian herself, was the frontier character known from Virginia City, Nevada, to Buffalo, New York, as "Calamity Jane," a rough, roistering, hard-drinking, former bullwhacker, camp-follower, likely prostitute, self-proclaimed army scout and putative "wife" of William Butler "Wild Bill" Hickok.

Her Dalton letter, together with many others allegedly written between 1877 and 1903 (the year she died), came to light in Billings, Montana, in 1941 when a woman who said her name was Jean Hickok McCormick made the letters public, McCormick said she was the daughter of Martha Jane Cannary and Hickok.

From the outset, the letters were regarded with suspicion. There is no verified example of Calamity Jane's handwriting extant, for one thing, and many regarded her too ignorant, if not entirely illiterate, to have written them. Moreover, her claim to have been legally married to Hickok has never been substantiated by any documentary evidence. (That she may have bore a child out of wedlock, however, has never been argued.)

But even the most skeptical of those who have read the letters wonder where all the information in them came from—so much of it verifiable, and reasonable, and sounding like something Calamity Jane would have written. Was McCormick, the daughter who Calamity allegedly gave away to the upbringing by a prosperous Englishman in 1895, the author of the letters?

Emory University professor Elizabeth Stevenson, in her 1994 book, *Figures in a Western Landscape,* says. "The letters are a document to move the reader. They create a character who is believable and haunting. This is not a cheap or cunning fraud, for the letters have the authenticity of art."

Jean Hickok McCormick died in Billings on February 22, 1951, ten years after she made the "Calamity Jane Letters" public and just six months before the death of J. Frank Dalton down in Granbury, Texas.

In Clay County, Missouri, where Jesse's birthplace is a museum and where an outdoor drama celebrates his life and exploits, the local Visitor's Bureau advertises its hero with the motto "The Legend Never Dies."

At least nobody can argue with that.

5

"I'm Billy the Kid"

The Case of "Brushy Bill" Roberts

"We of the jury unanimously find that William Bonney was killed by a shot in the left breast, in the region of the heart, fired from a pistol in the hand of Patrick F. Garrett . . ."

Thus did the coroner's jury, on July 15, 1881, in Fort Sumner, New Mexico Territory, report the death of Billy the Kid.

And thus began the trouble.

The jury's report was never officially filed, the original version of it disappeared, the people who signed it did not know Billy, and there were many who did know him who said flatly that the man Pat Garrett killed was not Billy and that the man buried in Billy's grave was not Billy.

Here was a ghostly echo. People said those exact things about Jesse James in Kearney, Missouri, only four years or so previously.

*Then, in 1949, an old man came forward, quite nervously.
Since there is no statute of limitations on murder he believed he
was still wanted for certain killings that had occurred seven
decades ago.*

He sought a pardon. "I want to die a free man," he said.

*He had a story to tell and of all the outlaw claimant stories,
Brushy Bill's was the best.*

🌿

The commonly believed story is that Henry McCarty, called "the
Kid" for most of his brief life and "Billy" after he took the alias
William Bonney, came out to New Mexico Territory as a
teenager, lived there about eight years, and died there with a bullet in the region of his heart at the age of twenty-one.

Why Billy the Kid is among that handful of Old West
names—Wyatt Earp, Buffalo Bill, George Armstrong Custer,
Butch Cassidy, Jesse James, Wild Bill Hickok, and Kit Carson
among them—that are instantly recognized around the world is
not clear. The Kid had no significant history. He never served in
war, never blazed a trail, never traveled beyond a few hundred
miles of his boyhood home, had no special talents, and knew no
one of importance. Until the spring of 1878 he was among a
multitude of nameless drifting ciphers and ne'er-do-wells in the
Southwest. He rose to a brief regional prominence in an obscure
territorial power struggle and by the summer of 1881 he was
dead, his own hometown newspaper celebrating the event by
proclaiming him a "vulgar murderer and desperado."

But somehow, his story has gripped us and won't let go.
Forty-five years ago a researcher published a bibliography of
Billy the Kid works and listed 437 books, major magazine articles, movies, plays, and songs. The number has at least doubled
since. There are books on Billy the Kid's childhood, books on
movies made about him, several "definitive" biographies, books
that argue about other books written about him, and two books
each on two men who cropped up long after Billy's death to
claim they were Billy.

He is, by a country mile or two, the most studied and written about outlaw of them all and there have been countless attempts to explain his appeal and durability. These range from the academic (he was a symbol of a vanished agrarian era in American history) to the vague (he represented a transitional period in our history, his life closing the past, his death opening the future) to the unsatisfactory (J. Frank Dobie's view that he was "an uncommon killer" who possessed "the art of daring.")

Others say it is his youth that captivates us, or his rebel spirit, or his loyalty to a cause, or the mysteries surrounding his brief, violent life. His best biographer, Robert M. Utley, has said, "Billy the Kid strides boldly across America's mental landscape, symbolizing an enduring national ambivalence toward corruption and violence." Maybe that is the key.

Whatever the case, 115 years after Pat Garrett gunned him down in a midnight raid on Pete Maxwell's place in Fort Sumner, he still strides boldly out there.

The Kid's last words were *"¿Quién es? ¿Quién es?"*—"Who is it? Who is it?" and to this day we ask that question about him.

The best historical investigators say he was born Henry McCarty in 1859, perhaps in New York City, of Irish immigrant parents. With his mother Catherine, Henry and his brother Joe lived briefly in Indiana, Kansas, and Colorado. In Santa Fe in 1873 Catherine married Civil War veteran William H. Antrim, a teamster, and the family soon removed to the frontier mining camp of Silver City in far southwestern New Mexico Territory, near the Arizona border.

Catherine died of tuberculosis in Silver City in the fall of 1874 and her sons were boarded with a local butcher during their stepfather Antrim's long absences. Henry seems to have drifted into trouble at the age of fifteen when he had minor brushes with the law over petty thievery, including one incident, a year after his mother's death, in which he stole a bundle of laundry from two Silver City "celestials" (Chinese). He was placed in jail but, given the run of the place, escaped by climbing up a chimney.

He fled west into Arizona Territory and for two years remained more or less lost to recorded history. It is believed that he worked as a teamster, cowhand, and hay-camp laborer in the Piñalero Mountains around Camp Grant and the town of Bonito, about 100 miles west of Silver City. In August 1877, in a Bonito saloon, Henry McCarty—soon to be called "Kid Antrim"—got into an altercation with Francis "Windy" Cahill, a Camp Grant blacksmith. This man, for reasons unknown, is said to have slapped the Kid and called him "a pimp," and Henry is said to have called Cahill "a son-of-a-bitch" and pulled a pistol from his belt. The blacksmith, who told the local lawman that he tried to wrest the gun from the young man but was "shot in the belly" for his efforts, died on August 18. A coroner's inquest found "Antrim, alias the Kid" guilty of "unjustifiable homicide."

The Kid was jailed, escaped, and fled back across the border to the Silver City vicinity, then, after drifting for a time through the Tularosa Valley, rode into Lincoln County in October 1877. Now a fugitive using the name "William Bonney," he found employment as a cowhand on a ranch owned by a wealthy young Englishman named John H. Tunstall.

Within four months of the day Tunstall's foreman Dick Brewer hired him, Billy stood in the epicenter of a bloody little power struggle later known as the Lincoln County War.

At the time of the Kid's arrival there, Lincoln County was the largest county in the United States. Its 5,000 square miles in south-central New Mexico Territory sprawled from the Texas line to the San Andres Mountains, its sparse population (about one person per square mile) scattered around the fringes of the arid Tularosa Basin and along the middle Pecos River.

The town of Lincoln, 200 miles south of Santa Fe, had been settled in 1849 by Mexican farmers who called the place Las Placitas (signifying the shops in a small town square or plaza) and later Bonito ("pretty," the same as the Arizona town in which the Kid killed Windy Cahill), after the stream that flowed nearby. In 1869, with the formation of the county named for the late president, the town, now the county seat, also became Lincoln.

The sinister cast of characters who would take part in one faction of the Lincoln County War had gathered in the town only a few years before the Kid's advent there. Irish-born Lawrence G. Murphy, a former army major and post trader at nearby Fort Stanton, came to Lincoln in 1869 and opened a general store and saloon that became known as "the House of Murphy" and "the Big Store." Murphy had an alliance with the "Santa Fe Ring," the clique of crooked politicians, including Governor Samuel B. Axtell, that controlled much of the economy and all the politics of the Territory, and Murphy soon had a monopoly on supplying beef and flour to Fort Stanton and the Mescalero Apache Indian Agency. And since he was unchallenged in his business dealings, he charged local ranchers and settlers exorbitant prices for foodstuffs and hardware.

Murphy eventually took on two partners, New Yorker James J. Dolan and another Irishman named John H. Riley. The mission this trio set out to accomplish was to eliminate the competition being offered by John S. Chisum, the "Lord of the Bosque Grande" and "King of the Pecos" whose great Jinglebob cattle outfit on the Pecos River near Roswell had fair-priced beef to sell.

Into this volatile arena came yet another competitor to the Murphy-Dolan-Riley combine. Alexander McSween, an asthmatic Canadian-born lawyer, moved to Lincoln in March 1875, bought an interest in a ranch, opened a bank, and built a store to challenge the House of Murphy. He had Chisum's support and financing from John Henry Tunstall, the twenty-five-year-old Englishman who had come west to make a fortune in the cattle business and who had set up his ranch on the Rio Felíz, southeast of Lincoln.

Inevitably, the McSween-Tunstall bank and store attracted Murphy-Dolan's once monopolized customers.

With Murphy out of the picture—he sold his interest to his

partners in 1877, returned to Fort Stanton, and died there a year later—James Dolan took steps to eliminate the Tunstall-McSween annoyance by obtaining, illegally, a writ of attachment on all the competitors' properties. Another of this early-day Irish Mafia, Lincoln County Sheriff William Brady, a man described by contemporaries as "generally honorable but subservient to the 'House,' " had the duty of serving the writ on Tunstall and in February 1878, sent a deputy and a posse of at least fourteen men to the Rio Felíz to do the deed.

Tunstall, meantime, had decided to ride up to Lincoln and try to negotiate some kind of settlement with the Dolan faction. He gathered some of his hands, including foreman Dick Brewer and young Billy Bonney, and set out on February 18.

Precisely what happened on the trail to Lincoln that late afternoon is not known, but by dusk the Brady posse had intercepted the ranchman and his men, there was an exchange of gunfire, and Tunstall died from bullet wounds in his head and chest.

With the match now touched to a trail of powder, the Tunstall-McSween bloc vowed to punish those responsible for the Englishman's death. The Kid, who said Tunstall "was the only man I ever worked for who treated me fairly," became an impassioned member of this group of avengers. At its peak numbering as high as sixty men and calling themselves "the Regulators," the band won an early victory by being deputized by a sympathetic Lincoln justice of the peace. Then, early in March, at a place in the foothills of the Capitan Mountains portentously called Dead Man's Draw, the Regulators drew first blood. They captured and killed three of Brady's possemen including William S. "Buck" Morton, believed to have fired the first rifle bullet into John Tunstall.

Governor Axtell now declared the Regulators outlaws and placed a $200 reward on each of their heads. This meager act had no deterring effect. On April 1, Billy and five other Regulators made their way into Lincoln and hid behind an adobe wall of a corral adjoining the Tunstall-McSween store. When Sheriff Brady and four of his deputies came walking down Lincoln's main street toward the courthouse and drew near the Tunstall corral, the Regulators opened fire. Brady, clearly the target of the ambush, was struck by eight bullets and died in the street along with one of his deputies. Billy took a slight gunshot wound in the thigh as he ran into the street to grab the dead sheriff's rifle but he and his compatriots made their way out of town relatively unscathed.

Four days after the Lincoln shootout a band of Regulators were camped at Blazer's Mill, southeast of Lincoln. In the group were the Kid, Dick Brewer, Lincoln County ranchers George and Frank Coe, and Charles Bowdre, a Southern drifter and McSween adherent. That April 5, 1878, a man named Andrew L. "Buckshot" Roberts rode his mule into the camp. Not much is known about Roberts except that he was young and very foolish. He is believed to have served in the Texas Rangers where in some nameless battle he took a shotgun wound that crippled his right shoulder and he may have been a deserter from the army out of Fort Stanton. One Lincoln County War historian says he operated a Murphy-owned store at South Fork, near the Mescalero Apache Agency, was a well-known Murphy-Dolan man, and probably had been among the possemen who killed Tunstall.

One thing seems certain: Roberts blithely rode into the Regulators' camp at Blazer's Mill to collect the reward offered for the apprehension of Sheriff Brady's killers. Quickly, Roberts found the tables turned on him. Dick Brewer demanded that he surrender and hand over his weapons, Roberts refused, and a gunfight followed. In the hail of bullets, Charlie Bowdre shot Roberts in the stomach but the fatally wounded man made his way into a small building, dragged a mattress to the doorway, and kept up a steady rifle fire on the Regulators. Roberts killed Brewer with a shot through the head and wounded four others—grazing the Kid with one shot—and died from his belly wound the next day. He was buried next to Brewer on the Blazer's Mill grounds.

In the three months that followed this affair, the tool of the Santa Fe Ring, Governor Axtell, asked President Rutherford B. Hayes to send federal troops to assist territorial officers in restoring law and order in Lincoln County. Soldiers from Fort Stanton actually were sent to Lincoln that summer of 1878 but only as observers. They departed on June 29 and the next month the great showdown of the war took place.

On July 14 some sixty McSween men, old and new Regulators, gathered at the lawyer's spacious home in Lincoln. Allied against them and headquartered in the Wortley Hotel, just down the street, were about forty Dolan supporters. These latter were led by the new sheriff, George W. Peppin, a former stonemason and Dolan employee who had been present in the street shootout on April 1.

For two days the factions fired sporadically at one another and shouted insults. On the fourth day of the siege, the commander of Fort Stanton, a pompous peacock of an officer and pro-Dolan man, Lieutenant Colonel Nathan Augustus Monroe Dudley, arrived in Lincoln with thirty-five men, a mountain howitzer, and a Gatling gun. He came ostensibly to protect the women and children of the town and soon after his arrival, the McSween forces began to evaporate, leaving the lawyer, his wife Susan, and about fourteen men bottled up inside the house.

On July 19, despite the efforts of Susan McSween to talk with Colonel Dudley, the house was set on fire, the wooden walls and fixtures inside the adobe structure burning slowly but inexorably. As darkness approached and with the situation growing desperate, the Kid organized an escape and he and four other Regulators slipped out of the house and into the dusk. Soon after, McSween tried to surrender but was shot down yelling, "Oh, Lord, Lord, save me!" Three other of his partisans were killed in the backyard of the flaming home.

The "Five-Day Battle," which cost the lives of McSween, five Regulators, and two Dolan supporters, brought the feud to an end.

In September 1878, President Hayes recalled Governor Axtell and replaced him with fifty-one-year-old Lew Wallace, once the youngest Union Army major general in the Civil War and soon-to-be author of the acclaimed biblical epic *Ben Hur, A Tale of Christ*. He came to the office with a long list of warrants for the arrest of Regulators, including one made out for "William H.

Antrim, alias Kid, alias Bonney," but in November issued an amnesty proclamation and journeyed from Santa Fe to Lincoln to interview participants in the recent conflict.

The amnesty decree did not apply to the Kid since he was under previous indictments in the territorial court for the killing of Sheriff Brady and in federal court for the killing of Buckshot Roberts. Even so, Governor Wallace was anxious to bring the whole nasty matter to an end and by letter promised Billy protection from prosecution in exchange for testimony on what he knew of the Lincoln County troubles and participants.

On March 17, 1879, occurred a bizarre scene: in the home of a justice of the peace in Lincoln, the refined Lew Wallace of Indiana, lawyer, musician, author, veteran of the Mexican War, hero of Shiloh and numerous other Civil War battles, and now governor of New Mexico Territory, sat in the candlelight of a low *jacal* (adobe hut) in the middle of nowhere tensely awaiting the arrival of a nineteen-year-old boy-outlaw.

The Kid came, Winchester in hand, wearing a new hat and a bright bandanna. He was about five feet eight, slender with small hands and feet, clean-shaven, and showing a toothy grin. He exuded some of the qualities Wallace had heard about: a likable but tightly coiled lad and clearly a tough one when crossed.

The details of the conversation are not known but in general the Kid agreed to testify in the matter of the murder of a McSween ally, the lawyer Huston I. Chapman, that occurred after the Five-Day Battle. Chapman had been shot to death on a Lincoln street on February 18, 1879, by one William Campbell, a Dolan partisan. Billy had witnessed the killing and true to his promise to Governor Wallace told what he saw before a grand jury. His testimony, however, did not result in a pardon.

With their base at old Fort Sumner, 100 miles northeast of Lincoln, the Kid and a few comrades undertook some cattle rustling—stealing from John Chisum, among others—and settled into a relatively ordinary life-on-the-run.

It was during this period that the Kid had his picture taken.

He posed in Fort Sumner with his Winchester carbine and .41 caliber single-action Colt revolver. The tintype, sometimes reversed to give the erroneous impression that he was left-handed, is believed to be the only genuine photographic image we have of him as an adult.

In late 1880 the final character in the Billy the Kid saga arrived in New Mexico. He was the new sheriff of Lincoln County, Patrick Floyd Jarvis Garrett, a tough, relentless, six-foot-five Alabama-born stringbean with a big mustache, a former trail driver and Texas buffalo hunter. Garrett's first duty as sheriff was to track down the Kid, upon whose head a $500 reward had been placed.

He lost no time. On December 19 Garrett and his posse were waiting in Fort Sumner when the Kid rode into the town with friends Tom O'Folliard and Charlie Bowdre, both veterans of the McSween house battle, and two other men. O'Folliard, a Texas drifter, was killed by the possemen, but the others escaped. Four days later Garrett and his deputies descended on an abandoned cow camp east of Fort Sumner called Stinking Springs where, in a small rock house, the Kid and four confederates were sleeping. In the opening skirmish, Bowdre, the man who had killed Buckshot Roberts at Blazer's Mill, was shot down and the miniature siege continued through the day. Finally, the Kid and the others surrendered. After a brief jailing in Fort Sumner, the prisoners were taken to Santa Fe, the Kid then removed to the town of Mesilla to stand trial in District Court for the murder of Sheriff Brady nearly three years before.

The trial took two days and on April 13, 1881, Judge Warren H. Bristol ordered the defendant to be taken to Lincoln and confined in the Lincoln County jail until May 13. On that date, between 9:00 A.M. and 3:00 P.M., the judge said, "the said William Bonney, alias Kid, alias William Antrim, will be hanged by the neck until his body be dead." (One account of the sentencing has the grandiloquent Judge Bristol banging his gavel and shouting, "You are sentenced to be hanged by the neck until you are dead, dead, dead," to which Billy responded, "And you can go to hell, hell, hell!")

❦

In Lincoln he awaited his execution in the second-floor jail of the county's new courthouse, the old Murphy-Dolan store. He was shackled with leg irons and handcuffs inside his cell and guarded—along with five other prisoners in the jail—by deputies Robert M. Olinger, a tall, weighty, long-haired man with a pock-marked face and a killer's reputation (he was under a murder indictment on the day he died), and James W. Bell, a former Texas Ranger with a great knife scar on the left side of his face. From all accounts, Olinger was the belligerent deputy. He seemed to take pleasure in tormenting his most notorious prisoner—including such acts as dramatically loading his shotgun outside the Kid's cell—while talking and laughing about Billy's impending date with the hangman.

Olinger had been warned by a friend that if not watched every moment, if given the remotest opportunity, the Kid would escape. The deputy's view on the matter was that the Kid had as much chance of escaping as he had of going to heaven.

In the early evening of April 28, 1881, with Sheriff Garrett out of town, Olinger took the five other prisoners across the street to the Wortley Hotel for supper, leaving Bell behind to guard the Kid. At about 6:00 P.M., Billy asked Bell to take him to the privy behind the courthouse. Upon their return, with Bell lagging behind, the Kid climbed the stairs, worked his small hand out of one of the manacles, turned, and swung the loose cuff at Bell's face, cutting the deputy with it. In the struggle that followed on the stairway, the Kid grabbed Bell's revolver and shot the deputy with it. Bell ran out the door and into the arms of a Lincoln citizen named Godfrey Gauss, sagged, and died.

The Kid meantime found Olinger's shotgun and stationed himself at a jail-floor window overlooking the yard at the side of the courthouse. Olinger, who heard the gunshots, emerged from the hotel, ran across the street, and entered the fenced yard. Above him the Kid is said to have said, "Look up, old boy, and see what you get." The deputy looked up and the Kid fired both barrels of the shotgun into the face and trunk of his nemesis. Olinger died instantly.

(One melodramatic and highly suspicious account of this incident has Gauss, the citizen standing with the body of the other deputy, shouting, "Bob, the Kid has killed Bell," whereupon Olinger looked up at the window and said, "Yes, and he's killed me, too.")

Gauss, who knew the Kid and frightenedly followed the escapee's orders, supplied a pick that Billy used to break the chain between his ankle irons and brought a saddled horse from a nearby corral. Meantime a crowd of Lincoln citizens had gathered but made no attempt to subdue the outlaw. The Kid apologized for killing Bell, then broke Olinger's shotgun over a porch railing and threw the pieces at the dead deputy, saying, "You are not going to round me up again."

Nearly an hour passed after the killing of Olinger when the Kid, his leg chains dangling and burdened with the side arms and rifles taken from the jail, was able to mount the skittish horse and ride out of Lincoln.

Instead of riding hell-for-leather for Mexico, Billy rode to Fort Sumner—where he had a girlfriend and several pals—and compounded this foolhardy act by making no effort to conceal his whereabouts. Garrett soon had reports that the Kid was roaming the country between White Oaks, the mining town near Carrizozo, and Fort Sumner, and had identified the Kid's friends in Fort Sumner and others who might be harboring the fugitive.

In Roswell, Garrett enlisted the help of two deputies. John W. Poe, a former deputy sheriff and town marshal in Texas, and Thomas K. "Tip" McKinney, a local cowboy, and on July 10 rode north to Fort Sumner. The trio arrived on the outskirts of the town on the thirteenth and spent the day trying to ferret out information on Billy's whereabouts. The sheriff was able to piece together scraps of information that the Kid might be staying at cattleman Pete Maxwell's place, a former barracks on the old army post. On the night of the thirteenth Garrett and his men crept into the barracks compound and found Maxwell's building.

They waited in a nearby orchard, then, just before midnight on July 14, 1881, Garrett, who left his two companions outside, moved carefully along the roofed porch and entered Maxwell's bedroom, woke the rancher up, and asked the Kid's whereabouts. Meantime, the Kid had emerged from his room to cut meat from a beef carcass hanging from the porch rafter some distance away and as he returned came face-to-face with John Poe, one of the deputies on the porch. Gun drawn, the Kid backed into Maxwell's bedroom. Inside the room he spotted the vague shape of Maxwell on the bed in the darkness and said, "Who are those fellows outside, Pete?" At the same moment, Garrett emerged from the shadows. Now, the Kid fell back and asked, "*¿Quién es? ¿Quién es?*" while pointing his revolver at the unknown figure in the dark. Garrett fired twice and heard a groan from the other side of the room. At the gunshot, Poe came barreling through the doorway. "Don't shoot Maxwell," Garrett yelled. "That was the Kid that came in there onto me, and I think I have got him." Poe said, "Pat, the Kid would not come to this place; you have shot the wrong man."

But Poe did not know the Kid, had never seen him before those scary seconds on the Maxwell porch.

Deluvina Maxwell, a Navajo woman who worked as Pete Maxwell's servant, brought a candle into the room. She knew Billy and identified him, as did Garrett.

The Kid died from a bullet just over his heart. His pistol and a butcher knife lay at his side.

The next day, a coroner's jury convened in Maxwell's bedroom, the seven citizens, several of them illiterate and signing the report with an X, reaching a unanimous verdict on the cause of "William Bonney's death."

On the afternoon of the fifteenth, Billy's corpse, neatly dressed, was placed in a wooden coffin and carried to the old military cemetery and buried next to two friends and fellow veterans of the Lincoln County War, Charlie Bowdre and Tom O'-Folliard. Garrett, his deputies, and many Fort Sumner citizens were in attendance.

Any notion that he was an obscure figure involved in an microscopic "war" in the remotest corner of the Western frontier was removed by the national press coverage that followed his burial. Typical of the attention given the story was this alliterative headline appearing on July 22, 1881, in the *Boston Daily Globe:*

"THE KID'S" CAREER
Life and Death of a Dare-Devil
Desperado
The Leader of the New Mexican
Banditti in His Castle
A Territory Terrorized by a
Beardless Boy in Blue Broadcloth

And in Billy's own home territory, three days after the *Globe* story, ten days after his burial, the first reports were trickling in that his bones were not resting in peace.

The *Las Vegas* (New Mexico Territory) *Daily Optic* reported on July 25 that the Kid's body had been dug up and brought to Las Vegas where an unnamed doctor removed and "cleaned" the skull, removed an index finger and "sent it east," and buried the remains in a corral.

It was an unlikely story but one that wouldn't die. In 1885 the *Silver City Enterprise* reported that the Kid's skull was in the possession of an Albuquerque man, and in 1892, when Pat Garrett got around to telling his story, he tried to put such rumors to rest. In his *Authentic Life of Billy the Kid,* an imaginative work ghostwritten by the itinerant New Mexico newspaperman Marshall Ashmum "Ash" Upson, Garrett stated, in what some believed too much of a protest:

I have said that the body was buried in the cemetery at
Fort Sumner. I wish to add that it is there to-day intact—
skull, fingers, toes, bones, and every hair of the head that
was buried with the body on that 15th of July, doctors,
newspaper editors, and paragraphers to the contrary
notwithstanding. . . . Again I say that the Kid's body lies
undisturbed in the grave, and I speak of what I know.

But if the bones lay "undisturbed," the spirit of Billy the Kid
did not. In the words of the eminent Southwestern historian C.
L. Sonnichsen, "Old desperadoes never die; they do not even
fade away. They arise from their ashes, full of strength and stories."

One example of Billy-as-Lazarus was the case of John Miller,
a man who lived for a time in Las Vegas and who later, with his
Mexican wife Isadora, settled in the wilderness at Ramah, a village near the Zuñi Pueblo in far west-central New Mexico, next
to the Arizona border. He worked as a farmer and horse trainer
most of his life and shared with only his closest relatives and
friends his secrets.

Miller was a small man of slight build, sloping shoulders,
slim hips, small hands, prominent ears, blue eyes under heavy
brows, and protruding front teeth. He had among his sparse possessions a pistol with twenty-one notches on the grips, some old
cartridges, a few photographs, a lead slug he said he dug out of
his own body, a pocketknife, and a jar filled with gold and silver
coins.

His appearance, secretiveness, and these seemingly unremarkable belongings, many believed, were proof that John Miller
was Billy the Kid. But even though Miller said toward the end of
his life that he wanted to "set the record straight," he died in the
Prescott, Arizona, Pioneer's Home, on March 12, 1937, without
divulging whatever secrets he had.

Eleven years later, in Hamilton, Texas, another Billy the Kid
stepped forward, as reluctant to talk as John Miller, but when he
was persuaded to tell it, having a whale of a tale to tell.

William V. Morrison, a Missourian and nonpracticing lawyer working as an investigator for a legal firm, found Billy the Kid's greatest claimant. A keen questioner, an indefatigable researcher, and a descendant of the Maxwell family of New Mexico, Morrison was captivated by a story told to him in 1948 by a client living in Florida named Joe Hines. This man had lived in New Mexico Territory in the 1870s, knew all about the Lincoln County War and its principals, and claimed to have fought for the Dolan faction at Lincoln. The old man stated unequivocally that Pat Garrett did not kill Billy the Kid in Fort Sumner or anywhere else and swore that the Kid was alive. But Hines stopped there. He would not reveal the whereabouts of the Kid or the name he was using.

Morrison, however, could not be stopped. He had to find out more about this man who people said was Billy the Kid, and the timing of his search turned out to be perfect: in 1948 an ancient named J. Frank Dalton cropped up in Lawton, Oklahoma, claiming to be Jesse James.

Morrison contacted Dalton and Dalton said Billy was living south of Fort Worth in the town of Hamilton where he was known as O. L. Roberts, sometimes called "Ollie" or "Brushy Bill."

Clearly, old desperadoes not only never died, they rose from their ashes and kept in touch with one another.

Morrison did his homework, wrote the old man he was coming, and paid his first visit to Roberts in June 1949. The man who greeted him at the door of his modest home wore a sleeveless sweatshirt, blue jeans, and cowboy boots. "I was amazed to see a man ninety years old in excellent physical condition," the lawyer later wrote, describing Roberts as about five feet eight inches tall, a wiry 165 pounds or so, his "blue-gray eyes dancing into my eyes, with right hand outstretched for a very firm handshake." The old man's hand, Morrison noticed, was quite small with well-shaped fingers, the wrists unusually large, forearms and shoulders heavy, forehead high, nose prominent. The lawyer took a special mental note on Roberts's large ears. "the left ear protruding noticeably farther from the head than the right . . ."

Morrison knew he stood on the threshold of a historical event. He went inside, met Mrs. Roberts, and in her presence remarked that it was difficult to believe he was talking to Billy the Kid. This embarrassed Roberts and he put off talking on the subject until the next day, when his wife would be visiting a neighbor. That day he told Morrison, "Well, you've got your man. You don't need to look any farther. I'm Billy the Kid."

In the eighteen months that followed, Morrison got all of Roberts's story. He took the old man on a remarkable "return" to Lincoln County and found the evidence so overwhelming that his interviewee was telling the truth that he petitioned the governor of New Mexico to issue an official pardon to Roberts for his crimes as Billy the Kid. This event, when it was played out in Santa Fe in November 1950, had unforeseen and disastrous results.

Roberts said his birth name was William Henry Roberts and that he was born in Buffalo Gap, Taylor County, Texas, on the last day of 1859. (The story of his New York origins, he said, was one he fabricated; presumably, too, he invented the name Henry McCarty.) He said his father had served with Quantrill in the Kansas-Missouri border wars and that he knew the Jameses, Youngers, and Daltons as a youth and that "We all have been lifetime friends." He also said he had been in Indian Territory in 1874, going there on a cattle drive by way of the "Chittem [Chisholm] Trail," and that in this time he got to know Belle Reed, later known as Belle Starr, and that he worked as a horsebreaker for John Chisum in New Mexico.

In the Morrison interviews and in letters he subsequently dictated, Roberts zeroed in on the events of the Lincoln County War and his—Billy's—role in it. Morrison was especially impressed that his claimant, barely literate, could have such a wealth of details on the history of the war that could not have been gained from books.

Roberts told of the shooting of Sheriff Brady on April 1, 1878, saying that Brady was "gunning" for him with warrants for cattle rustling. He denied killing Brady in front of the McSween-Tunstall store in Lincoln but admitted he took a shot at Billy Matthews, the county clerk who was with Brady and his deputy on the street, and said Matthews shot back and that a rifle bullet nicked his right hip. He said others were shooting when Brady fell.

As to the killing of Buckshot Roberts at Blazer's Mill, Brushy Bill's temper rose a moment: "He was an outlaw before he went to that country," he said. "He was a snake, too, he was. But he got what was coming to him that day at Blazer's place."

Roberts told Morrison countless details that later turned out to be significant—many of them seemingly unknown to anyone other than Billy. For example, Roberts said that while the prominent New Mexico lawyer Albert J. Fountain represented him on the territorial charges in Mesilla, he, the Kid, had no money to pay the attorney. He said he tried to get some cash by selling his most valuable possession, his horse, which he had left in the care of a friend in Las Vegas. "They didn't sell my mare up at Scott Moore's in Las Vegas," Roberts said. "He was a friend of mine, but now he said I owed him money for board."

Subsequent investigation disclosed that the Kid wrote a letter on April 15, 1881, to another friend, Edgar Caypless, saying, "The mare is about all I can depend on at present so I hope you will settle the case right away and give him [Fountain] the money."

In 1950 Morrison drove Roberts from his Texas home to New Mexico. In Lincoln the old man at first refused to enter the courthouse where, seventy years earlier, the Kid has been jailed and where he had killed deputies Bell and Olinger. As they were about to drive out of town. Roberts had a change of heart and agreed to visit the courthouse providing he and Morrison could do so alone. Once inside, Brushy Bill was puzzled over the changes in the building since 1881. He pointed out that the outside stairway didn't exist in the old days. He said that the upper floor was completely different from the day he sat on a soapbox in his cell while Deputy Olinger ostentatiously loaded his shotgun. Roberts remembered the deputy snarling, "Kid, do you see these buckshot I am loading into these two barrels, twelve in each barrel? Well, if you try to make a break, I'll put all twenty-four between your shoulder blades."

Roberts said that Deputy Bell "was a nice man. He treated me like an ordinary prisoner." But Olinger, he said, taunted and threatened him constantly and "treated me like a dog."

He told Morrison that his enmity for Olinger dated earlier than the taunting at the Lincoln jail. "He murdered the Jones boy in cold blood." the old man said bitterly. "I promised the father that I would even the score with Olinger for the murder of his son . . . I was eager to kill him, but I did not want to kill Bell."

(Olinger, who was among the besiegers of the McSween store in July 1878, had been marshal of Seven Rivers in Lincoln County. In September 1879, he had accompanied Deputy Sheriff Milo Pierce in tracking a cattle rustler named John Jones to a cow camp. After Jones fired his rifle at the lawmen, Olinger killed Jones with three pistol shots—one of which struck Pierce and gave the lawman a lifelong limp.)

Roberts told Morrison that when Olinger came across the street from the Wortley Hotel that April 28 in 1881, he came around the corner of the building directly below where the Kid waited. Roberts said he shouted down. "Look up, Bob, I want to shoot you in the face with your own buckshot. I don't want to shoot you in the back like you did other men, and the Jones boy." After this, he told Morrison, "I fired the twelve into him. I wanted him to get all of them like he had promised to give them to me. I wanted him to know that I was the man who was killing him. This was the happiest moment of my life."

Roberts claimed he knew Pat Garrett was in Fort Sumner on July 14, 1881, and that at a dance the Kid attended the night before, his friend Jesús Silva warned him to leave town. He said he spent the day of the fourteenth with Celsa Gutiérrez, daughter of Garrett's brother-in-law, and added, "Nearly all the people in this country were my friends and they helped me. None of them liked Garrett."

That night, Brushy Bill said, he and his "partner," a man named Billy Barlow, were at Silva's place and that Jesús had agreed to fix a meal for them if somebody would go over to Maxwell's house and fetch some meat from a beef carcass there. Roberts said Barlow agreed to go on the errand and that not long after, "I heard gunshots at the Maxwell house, ran into the yard and began firing at shadows."

He told Morrison, "One of the first shots had killed my partner on the back porch" and said other shots by Garrett, Poe, and McKinney grazed him in the mouth, left shoulder, and the top of his head and that he stumbled to an adobe behind the Maxwell home. There, he said, a Mexican woman tended his wounds, putting tallow on his scalp to stanch the blood flow from that wound and helping him reload his .44s.

Roberts was emphatic that the man Garrett killed was Barlow and that soon after the shooting, Celsa Gutiérrez told him that Garrett and his men were passing the body of Barlow off as the Kid.

Celsa, he said, brought his horse to him and he rode out of Fort Sumner with a man named Frank Lobato at about three that morning. He recalled staying at a sheep camp the next day, then at another south of the town while his wounds healed enough for him to move on. Around the first of August he rode to El Paso where he had "lots of friends," then, he said, "I crossed the Rio Grande north of town and went into Sonora, Mexico, where I was acquainted with the Yaqui Indians. I lived with them nearly two years."

Roberts accounted for his seventy years on the run in a far more condensed fashion than he did his comparatively brief twenty-one years as Billy the Kid although the long part of his life was no less eventful, or incredible, than the short part. Without dates and only a few named years, durations, or details, he said he took the name "Texas Kid," hid out at Belle Starr's place in Indian Territory (where he said he met J. Frank Dalton—the man who would be Jesse James—for the first time), worked breaking horses in Texas, then traveled the Black Hills of the Dakotas. He later joined the Pinkerton Detective Agency and hunted horse thieves in the Red River country of Texas and Oklahoma. He served as a marshal under Judge Isaac C. Parker out of North Platte, Nebraska, took horses to Argentina, and later shipped out to the Shetland Islands to "catch ponies." In 1898 he joined Roosevelt's Rough Riders under an assumed name and served in Cuba in the Spanish-American War. He organized a Wild West Show in Texas in 1902. He served with the forces of Venustiano Carranza and later with Pancho Villa during the Mexican Revolution. He took part in breaking up a gang of bank robbers holed up in the Sabine River bottoms of Texas. He married thrice and used a dozen aliases.

꙰

There were, of course, enormous holes in Brushy Bill's story.

There was (and is) no historical record whatever on "Billy Barlow," the man Roberts said Garrett killed at the Maxwell place. Roberts seemed to know little about his "partner" other than that he came into New Mexico Territory in about 1880, had taken no part in the Lincoln County troubles, was a bit younger than the Kid but about the same general size.

Nor was Roberts helpful in explaining why Pat Garrett would shoot Barlow, claim he was the Kid, and enlist the help of others—some of whom knew Billy on sight—to conspire with him. And there were questions Morrison either didn't ask or which elicited answers he didn't record: Wouldn't passing off Barlow as the Kid have required collusion with the Kid himself? What if the Kid were to show up somewhere and make a laughingstock of Garrett?

And why did Roberts wait so long to tell his tale? Was it because he genuinely feared confessing his crimes and facing imprisonment, as he said, or was he merely inspired by the recent and much publicized example of J. Frank Dalton's Jesse James claims in Oklahoma? And what about the similarity between the name "Charlie Bigelow," the man Dalton said Bob Ford killed, and "Billy Barlow," the man Roberts said Pat Garrett killed?

The lawyer apparently didn't ask Brushy Bill when he had last been in touch with Dalton, but the peculiar timing of their revelations must have bothered him.

Morrison knew he had problems with such questions—plus hundreds of others from descendants of Garrett, Poe, and McKinney, from old Lincoln County families, from historical scholars and researchers, but he proceeded with plans to seek a pardon from Thomas J. Mabry, the governor of New Mexico, for Roberts's crimes as Billy the Kid.

This was the only thing Brushy Bill requested of Morrison: "I want a pardon so I can die a free man" he had said early in his friendship with the lawyer.

Miracuously, Governor Mabry agreed to meet with Morrison and Roberts on November 28, 1950. The lawyer came prepared with seventeen parcels of legal materials—transcriptions of his interviews, investigative findings, depositions, and several notarized statements from people who had known the Kid and who testified that Roberts and the Kid were one and the same.

Among the latter were a couple of very interesting, if not wholly convincing, stories.

Severo Gallegos of Ruidoso, New Mexico, testified on paper that as a boy he was playing marbles under a tree near the Lincoln County Courthouse when Billy the Kid shot deputies Bell and Olinger. Gallegos said the Kid, as he prepared to ride out of town, asked him to bring a rope (for some unstated purpose) and Gallegos said he did so. He saw the Kid up-close. He told Morrison, "Your man talks like Billy; he looks like Billy; he has small hands and large wrists, small feet, large ears, stands and walks like Billy; but he is not old enough to be Billy." Gallegos wanted another look at Roberts, telling Morrison that if he could look closely into his man's face, he would know because Billy had small brown spots in the blue of his eyes. Morrison brought Roberts around and Gallegos got his close look. "That is Billy the Kid, all right. Only Billy had eyes like that," he said.

Another deposition came from Mrs. Martile Able, widow of John Able, one of Billy's friends in Lincoln County War days. Mrs. Able was eighty-nine and bedfast when visited by Morrison and Brushy Bill in El Paso. She later told a reporter she had not seen Billy since some time before Pat Garrett claimed to have killed him. She said when Morrison brought Roberts to her as she lay in bed, the lawyer asked. "Do you know this lady?" and Roberts said, "Sure, that's John Able's wife." Mrs. Able had no doubt this was the young man she knew as Billy Bonney.

The meeting with Governor Mabry turned out to be a sad fiasco. Roberts was supposed to meet privately with the governor and state his case, but Mabry's staff clearly didn't take the proceeding seriously and viewed it as a publicity gimmick and photo op. They invited the regional press, radio stations, numerous historians, civic leaders, police authorities, and friends of Mabry's, plus such significant personages as Pat Garrett's sons Oscar and Jarvis, Tip McKinney's son, and even a grandson of Sheriff James Brady.

At a "press conference" cobbled together by the statehouse staff, old Brushy Bill was trundled out, white as a sheet, his eyes nervously searching the crowd as Mabry introduced the guests of honor. When reporters began firing questions, Roberts crumbled. He could remember nothing, not even Pat Garrett's name, and said he hadn't killed anybody in escaping from the Lincoln County jail, that he just got on his horse and rode away.

The guests were indignant. Oscar Jarvis seemed to speak for them all when he said, "I do not wish to dignify this claim with any questions."

Roberts, whose fright seems to have brought on a heart attack or a small stroke, had to be removed from the room. He lay awhile in a private chamber in the statehouse until he had recovered enough to return home.

Governor Mabry's announcement came as no surprise. "I am taking no action, now or ever, on this application for a pardon for Billy the Kid because I do not believe this man is Billy the Kid."

Morrison got Roberts home to Hico, a town just north of Hamilton where he had settled, and there the old man took to his bed for three weeks. He rallied enough to walk to the post office to deliver some letters for his wife, but suffered a fatal heart attack in front of the building on December 27, 1950. He was, by his own reckoning, ninety-one.

His story did not die with him.

Not long after Brushy Bill fell dead on Main Street in Hico, Morrison took his armload of interviews, depositions, and legal briefs and paid a visit to Dr. Charles Leland Sonnichsen, the brilliant Harvard-educated English professor and historian at Texas Western College in El Paso. Sonnichsen knew about the Lincoln County War and counted among his friends some of the greatest authorities on it and on Billy the Kid—Colonel Maurice Garland Fulton, William Kelleher, Eve Ball, and Robert N. Mullin, none of whom believed Roberts's story. But Sonnichsen, naturally dubious of the old man's claim himself, saw in it, and in Morrison's enthusiasm, material for a book. The result was a small but respectable collaborative effort, *Alias Billy the Kid* (1955), a fair and balanced work in its recounting of Roberts's story and a book once thought to be the last word on the subject of Billy's greatest claimant.

But thirty-five years after that seemingly definitive book, some startling scientific findings renewed the argument on whether or not Brushy Bill Roberts and Billy the Kid were one.

The work came as a result of research done by the Austin, Texas, novelist Frederic Bean, who became enthralled by the Roberts story and decided it warranted some scientific investigation.

Bean knew that the exhumation of the Kid's grave in Fort Sumner was unlikely to provide any evidence and would probably not even produce any bones due to the repeated floodings of the nearby Pecos River. In any event, no known blood relatives of the outlaw survived and so DNA testing was not an option, as it had been with the Jesse James case.

But there was at least one authentic photograph of the Kid at age twenty-one, another believed to be the Kid as a kid, and some images of William Henry "Brushy Bill" Roberts, boy and man. What about photographic analysis?

In 1990 Bean asked the University of Texas at Austin's Laboratory for Visual Systems, an arm of the Department of Electrical and Computer Engineering, to have a look at the images.

Four photographs were studied: that of young Billy, one of young Roberts, one of old Roberts, and the famous 1880 Fort Sumner tintype, owned by the Lincoln County Historical Trust (and identified as LCHT). The images were scanned, "improved"—getting rid of the "noise," the scratches and blemishes on the old tintype photo of the Kid—digitalized, and computerized. A photo of Mikhail Gorbachev and a known fake image of the Kid were added as comparison controls.

Comparisons were made in nine areas criminologists employ in identifying suspects from photos, areas involving unchanging basic bone structure: distance between the pupils of the eye, breadth of the eye internally and externally, breadth of nose and mouth, bizygomatic (cheekbone) breadth, distance between mid-lip and chin and mid-lip to nose, and nose length. (Ears are not measured since they are cartilaginous and can be altered, occluded, bent, and changed with age and other factors.)

"The fundamental research of the system used was by Townes (1976) and Kaya, Kobayashi (1972)," the Texas engineers wrote to Bean, adding that the "computerized pattern recognition systems" are "statistically proven for a 92% success rate in face recognition."

The comparisons produced some extraordinary findings in the Billy-Brushy case.

The LCHT photo of Billy and one of Roberts in his eighties were an amazing match in most categories. The margin of error, in which the lower the number the greater the match, was 17.7 pixels (picture elements) in comparing these two images. The photos of young Roberts and the LCHT image produced a somewhat greater (29.2) margin; a known fake image of the Kid produced a 79.6 margin and the Gorbachev photo compared to the LCHT tintype produced a 178.3 difference.

The computer engineers said the similarity between the facial structure of Roberts and the man in the LCHT tintype "is indeed amazing." The main sources of difference, the bizygomatic breadth and the mid-lip to lower chin distances, can be explained, they said, by weight gain and dental work.

If Brushy Bill Roberts was not Billy the Kid, then who was he?" asked Sonnichsen and Morrison at the end of *Alias Billy the Kid*.

It is the best of questions on the best of all the outlaw claimants, a man whose story inspired Sonnichsen's final word on the subject: "If it were not true, it ought to be."

DISAPPEARANCES

6

Bandit Laureate of the Mother Lode

A Tentative Good-bye to Black Bart

The Lewis Disbrow farm lies a mile out on Wyckles Road in Warrensburg township, five miles north of Decatur, Illinois. It is a calendar-photo place with its orange-roofed barn and corn and soybean bins, two-story white clapboard house, maple trees and big pumpkin field nearby.

The Disbrow place has been designated a Centennial Farm by the State of Illinois—the family has been farming there over 130 years—but it has another distinction as well: the celebrated California stagecoach bandit Charles E. "Black Bart" Boles homesteaded on this land in 1862 and Lewis Disbrow's orange business card attests to it. It reads "Black Bart Pumpkin Patch."

There are not many traces of the gentleman bandit extant— some Wells Fargo reward posters, the funny poems he left at some of his heists, the Disbrow farm where he abandoned his

*family. Black Bart was good at leaving few traces, so good we're
still trying to figure out what happened to him.*

Among the great highwaymen of romantic legend, Robin Hood
had his Merry Men and Alfred Noyes's nameless hero "came
riding—riding—riding—up to the old inn door."

Black Bart did not resemble these immortals in the remotest
way—he had no men, least of all merry ones, nor even a horse
except for shanks' mare—yet in an eight-year period he made a
name for himself (literally) and carved a deep niche in Gilded Age
California history as the harmless, horseless, whimsical nemesis
of Wells Fargo and bandit-laureate of the Mother Lode country.

When investigators confronted him outside his hotel in San
Francisco in November 1883, he was using the name C. E.
Bolton and to his captors he looked nothing like the down-and-
out, shifty-eyed, Dynamite Dick-variety desperado they were ac-
customed to. Instead, here stood, leaning on a cane but militarily
erect, a kindly, graying old duffer with a grand walrus mustache,
a jaunty derby hat on his head, and dressed to the nines in a
tailor-cut salt-and-pepper suit, waistcoat, and cravat.

He appeared every inch the prosperous mining man he
claimed to be. And if he wasn't, the operatives who nabbed him
must have thought, who *was* he?

In harmony with true legendry, in which little is in focus and
myth and outright fiction rules fact, only the eight years of Black
Bart's outlaw career has any historic documentation; the rest of
his life—the beginning, a ten-year period in the middle, and the
end of it—is a take-your-pick grab bag of speculation and sup-
position.

His name was probably Charles E. (middle name unknown)
Bolles, Boles, or Bowles, and it appears he was born in Norwich,
Norfolk County, England, in about 1829 and emigrated with his
family to the United States in 1830. The Boles clan, with perhaps
seven children among them, settled in Jefferson County in upstate

New York, on farming land near Watertown and not too far inland from Lake Ontario.

In 1850 Boles made his first trip to California, a year-late "forty-niner," traveling overland with his brother David to the goldfields around the American River and Sacramento, working claims in the Sierra foothills, in Butte, El Dorado, and Tuolumne counties. David Boles apparently died in California, precisely when and under what circumstance we do not know, and was buried at the Yerba Buena cemetery in San Francisco.

Charles returned to the farm in New York in 1852 and may have returned to California later that year, probably by himself and via the Panama-Chagres River route.

There can be little question that Boles did some kind of mining in California before his real debut in recorded history in the summer of 1875. He may even have had some minor success at it—enough, at least, to finance a probable return to the state in 1852 and subsequently to finance his homesteading ventures.

In 1854 he married Mary Elizabeth Johnson, the ceremony probably taking place near the Boles farm. We know nothing about his wife except that in later years she showed a saintly restraint when questioned about her absentee husband. For his part, Boles, in his mawkishly sentimental letters to her, appears to have genuinely cared for Mary despite the fact he would desert her and their children in 1873 and never, so far as is known, return to her and his familial responsibilities.

While his nineteen years as husband-at-home with Mary is a virtual blank, there is evidence he took her to Iowa on a brief farming venture and that in 1855 he was farming and homesteading in Macon County, Illinois, near Decatur. At least two daughters were born to Charles and Mary during this period and it was in Decatur that he enlisted, on August 13, 1862, in the 116th Illinois Volunteers, an infantry regiment. His papers listed him as age thirty-three, five feet eight inches in height, with gray eyes, said he was born in Norfolk County, England, and gave his occupation as farmer.

His Illinois regiment became part of General William T. Sherman's Fifteenth Army Corps in Memphis and Boles had his baptism of fire at the battle of Chickasaw Bayou, Mississippi, near Vicksburg, on December 27–28, 1862. During the battle and siege of Vicksburg, he served under Colonel (later Brigadier General) Giles A. Smith, who Boles may have known earlier in his life. Smith, the same age as Boles, was also a native of Jefferson County, New York, and had been a hotel proprietor in Bloomington, Illinois, fifty miles north of Decatur, at the outbreak of the war.

During the Atlanta campaign, Boles was wounded in the abdomen in a battle near Dallas, Georgia, north of Atlanta, in May, 1864, and was hospitalized for a time. He rejoined his unit in time to participate in Sherman's scorched-earth march to the sea and was mustered out with his regiment on June 7, 1865.

Between the end of his Civil War service and the first stagecoach robbery attributed to him, there is a decade-long gap in the historical record of Charles E. Boles.

Between June 1865, and July 1875, he is believed to have returned to his Decatur homestead briefly, drifted to Iowa, then to Minnesota. He may have left Mary and their children (now said to number four daughters) for a gold-mining venture in Montana Territory in 1867, in Idaho in 1869, and back to Montana in 1871.

It appears that he abandoned his wife and children in 1873 if not before, and returned to California where, for a time, he was engaged in legitimate mining work of some kind.

Mary settled in Hannibal, Missouri, in 1880, where at least one of her daughters had preceded her. She lived with her daughter and worked as a seamstress and the Hannibal City Directory listed her as a "widow."

Whatever mining activities Boles undertook upon his return to California must have ultimately failed and there is a hint that he developed a particular antipathy toward the prevailing giant of the Western freight business. When he began robbing stagecoaches he selected Wells Fargo coaches exclusively and when during the course of one of these robberies a female passenger threw her purse out of the coach window, Boles returned it politely, thanking the owner and saying "I honor only the good office of Wells Fargo."

More than likely, however, Boles preferred Wells Fargo for the same reason Willie Sutton preferred banks: it was where you found the money.

(Henry Wells and William G. Fargo formed the express company in 1843 in New York and made their fortune when they expanded into California in 1852, opening their first office on Montgomery Street in San Francisco. The company grew rapidly from a small, efficient business guarding bullion from the California goldfields to the east, to a corporate monolith buying out all its competitors, operating banks and a mail service and creating a monopoly on long- and short-distance freight west of the Mississippi. By 1859 Wells Fargo had 126 offices in the West, was using steamers from San Francisco Bay to carry freight around Cape Horn to Eastern ports, riverboats on the Sacramento, railroad cars, heavy freight wagons, mule trains, men on snowshoes in the Sierras, and—the principal symbol, if not the most important conveyance of the company—stagecoaches. If you shipped anything—mail, goods, ore, bullion, cash, or passengers—in or from California in the pre-railroad era, chances are you shipped by Wells Fargo.)

Boles's first recorded act of road agentry occurred on July 25, 1875, in Mark Twain's "Celebrated Jumping Frog" region of Calaveras County, southeast of Sacramento. In a daring and imaginative act, Boles simply stepped out of the roadside brush, aimed a shotgun, and stopped a Wells Fargo stagecoach near the town of Copperopolis. The double barrels provided the main instruction but Boles's appearance alone must have given the driver, a man named John Shine, pause: here stood a bandit wearing a linen duster, a flour sack with eyeholes cut from it over his head, and other sacks bound around his feet. Moreover, the robber appeared to have partners lurking in the bushes for he gestured to the edge of the trail to the manzanita shrub where several guns appeared to be aimed toward the coach. Then he pointed at the driver and said politely, "Please throw down the box," and over his shoulder to his phantom cohorts, "If he dares to shoot, give him a solid volley, boys!"

Shine's ten passengers—eight women and children and two men—waited, no doubt fearful for their lives and possessions. One woman offered the bandit her purse, which he declined. Then Boles instructed Shine to "drive on" and as the driver moved forward he glanced back and saw the robber cracking open the stage's familiar green-painted lockbox with an ax.

Boles's take in that first robbery was $174 in gold notes. Unknown to the amateur bandit, the stage also carried an iron safe bolted to the floor under the seat in which lay $644 in gold and coins.

When Shine (who, coincidentally, had also served in an Illinois regiment in the Civil War) returned to the scene a short time later, accompanied by a posse from Copperopolis, he found that the "guns" sticking from the bushes were merely whittled sticks. The bandit had acted alone and had escaped on foot without a trace, his bagged feet leaving no tracks.

Boles robbed at least two other Wells Fargo stages, in Yuba and Siskiyou counties, over the next two years, neither of which netted him much money (the Yreka stage in Siskiyou County carried only about $82), leading some to speculate that the highwayman may have had some other, legal source of funds, perhaps from some mining property or partnership.

Whatever the case, his caper on August 3, 1877, was particularly auspicious: he kept his flour-sack disguise, dropped the ploy about having comrades in the bushes, and, most significantly, first introduced the name that made him immortal in Old West history: Black Bart.

Again, he stopped a Wells Fargo stage, this time shifting his operation to the coastal area north of San Francisco in Sonoma County between Point Arena and the Russian River. From the strongbox he took a bit over $300 in cash. When the county sheriff came to investigate the scene of the robbery, the smashed strongbox was found to contain a waybill, on the back of which, in a weird and obviously disguised handwriting, the highwayman had left a clever message. It read:

> I've labored long and hard for bread
> For honor and for riches
> But on my corns too long you've tred
> You fine-haired Sons of Bitches.

The signature below the verse read "Black Bart, the PO8."

A year later Boles-as-Bart struck again—both with a Wells Fargo robbery and a poem. On July 25, 1878, the stage heading to Oroville, north of Sacramento, was robbed of $379 in cash, a diamond ring, and a gold watch. This time, the verse left in the box seemed a bit more philosophical and even a bit fatalistic:

> here I lay me down to sleep
> to wait the coming morrow
> perhaps success, perhaps defeat
> and everlasting sorrow
> let come what will, I'll try it on
> my condition can't be worse
> and if there's money in that box
> 'tis munny in my purse.

Boles's road agentry territory, covering a 350-mile stretch in ten counties, ranged from Calaveras County on the south to Jackson County, Oregon, on the north, from the Sierra Nevada foothills to near Fort Ross on the Pacific Coast. For a man without a horse, and in a time before bridges spanned San Francisco Bay and the larger waterways to the north, he covered a lot of ground—traveling by ferryboat, riverboat, railroad, stagecoach, and on foot.

His robberies followed a pattern: he selected rises on the road on which the horse teams had to slow, enabling him to emerge leisurely from the brush into the roadway, his shotgun leveled.

He rarely said more than "Throw down the box" and "Get along, now," the latter phrase after he had taken the box, or (in the case of the strongbox "safes" bolted to the floor of the coach under the driver's feet) smashed it and taken its contents.

He was never known to actually fire the shotgun or the Henry rifle he carried slung over his shoulder and later told authorities he never loaded them.

His "take" varied widely in the twenty-nine robberies attributed to him in his eight-year career and although one job is said to have netted him nearly $5,000, the average score was under $500 (even that a princely sum in 1880). On one occasion, when the lockbox had a paltry few dollars in it, Boles left this good-natured verse (which may be spurious although the rhyme and humor are certainly Bartean):

> So here I've stood while wind and rain
> Have set the trees a-sobbin'
> And risked my life for that damn stage
> That wasn't worth the robbin'.

Bay Area newspapers, especially feisty young William Randolph Hearst and his *San Francisco Examiner,* loved Bart and depicted him as waging a David vs. Goliath battle against Wells Fargo. Others were not so amused: California's Governor William Irwin announced a reward of $300 "for the capture and conviction of the bandit known as Black Bart," the federal government got into the act, authorizing the Post Office (some of whose mail had been taken in the robberies) to add $200 to the reward, and Wells Fargo, least amused of all, added its own $300 and printed posters announcing:

$800.00 Reward!
Arrest Stage Robber!

The wanted posters carried a facsimile reprint of Bart's poems and his signature but despite these measures, neither the reward

money nor the posters brought in a single clue as to Bart's identity or whereabouts.

What brought the bandit down involved the combination of
two clever and persistent investigators and Bart's own blunder.

James B. Hume, Wells Fargo's chief detective, had an impressive
record in California and Nevada before he joined the freight
company in 1873. In both appearance and actions he had all the
characteristics of a model Western lawman: tall, handsome, modest, reticent, quietly efficient, as dogged as Inspector Javert in
pursuit of Jean Valjean, and resourceful in his use of modern detection methods, including the new science of ballistics.

Hume had been trailing Boles almost from the beginning of
the bandit's career, visited the sites of all the holdups and patiently put together some valuable information. Witnesses in settlements near the scenes of the robberies described seeing a polite,
friendly man in his fifties, about five feet eight in height with
brownish-gray hair, a fierce gray mustache and matching goatee.
Several said he carried a bedroll (which Hume correctly guessed
carried the duster, flour sacks, shotgun, rifle, ax, pry bar, and
loot) as he passed through on foot and disappeared. Hume made
special note of the reports by several witnesses that the man's
boots were neatly slit at the toes as if to relieve corns or
bunions—small wonder, given the territory the bandit covered in
his hikes from the Sierras to the northern California coast and
even into Oregon.

Another piece of information Hume placed in his meticulous
dossier on Black Bart derived from a Wells Fargo robbery attempt on the early morning of July 13, 1882, near Laporte, in
Plumas County. Here the highwayman, wearing a duster, flour-
sack mask, and a floppy black hat, ran out of the brush and tried
to take hold of the reins of the three-horse stage team. The star-
tled driver "whooped up" the horses suddenly and the team ran
a few yards until the frightened lead horse ran the team off the
road. As the robber approached, Wells Fargo messenger George

Hackett, riding on the box beside the driver, fired his own shotgun at the would-be bandit. The load of buck tore off Bart's hat and he loped away down a hill. Hackett got a glimpse of his fleeing quarry, a man with gray-streaked hair and a bald spot on his head.

(Boles thus missed the robbery of his life: the Oroville-bound stage had $18,000 in bullion on board.)

But Hume's first real break in his investigation occurred on November 3, 1883, when Boles robbed a Wells Fargo coach headed from the town of Sonora to Milton, in Calaveras County. It was the classic instance of a criminal returning to the scene: this heist occurred on the precise spot as Bart's debut robbery over eight years earlier.

He had apparently traveled to Calaveras County from San Francisco via Stockton, took the train to Milton and a stage to Sonora, then camped along the Stanislaus River, near the stage road.

The driver that day, Reason McConnell, had stopped at the Reynolds Ferry Hotel on the Stanislaus and there agreed to give nineteen-year-old Jimmy Rolleri, son of the hotel manager, a ride. The boy wanted to go deer hunting in the gulch along the stage road and so took a .44 Henry rifle with him.

McConnell had a healthy sum in the big green strongbox bolted to the floor of the driver's compartment. Inside were 228 ounces of "amalgam"—a mixture of silver and mercury—in a conical-shaped cake worth over $4,000, plus over $500 in gold dust and coins.

After letting young Rolleri out to hunt in the brush, McConnell leisurely drove his team on. Atop a rise called Funk Hill, a few miles east of Copperopolis—the exact place where John Shine's stage was robbed in July 1875—Boles walked out from behind a roadside boulder, raised his shotgun, and ordered the driver to stop. McConnell later described how the bandit blocked the coach wheels with stones, then ordered the driver to unhitch the team and take the animals down the road a piece. McConnell heard the robber chopping at the strongbox with his ax, then spotted Rolleri stalking deer through the brush. He waved the boy down and the two walked back toward the coach. When Boles spotted them, Rolleri's Henry at the ready, he slung a sack over his shoulder and took off on a run.

McConnell took the boy's rifle and got off two shots, hitting nothing. Rolleri then took the Henry and fired once, nicking Boles across the knuckles of his hand.

At Copperopolis McConnell contacted County Sheriff Ben Thorne at San Andreas and wired Wells Fargo in San Francisco. The company sent detective Harry N. Morse, whom James B. Hume had hired to assist on the case, to the scene of the robbery. The two men followed the trail taken by Boles—whose identity, of course, they did not know—and along the road and in the brush picked up several items dropped by the bandit: a derby hat, some sugar, crackers, a belt, a binocular case, a magnifying glass, a razor, and two flour sacks.

More important than these, Morse found a bloodstained handkerchief knotted around a handful of buckshot. The rag bore a laundry mark: Fxo7.

In an astonishingly swift example of frontier justice, in eighteen days following his robbery of the Sonora-Milton stage, a judge's gavel and a prison door slammed on Charles E. Boles, aka Black Bart.

Hume and his man-on-the-scene, Morse, were real detectives in a time when law work, outside the Pinkerton Agency and Wells Fargo operations, consisted principally of gathering posses, serving warrants with a six-gun, and preventing mobs from lynching the miscreants. Few lawmen in 1883 put their nose on the carpet and searched for clues in the manner of a Sherlock Holmes (who had not yet surfaced: his first adventure was published in 1887) and not many did the legwork that ended Black Bart's escapades.

Harry Morse's career as a lawman surpassed even that of his boss, the dauntless Jim Hume. A forty-eight-year-old New Yorker and onetime merchant seaman, Morse had come to California as a forty-niner and had been elected sheriff of Alameda County in

1863. He served seven terms, survived several gunfights, had a reputation as an expert tracker, a long-distance pursuer, and one who used detection as well as his guns and fists in maintaining law and order in his jurisdiction. In 1874 he assisted in the search for the notorious outlaw Tiburcio Vásquez that led to the bandit's arrest and execution, and after his fourteen years as sheriff he set up a detective agency in San Francisco that eventually employed sixty carefully selected men. So great was Morse's reputation as a manhunter and detective that Hume hired him expressly to help solve the Black Bart case.

Hume and Morse knew that the laundry mark, their only genuine clue to the long roll call of Wells Fargo stage robberies they attributed to the man they knew only as Black Bart, could unlock the case. Morse spent a week visiting the laundries in the Bay Area—working from a list of ninety of them. He struck paydirt when he dropped into the California Laundry, which shared space with a tobacconist on Stevenson Street, a few blocks from Wells Fargo's San Francisco office. The laundry proprietor identified the Fxo7 handkerchief mark as that assigned to one C. E. Bolton, a mining man who lived in a hotel called Webb House on Second Street, a man whose landlady said was "an ideal tenant. So quiet, so respectable and so punctual with his room rent."

Morse and his agents staked out the hotel. They did not have long to wait. In the late afternoon of November 9, six days after the robbery, the man who called himself Charles E. Bolton emerged from his rooms and sauntered alone down the street swinging his cane. Morse had the tobacconist, T. C. Ware, introduce him to the nattily dressed suspect and using the ploy that he needed help in identifying some ore he had nearby, took Boles to his Wells Fargo office where Hume awaited.

Morse later described his man as "elegantly dressed," wearing "a natty little derby hat, a diamond pin, a large diamond ring on his little finger and a heavy gold watch and chain," and observed, "One would have taken him for a gentleman who had made a fortune and was enjoying it. He looked anything but a robber."

Under Hume's questioning, Bolton gave his age as fifty-five

and, at first, said simply that he was a mining man although he did not identify any mining property by name or location with which he was involved.

Hume noticed the man had had scabs along the knuckles of one hand.

After a time Bolton refused to answer further questions but there being no Miranda warnings in 1883, nor any search warrant laws, and since suspects then were considered guilty until proven innocent, Bolton was taken into custody by a San Francisco police captain. He was then led back to Webb House where the police officer and Wells Fargo agents searched his apartment.

Morse quickly found what he needed: a sample of handwriting that matched that of a Black Bart poem plus a handkerchief and other items bearing the California Laundry's Fxo7 mark.

The man who continued to identify himself as Charles E. Bolton was now officially under arrest and taken by train to Stockton for arraignment and overnight jailing, then by train to Milton and by buckboard to San Andreas. Morse, along with Calaveras County Sheriff Ben Thorne, questioned the prisoner unrelentingly and after five hours of grilling Bolton began to crumble. He took exception only to being described as a "common criminal" ("I am a gentleman," he insisted) and at one point asked the question that sealed his fate: "Suppose that a man who had committed a robbery made a clean breast of the affair and made full restitution. Might he expect to escape a prison sentence?"

Morse said it was not possible but that a confession would be taken into consideration by the sentencing judge.

At last, Bolton confessed—but only to the Funk Hill robbery—and agreed to take the lawmen to the spot where he buried the amalgam. The silver was recovered, together with some gold coins and dust, and Bolton returned to San Andreas in the custody of Sheriff Thorne.

(The San Francisco Newsletter reported: "The arrest of Black Bart, the hero of twenty-three stage-coach robberies, appears to develop the fact that in the placid intervals during which he was not employed in the cheerful pastime of leveling double-barreled shot-guns at stage-drivers and corraling treasure-boxes, he lived in San Francisco and passed for a mining man. This apparently disarmed suspicion where naturally enough it ought to have excited it.")

At some point in the questioning, Boles-Bolton, who continued to deny *he* was Black Bart (probably fearing that such an admission would result in his being charged with all the robberies attributed to the "PO8"), nevertheless told Wells Fargo investigators the origin of the name. He said it derived from a character in a novel, *The Case of Summerfield,* published serially in a Sacramento newspaper some years earlier. The leading character in the novel, with whom Boles obviously felt a kinship, was Bartholomew Graham, a Civil War veteran, desperado, and Wells Fargo bandit known as "Black Bart."

Boles-as-Bolton, convicted of a single count of armed robbery—that of the Sonora-Milton holdup—was sentenced in a San Andreas court on November 17 to six years imprisonment. Newspapers speculating on the light sentence guessed that the court took into consideration the age of the defendant (he was fifty-four), the fact that no evidence existed that he ever fired his shotgun or robbed a stage passenger, and that he cooperated with authorities.

He entered San Quentin Prison on November 21, 1883, listed as Prisoner 11046, Charles E. Bolton. But while he never confessed to authorities that he was Black Bart nor that his birth name was Charles E. Boles, he admitted all in letters he wrote to his family. "Yes, it is only too true," he wrote his brother in New York a month after his imprisonment, "I am your brother, lost & in disgrace," and San Francisco area reporters soon ferreted out his identity, even tracing his wife Mary to Hannibal, Missouri, where she had moved in 1880. He told a Stockton reporter, "The shame of my old friends finding me out hurts me more than all. . . . I never drink, smoke, or chew; all my friends are gentlemen. . . . To be sure, I can't claim to be perfect. They say I will rob a stage occasionally. But no one can say that I ever raised my gun to do anyone harm."

Even before his capture, Black Bart's exploits were a favorite subject of San Francisco newspapers, especially Hearst's *Examiner,* and soon the national press. Not long after his imprisonment, Beadle & Adams, the great dime-novel publisher, issued a book, *The Gold Dragon, or, the California Bloodhound: A Story of PO8, the Lone Highwayman,* which, while having little resemblance to anything in the Boles/Bart story, succeeded in spreading his notoriety from coast to coast.

ॐ

In San Quentin, after a twenty-year silence, he began writing to his wife in Hannibal, letters filled with obsequious sentimentalities and pious, self-serving confessions. He said he would rejoin her and the children when he was released, but after he was freed begged off any immediate reunion, promising eventually to come home when he would not be a "burthen" to her.

There is no record that he ever saw Mary and his children again.

He served four years and two months of his sentence, earned an early, good-behavior release on January 21, 1888, and walked out of the prison with the suit he wore when he entered it together with his gold watch, cane, and five dollars in cash. At an impromptu press conference he thanked San Quentin officials for their kindnesses to him and spoke of his faithful wife and three grown daughters and his longing to be reunited with them.

Boles, now sixty, returned to San Francisco for a time, living in a shabby boardinghouse (which Wells Fargo kept under surveillance during his stay there) sustained by money he had secreted from authorities or from some other, never identified source. He was also spotted by alert Wells Fargo agents in the towns of Modesto, Merced, and Madera.

In February 1888, he traveled southeast to the town of Visalia, between Fresno and Bakersfield, and registered on the twenty-eighth at the Palace Hotel there. Then, a few days later, he left the hotel and never returned.

Wells Fargo, which had watched Boles after his release from prison, clearly suspicious that despite his age he might return to his road agentry career, investigated his disappearance and the intrepid James B. Hume traveled down to Visalia. In Boles's room was found a valise containing cans of corned beef and tongue, crackers, jelly, some sugar, two neckties, and a pair of cuffs bearing the Fxo7 laundry mark.

As for Boles, he was never seen again.

What became of him?

Stories—most of them harebrained—abound: he moved to Harrisburg, Pennsylvania, and married a childhood sweetheart with whom he corresponded while in San Quentin, doing so apparently without benefit of a divorce from Mary Elizabeth; he kept more Wells Fargo money than he returned and lived a life of luxury in Mexico or New Orleans or perhaps St. Louis or New York City. (A New York newspaper allegedly carried Boles's obituary in 1917 but the notice has never been found.) He was spotted in the Klondike during the great Yukon gold rush of 1896 and in several Western towns where he had returned to work as a farmer.

Among the intriguing tales was that which placed Boles in Olanthe, Kansas, south of Kansas City. A thief had been arrested there who was identified by local law authories as Black Bart. James B. Hume dispatched an operative, Jonathan Thacker, to Olanthe to investigate and while the thief in fact turned out to be a former Wells Fargo bandit who had served time in Folsom Prison, the man was not Black Bart. Thacker, however, did return to San Francisco with a Bart story. He said he had learned that after his release from San Quentin, Boles roamed around Utah, Montana, and Idaho, then made his way to Vancouver and sailed for Japan. Thacker even provided the name of the steamship that took Boles to the Orient—the *Empress of China*—and added this closing-the-book remark, "He is in that country now, and at any rate, he is straight as a string."

One persistent and patently preposterous rumor, fomented by Hearst's *San Francisco Examiner,* had it that Boles resumed his career as Wells Fargo nemesis after his release from prison—there were apparently a few northern California robberies in the late 1880s that seemed to match his style—until the company awarded him a $125-a-month "pension" for agreeing to leave their vehicles alone.

Wells Fargo, throughout 1888, did continue to list "Bolton" as a suspect in certain stage holdups and issued a detailed circular giving his height as "5 feet 8 inches in stockings," his shoe size (No. 6), hat size (7-1/2), weight (160 pounds), and such details, including the scar from his Civil War wound, as these: "does not use tobacco in any form, nor intoxicating liquors or opium. High forehead . . . eyes, light blue and deep-set; nose, rather prominent and broad at base . . . two lower teeth missing in center . . . forearms quite hairy; heavy tuft of hair on breast; gunshot wound opposite navel on right side; well muscled; has been troubled with throat disease and voice at times seems somewhat impaired."

The circular, which contained more precise and probably accurate information on Boles than any other document, called him "a thorough mountaineer, a remarkable walker, and claims he cannot be excelled in making quick transits over mountains and grades," and observed that Boles was "a cool, self-contained talker with waggish tendencies; and since his arrest has . . . exhibited genuine wit under most trying circumstances."

Nine months after her husband was last seen in Visalia, California, Mary Elizabeth Boles was interviewed by a Hannibal, Missouri, newspaper and said, "I believe he is engaged in mining in some secluded spot in the mountains, though of course I do not know. He may be dead. God only knows."

Mary never seems to have had any rancor toward her wayward husband.

Curiously, from 1892 to her death on March 6, 1896, she had listed herself in the city directory as a "widow."

In 1948 Hollywood provided the most fabulous of all theories on his career. The Universal film *Black Bart,* starring Dan Duryea as Bart, had him a respectable rancher who robbed stagecoaches for the fun of destroying the Wells Fargo company. Additional spice was added by having Bart involved with the celebrated courtesan Lola Montez (played by Yvonne DeCarlo).

California journalist and gold country historian George Hoeper, a resident of Calaveras County, offers a theory that Black Bart may indeed have returned to his old profession and ended up dead in the Comstock Lode region of Nevada. Hoeper has found evidence that in the summer of 1888, a masked bandit attempted to rob a stagecoach out of Virginia City headed for Reno, was killed by shotgun blasts and buried in a shallow grave alongside the road. When the stage driver brought lawmen to the scene and the body was uncovered it was said the corpse resembled photos and sketches of Black Bart.

The grave was covered again and, unmarked, disappeared into the landscape.

If it *was* Black Bart in the vanished grave, he could not have planned a better sort of "PO8'ic" justice.

7

The Mad Hatter and the Assassin

Boston Corbett and John Wilkes Booth

He may have been—may have been—the Jack Ruby of his day, the killer of a killer of a president of the United States.

Ruby's shooting of Lee Harvey Oswald on November 24, 1963, in the basement of the Dallas jail was witnessed by reporters and cops—and broadcast live on television. But Boston Corbett's shooting of John Wilkes Booth on April 26, 1865, in a tobacco barn a few miles south of Port Royal, Virginia, attracted controversy from the get-go. While he was celebrated for a time as Booth's killer, his place as a minor figure in the Lincoln assassination remains in question over 130 years after the event.

Corbett shot somebody who was standing in that burning barn, but was it Booth?

If not Booth, who?

If not Booth, what happened to Booth?
And what happened to Corbett?

He arrived in Concordia, county seat of Cloud County, Kansas, in 1878, jouncing over rutted dirt roads in a buckboard pulled by a pony he called "Billy." He was small and wiry with a thin and straggly mustache and chin whiskers, wore a faded homespun linsey-woolsey shirt and baggy trousers held up with a old army belt from which two big pistols flapped in scuffed holsters at his sides. Everyone who saw him remarked on his hair—parted severely in the middle of his head and pulled behind his ears to hang down in straight black locks to his shoulders—and his burning brown eyes, unblinking and scary, fueled as if by some interior fever.

He said he was taking up farming on eighty acres of land a few miles northeast of Concordia along the Republican River and he built a crude dugout on his property and hired some men to plow the ground and plant corn. But he seemed to do little farming, had no stock other than his faithful pony, and no farming implements. He also had no friends and made no attempt to attract them: indeed, he welcomed no one on his property and waved his pistols at those who ventured too close to his dugout. He lived as a hermit, a strange existence for one who, as it soon became known, had a record as a seasoned fire-and-brimstone evangelist, one of the "shouting brethren," as a Topeka newspaper described him after he began calling sinners to task at the Methodist Episcopal Church in Concordia.

When he stood before that small congregation for the first time, soon after he took up his lonely residence on the outskirts of Concordia, it became clear that he was the militant messenger of a singularly angry God. In his preaching he would throw his arms out crucifixionlike, toss his long hair from side to side in a spasm of religious ardor, and recount his days as a "down-and-outer," how he "came to Christ," was baptized, heard voices, and saw angels. He told of seeing signs in the sky that read "Repent, for the Day is at hand!" and of going off to war to kill Confederates. He said he marched into battle with a single thought in mind: "I will say to them 'God have mercy on your souls'— then pop them off."

He made no secret of his past: indeed, his notoriety had preceded him even to remote Concordia and his name and his single celebrated act, just thirteen years ago, drew curious crowds to his revivals.

People came not so much to hear his fevered messages of sin and redemption as simply to see him in the flesh: Boston Corbett, Lincoln's Avenger, the strange, fiery little preacher-soldier who killed John Wilkes Booth.

What little is known of Boston Corbett's life before April 26, 1865, has been pieced together from Corbett's own often confused and contradictory testimony, the recollections of his few acquaintances and fewer friends, and from Union Army records and newspaper accounts.

He was born Thomas H. (or P.) Corbett in London in 1832, emigrated with his parents to Troy, New York, in 1839, and as a youth, he said, "struggled in poverty for an education, became a fair scholar and fluent speaker."

In Troy, at a young age, he learned to be a hat-maker in a time when the dire occupational hazard of that trade remained undiscovered. In the 1850s, when Corbett was learning his craft, most of the felt for hats was made from coney (rabbit), muskrat, and beaver fur and one of the most important felt-making processes, known as "carroting," was the soaking of the fur in open vats of nitrate of mercury. The inescapable inhaling of the vapors from this evil brew affected the brain. Hallucinatory episodes, twitches and tics (known as "hatter's shakes"), and outright psychoses were often the product of the hatter's labors and were most certainly the root of Corbett's undoubted madness.

(The phrase "mad as a hatter" seems to predate hat-making and may come from "atter" or "adder," the poisonous snake whose bite was believed to cause insanity. But the phrase, made famous by the character in *Alice in Wonderland*, has a pertinent, if accidental, accuracy applied to the early hat-making trade.)

He worked in the trade in Troy and Albany, in Richmond, Virginia, and in Boston and New York City for several years and is said to have married during this period, losing his wife and baby in childbirth. After this tragedy, he became a derelict, began drinking heavily, and strayed into religion after attending a revival meeting in New York.

In 1857, while working in Boston, Corbett was baptized, apparently into the Methodist Church, and the experience so moved him he adopted the name of the city where he found his faith.

He was by now a local eccentric. He wore his hair long "because all the pictures of Christ represented Him wearing long locks," and preached extemporaneously to any passerby who paused in curiosity.

Corbett's religious fanaticism, loud but harmless (newspapers called him the "Glory to God Man"), took a violent turn in the summer of 1858. After a revival meeting at a North Square church in Boston he was propositioned on the street by two prostitutes. The experience so unhinged him that he returned to his cheap boardinghouse room, pored over chapters 18–19 of the book of Matthew ("And if thine eye offend thee, pluck it out and cast it from thee. . . . and there be eunuchs, which have made themselves eunuchs for the kingdom of heaven's sake"), and castrated himself with a pair of scissors. He was treated at Massachusetts General Hospital from July 16 to August 18.

His whereabouts for the two and a half years that followed his hospitalization is unknown, but he returned to New York state at some point in this period and in April, 1861, enlisted as a private in Company I, Twelfth New York Militia.

His habitual disciplinary problems began before the ink dried on his enlistment papers when he heard Colonel Butterfield, commander of the militia regiment, unleash an outburst of profanity toward his raw recruits. Corbett upbraided the colonel for using the Lord's name in vain and for this was marched off to the guardhouse. A few days later Butterfield offered to release him if he would apologize for his insubordination but Corbett refused, saying, "No, I have only offended the colonel while the colonel has offended God and I shall never ask the colonel's pardon until he himself has asked the pardon of God."

Somehow Corbett got through all this and in August 1863, he reinlisted, this time in Company L, Sixteenth New York Cavalry. Soon he was promoted to corporal and later rose to the rank of sergeant, despite his service record listing many disciplinary problems. He fought a losing battle in haranguing fellow soldiers for their use of profanity; he held unauthorized prayer sessions and argued with his superiors. New York Cavalrymen remembered their odd comrade for his periodic punishment tours in which he carried a knapsack filled with bricks around the guardhouse.

But those who commanded him saw in him a fierce and resolute fighting man and at least one notable enemy officer experienced and admired this attribute.

In June 1864, Confederate raiders under John Singleton Mosby cornered a squad of Union troopers, including Corbett, at Culpeper Courthouse in Virginia. The "Glory to God Man" refused to surrender, found cover, and opened fire on Mosby and his twenty-six raiders. Only when his ammunition ran out did Corbett give up. Mosby was impressed.

Corbett and his comrades were sent to the newly opened and already notorious Andersonville prison in Georgia. He endured five months incarceration there, three of them in an outdoor compound. On November 19, 1864, he was released in an exchange of prisoners and his superiors then assigned him to an army hospital in Annapolis, Maryland, to recover from exposure, malnutrition, and scurvy.

There is no clear record of Corbett's duties or whereabouts at the end of 1864 and the first four months of 1865, but he had returned to the Sixteenth New York Cavalry by April that year and was said to be the first man to volunteer for service in the pursuit of President Lincoln's assassin, John Wilkes Booth.

On April 15, the day Lincoln was murdered, Colonel Lafayette C. Baker, head of the War Department's secret police in Washington, took command of the mission to find and arrest the assassin and his conspirators. His specific orders from War Secretary Edwin Stanton stated he was to "capture but not to shoot Booth."

Baker's intelligence network picked up information that Booth and conspirator David Herold had been spotted crossing the Potomac from Maryland into Virginia and the eager and erratic colonel quickly put together a search force of twenty-six men. These were volunteers from the headquarters detail of Corbett's regiment, the Sixteenth New York Cavalry, then stationed at Vienna, Virginia, twelve miles out of the capital. Lieutenant Edward P. Doherty was assigned to lead the search team with Lieutenant Colonel Everton J. Conger accompanying. Corbett recalled later that he volunteered for the search party because he knew that as a reward for his prayers, Booth would be delivered into his hands.

The officers, men, and horses were boarded on the steamer *John S. Ide* on April 24 to make their way down the Potomac from Washington.

Unknown to the search party, that very day Booth and David E. Herold, a nineteen-year-old pharmacist's clerk later described as "doltish" and having the intellect of an eleven-year-old, had journeyed to the Rappahannock concealed in a wagonload of hay. With the assistance of three ex-Confederate soldiers they were ferried across the river to Port Royal and rode on horseback the three miles down the road toward Bowling Green to the farm of a known Confederate sympathizer named Richard Garrett.

On the twenty-fifth, Doherty, Conger, and their troopers rode overland to Port Conway on the Rappahannock and questioned a ferryman named William Rollins. Rollins told of two men, one crippled, who had crossed the river to Port Royal the day before, heading for Bowling Green, about fifteen miles to the south. The ride to Bowling Green—during which the Federal troopers passed the Garrett farm where Booth and Herold watched them from a stand of pine trees—proved to be a wild-goose chase. But Doherty did find there a young Confederate veteran named William Jett who had accompanied the fugitives across the Rappahannock and said the men were hiding out on a farm owned by Richard Garrett, three miles inland from Port Royal.

The search force now backtracked, Corbett riding at the rear of the column, and at about two o'clock on the morning of April 26 arrived at the farm. Doherty deployed his men around the property and the farm owner was summoned and questioned by Colonel Conger. Richard Garrett professed ignorance of Booth's whereabouts but when a noose was slung around his neck his son stepped forward and said Booth and his friend were sleeping in the barn.

Booth and Herold were ordered to surrender. Herold complied, stumbled out of the barn, and was tied to a tree, but Booth remained inside, shouting, "Well, my brave boys, prepare a stretcher for me!" Pine boughs were brought forward and piled around the barn yet Booth, propped up on two crutches and with a carbine at his hip, still refused to lay down his weapon and give himself up. Someone tossed a handful of burning straw into the barn and soon the structure was aflame and pouring smoke.

Corbett, meantime, stood among Doherty's troopers stationed at a point on the outbuilding's perimeter where, through a gap in the barn's siding, he could see the lone figure inside. He said at the conspiracy trial a month later that he had never seen Booth before but that the man in the barn had a broken leg and made "desperate replies" to the Federal officers who demanded his surrender. He testified in a May 1, 1865, statement:

> I saw [Booth] in the act of stooping or springing, and concluded he was going to use his weapons. I immediately took steady aim upon him with my revolver and fired— shooting him through the neck and head. He was then carried out of the barn before the fire reached him; was taken to the Piazza of the house . . . Lt. Doherty, and the detective officers who were in front of the barn, did not seem to know that I had shot him, but supposed he had

shot himself, until I informed Lt. Doherty of the fact—showing him my pistol which bore evidence of the truth of my statement, which was also confirmed by the man placed at my right-hand who saw it.

(On other occasions Corbett would say that he did not want Booth to be roasted alive in the barn and that "Providence directed me.")

Whatever the case, the shot he made was an extraordinary one considering the distance, the weapon, the smoke and fire within the barn, and the confusion outside it. The bullet struck Booth in the back of his head (at almost the same spot as Booth's derringer bullet had struck Lincoln), severing his spinal cord.

The assassin was dragged from the burning barn and placed on a mattress from the Garrett house. He was scarcely recognizable as the darkly handsome actor who posed for *cartes de visite* only a few weeks before. He was filthy, his hair in tangles, an eleven-day growth of beard concealing his emaciated face. He told his captors, "Tell Mother that I died for my country," then, paralyzed, asked that his arms be raised so he could see his hands. "Useless . . . useless" were his final words. He died a few minutes after 7:00 A.M.

Booth's body was sewn in a saddle blanket and taken by wagon to the Rappahannock, placed on a tugboat that transferred it to the ironclad *Montauk*. On board, Surgeon General J. K. Barnes, working under a canvas awning, supervised a necropsy on the corpse after which Booth's remains were conveyed to Greenleaf Point, site of a former Federal penitentiary now used as a storage building of the Washington Arsenal. Secretary Stanton sent a coroner to examine the body and Booth was identified from a tumor scar on the back of his neck, from a tattoo "JWB" on his hand, and from gold fillings in his teeth. There was some confusion over which leg had been broken in the leap to the stage of Ford's Theater, but at least ten witnesses testified to the identity of the body as that of John Wilkes Booth.

The assassin's corpse, placed inside a wooden rifle case, was buried in a shallow grave under the warehouse floor on the night of April 27.

From the day the body was brought down the Potomac to the capital, the rumors began: *somebody* was shot and killed at the Garrett farm, *somebody* was buried under the floor of the arsenal . . . but not John Wilkes Booth. These will-o'-the-wisp rumors would be repeated, always with some new and startling "evidence" added, for forty years and would never completely be stilled.

Over the years there would be at least twenty men claiming to be the assassin. Booth was "sighted" in Leadville, Colorado; Fresno and San Francisco; Canada, England, Shanghai, India, Ceylon, the Pelew Islands in the South Pacific; in China serving with General Gordon in the Taiping Rebellion, and in Mexico during Emperor Maximilian's regime.

Booth's granddaughter, Izola Forrester, came to the conclusion in her 1937 memoir that the Lincoln assassination had been "instigated by men in the Order of the Knights of the Golden Circle, said to have been a branch of Freemasonry," and that Booth "escaped from the Garret farm through the aid of the Order and lived in exile until 1879."

(The Knights of the Golden Circle, a radical pro-slavery, pro-South secret society that flourished during the Civil War and Reconstruction era, was eventually "exposed" in the *Louisville Journal*. The newspaper claimed that among its members were Vice President Andrew Johnson, Confederate President Jefferson Davis, many influential congressmen and senators, and generals on both sides in the war. The *Journal* called the order "the Invisible Government of the North and South.")

After the Garrett farm incident Corbett was placed under arrest by Colonel Conger, Doherty's superior officer in the search party. The charge was breach of military discipline "in firing without

Doherty's order and in defiance of Gen. Baker's order" and Corbett may have been placed under guard along with David Herold on the *Montauk* during the return to the capital.

Back in Washington, Corbett awaited court-martial but upon hearing the story of the incident, War Secretary Stanton ordered the sergeant's freedom. "The rebel is dead," Stanton announced theatrically, "the patriot lives . . . the patriot is released."

On August 17, 1865, Corbett mustered out of the army (Lieutenant Doherty having commended him by saying "In military capacity he is second to none in the service") and moved to Danbury, Connecticut. There he found work, again in the hat trade, and supplemented his income with occasional lectures, illustrated with lantern slides, on his exploit as "Lincoln's Avenger."

In Camden, New Jersey, where he cropped up in the late 1860s, he was known as a "Methodist lay preacher," and soon became full-time minister at the Siloam Methodist Episcopal Mission there. A Philadelphia reporter who found him in Camden wrote that Booth's slayer lived alone in a little house, did his own cooking, and "preaches and exhorts himself and uses a Windsor chair for a pulpit."

During Corbett's Camden ministry, President Andrew Johnson permitted Booth's brother Edwin to disinter John Wilkes's body from the arsenal-warehouse grave and rebury him in the family plot in Baltimore's Greenmount Cemetery. Edwin seemed to be prepared to make the definitive identification of the body and to lay the "Booth lives" rumors to rest. In February 1869, the grave was opened. But Edwin could not bear to look at his brother's remains, much less identify them, and a Baltimore newspaper soon after reported that the body displayed a broken *right* leg (it was the left Booth broke at Ford's Theater) and no bullet wounds.

The "Booth lives" stories were given new life.

From the beginning, even among those who did not question that the assassin had died at the Garrett farm, the debate continued as to whether or not Corbett actually fired the fatal shot that killed Booth or whether Booth committed suicide or escaped. Some believed Colonel Conger made the shot from a corner of the barn. (He received a suspiciously high $15,000 of the combined $75,000 offered for Booth's and Herold's capture.) Others believed Lieutenant Edward Doherty had done the shooting and point out that he received $5,250 of the reward money and was never questioned at the conspirator's trial. Izola Forrester, Booth's granddaughter, wrote in 1937 that Corbett's claim to have made the fatal shot was "a dramatic seizing of honor which brought him no punishment, but a share in the final award of money, and an established position before the public in the North, on which he capitalized, by delivering for several years lectures on how he killed Booth." And an early Lincoln assassination authority, David M. DeWitt, wrote in 1903 that testimony showed that Corbett was at least thirty feet from the barn when the shot was fired that killed Booth. DeWitt concluded, "Corbett's story, highly improbable, because of the relative position of the parties, and uncorroborated by the testimony of a single witness out of the twenty-four comrades presumably on the watch, seems to have been accepted without question."

But an investigator-author named Byron Berkeley Johnson, who knew Corbett well, who had dinner with him after his release from custody, and who took Corbett to Matthew Brady's studio in Washington to have his portrait made, wrote of those who denied Corbett's deed: "It might as truthfully be said that Booth did not shoot Lincoln." And even John G. Nicolay and John Hay, who had unlimited access to the records, credit Corbett with killing Booth in their ten-volume biography of Lincoln published in 1890.

For his part of the government's reward for bringing Booth "to justice," Corbett received $1,653.85. His petition for a federal pension for his service in the Union Army, specifically for his work as a volunteer in the dangerous business of tracking down Lincoln's assassin, came through in 1882. He was granted $7.50 a month in appreciation of his "services" to the United States.

❦

What drew Boston Corbett to Kansas in 1878? And why Kansas, specifically Concordia, of all places?

The answers, like those on Corbett's life from beginning to end, begin with "perhaps" and "maybe." Perhaps he knew some former Union soldiers or fellow Andersonville prisoners in the area. Perhaps he was running away from something such as letters he allegedly received from unreconstructed Confederates that notified him he would suffer for killing the great patriot Booth. Maybe he wanted to escape the incessant notoriety he received from Eastern newspapers, even thirteen years after the event. Maybe he was curious about heartland America, a place he had never been, and saw it as a fertile field for his evangelism.

As for the facts of Corbett's Kansas period, what is known from the actual historical record is sparse and sad and all of it points to a deteriorating mental state.

In November 1885, he was arrested for threatening with a pistol some boys playing baseball on the Sabbath in a pasture near his property. The case was dismissed by the county attorney.

A year after this incident, through the efforts of the Grand Army of the Republic and a state legislator from Cloud County, Corbett was hired as an assistant doorkeeper at the Kansas House of Representatives in Topeka. He reported for duty in January 1887, and lasted a month before his brain's demons caught up with him.

In a 1913 account gathered by Byron Berkeley Johnson, this report was given of Corbett's conduct in the Topeka legislative chambers: "On February 15 [1887], laboring under the impression that he was being discriminated against by other officers of the House, Mr. Corbett drew a revolver and, running the officers from the building, created such a commotion that it became necessary to adjourn the Legislature. He was finally seized by police officers, overpowered and was taken before the probate judge, where he was adjudged insane on the following day."

Contemporary newspaper reports in the Kansas capital said that Corbett believed the other doorkeepers and officers of the

Legislature were laughing at him behind his back, that he first drew a knife and threatened a janitor, then pointed a revolver at the House sergeant-at-arms and, proceeding to the House gallery, succeeded in causing lawmakers, staff, and workers to flee for their lives. Another account says he drew two large revolvers and "With his very best evangelistic voice he informed the Legislators that God demanded their lives, and promptly cut loose with both guns."

Prairie justice abided no wasting of time. The day after the fracas, Corbett was brought before a judge. Topeka District Attorney Charles Curtis (later vice president of the United States under President Herbert C. Hoover) spoke for the state and a quick verdict came down: Corbett was to be committed to the Topeka Asylum for the Insane.

He failed on his first attempt to escape but on May 26, 1888, he succeeded. Walking around the asylum grounds with other inmates on that day, Corbett saw a pony belonging to the young son of the superintendent tied up in front of the hospital office. He returned, stole the horse, and rode away.

A week later, as flyers were posted everywhere and posses combed the state for him, Corbett surfaced in Neodesha in the southeastern part of the state. There, it was reported, he met a local school superintendent named Richard Thatcher and one Irvin DeFord, son of a soldier who had known Corbett at Andersonville. Thatcher and DeFord are said to have supplied Corbett with a fresh horse, food, and money and it is their testimony, filtered through others, that Corbett said he had been "shamefully mistreated" and intended fleeing to Mexico.

He may have. He was only fifty-six years old and in good physical health and Mexico was the perfect place to do what he did—disappear.

There is not a single substantiated sighting of Corbett or shred of real evidence about him after June 1, 1888, the date he rode away from Neodesha. A Judge Huron, appointed Corbett's "guardian" by the court that had pronounced him insane, tried

to track his ward but to no avail. He did, however, ruin one imposter's career. In the early 1900s, Huron investigated the case of
a man who filed for a pension under the name Boston Corbett.
The judge determined that the claimant was six feet tall and
under fifty years of age (Corbett was five feet five inches tall and
would have been sixty-eight years old in 1900) and succeeded in
sending the man to a penitentiary in Georgia.

Other imposters cropped up periodically. In September 1905,
the *New York Sun* carried a story about a man in Dallas, Texas,
claiming to be Corbett. He turned out to be a fraud. In November 1913, another "Boston Corbett," much too young (Corbett
would have been eighty-one), turned out to be a patient in the
government hospital for the insane in Washington, D.C.

Corbett was sighted in the South, West, and Southwest, in
Mexico, South America, and even in the "Oriental Seas" by the
captain of a privateer who had the story from a professor in
Bombay, India. The sightings of him in exotic places rivaled those
of John Wilkes Booth.

In 1901 a writer and collector of Lincolniana named Osborn
H. Oldroyd wrote in a privately published book about the Lincoln assassination that in the 1890s Corbett was earning a living
as a traveling patent medicine peddler and made his home in
Enid, Oklahoma. A 1913 story in the *Boston Herald,* perhaps derived from Oldroyd's account, also claimed that Corbett became
"a patent medicine peddler and was residing in Enid, Oklahoma," at the time of his death. In the 1920s historian Lloyd
Lewis investigated Corbett's disappearance and concluded that
Oldroyd's story contained some inaccuracies but that "the evidence of Corbett's residence in Enid may have been more accurate."

Enid, not far south of the Kansas state line and only about 150
miles southwest of Neodesha, where he had been last seen, is
where the strange story of Boston Corbett takes its strangest
turn. To trace it, we have to turn the calendar back to 1870.

In that year a Memphis lawyer named Finis L. Bates moved

to the town of Granbury, Texas, near Fort Worth, and had as one of his first clients a saloonkeeper, a "ruffian with sporting instincts," as one writer had it, named John St. Helen. This man, when he fell ill in an asthma attack and thought he was at death's door, told Bates, "I am dying. My name is John Wilkes Booth and I am the assassin of Abraham Lincoln. Get a picture of myself from under the pillow. I leave it with you for future identification. Notify my brother Edwin of New York City."

St. Helen recovered from his illness and during his convalescence told Bates more of his story. Among his revelations, he said that Andrew Johnson had instigated Lincoln's murder and that he had conferred with the vice president for over an hour on April 14, the day of the assassination. He said that Johnson had arranged for General Grant to be out of the capital on the fourteenth and had arranged for Booth's escape into Virginia. St. Helen told his astonished attorney that the man killed in the Garrett tobacco barn was a Confederate sympathizer who had accompanied him and Herold to the farm, and that he, St. Helen/Booth, had never been in the barn and had, in fact, escaped to Texas where he assumed his new identity.

Not long after telling this tale, St. Helen disappeared from Granbury. Bates, who said he didn't believe his client's tale and took no notes (he would, however, remember the entire conversation thirty years later), eventually moved back to Memphis where he spent his free time investigating St. Helen's claim. He traced the man to Fresno, California, then lost the trail. He had a tintype photograph of St. Helen and used it to collect "evidence" that his former client was Lincoln's murderer. (Among the scraps of this evidence was the story that another Memphis lawyer, former Confederate General Albert S. Pike, had caught a glimpse of St. Helen in Fort Worth and exclaimed, "My God, Booth!")

In 1900, thirty years after hearing St. Helen's "deathbed" confession, Bates made a formal inquiry to the U.S. War Department claiming he had discovered "conclusive evidence" proving Booth had escaped capture in 1865. Thereafter he assailed the Department with petitions, reminding, somewhat suspiciously, that Secretary Edwin Stanton had offered a $50,000 reward for the capture of Lincoln's murderer and offering the opinion that the reward was "yet valid and subsisting."

In January 1903, the lawyer read a newspaper story about the suicide by poisoning, in Enid, Oklahoma, of a man known as David E. George, a local barfly and house painter who had claimed to be John Wilkes Booth. Bates took a train to Enid and there found the corpse of George still on display in Penniman's Undertaking Parlor, embalmed, dressed, and unclaimed.

Bates was satisfied that David George and John St. Helen were one and the same man.

In a bizarre turn of events, Bates ended up buying the corpse and having it shipped to Memphis where he placed it in his barn. In 1907 he wrote a book about the case with the tortured title *The Escape and Suicide of John Wilkes Booth, or the First True Account of Lincoln's Assassination, Containing a Complete Confession by Booth, Many Years After His Crime*. In this work Bates revealed that after the assassination, St. Helen/Booth escaped to Mexico where he lived for a time disguised as a priest. Bates said his former client then moved on to California where he met his mother and brother Junius in San Francisco—this in 1866 or 1867—thereafter drifting to Texas under the adopted name of John St. Helen.

The book sold 70,000 copies.

Bates displayed the mummified remains of St. Helen to friends, offered it to Henry Ford for $100,000, and finally leased it to a carnival promoter who went broke and ended up in Declo, Idaho. This man occasionally placed the mummy on his porch in a rocking chair and charged a dime to passersby to view it.

Finis Bates died in 1923 and the mummy of "John Wilkes Booth" cropped up around the country in carnival circuits until the 1930s when it disappeared.

Weird and complex twists, most of them utterly absurd, lurk everywhere in the Corbett-Booth story.

Take for example the proposition that Jesse James killed John Wilkes Booth.

The town of Granbury, where Bates first met John St. Helen in 1870, and the Knights of the Golden Circle, the organization cited by Booth's granddaughter as aiding Booth's escape from the Garrett farm, are both to be found in the story of J. Frank Dalton. He was the ancient who cropped up in Lawton, Oklahoma, in 1948 claiming to be Jesse James (see Chapter 4) and who died in Granbury in 1951.

According to Dalton's chief promoter, a man named Orvus Lee Howk, Jesse James (under the name J. Frank Dalton) headed the Knights of the Golden Circle, in which Booth was a member, in Texas at the time of Booth/St. Helen's confession to Finis Bates. And Howk, at some period before his death in Arizona in 1984, gave a startling version of Booth/St. Helen/George's death in Enid, Oklahoma. He said Frank Dalton (who presumably knew St. Helen in the years the Booth claimant lived in Granbury) and the Knights of the Golden Circle were upset over St. Helen's "confession" of being Booth, made to the Memphis lawyer Bates in 1870. The Knights apparently waited more than twenty-five years to locate St. Helen, but found him at last, in Enid, where he was living as David E. George.

There, Howk said, Dalton administered arsenic to George in a glass of lemonade—enough of the poison to fell a horse.

It was the arsenic, Howk said, that aided in the mummification process of George/Booth's corpse.

Did Boston Corbett, vaguely associated with the town in the 1890s, and with at least one newspaper claim that he died there, go to Enid to meet or confront the man who claimed to be John Wilkes Booth? It seems a miraculous coincidence that the man who claimed to be John Wilkes Booth and the man who was credited with killing John Wilkes Booth both had a contemporaneous association with a town as obscure as Enid (which was not incorporated until 1893), in Oklahoma Territory.

One writer who spent some time investigating Finis Bates's claims about Booth/St. Helen/George was William G. Shepherd whose "Shattering the Myths of John Wilkes Booth" appeared in *Harper's Magazine* in November 1924, a year after Bates's death. Among other findings, Shepherd said Booth's and St. Helen's handwriting did not match and that St. Helen's eyes were blue, Booth's a deep brown. He found, he said, no scintilla of evidence that St. Helen and Booth were one and the same man.

But, as Lloyd Lewis wrote, "Myth-makers are welcome to play with it. How satisfying to them to tell a tale about Boston Corbett, the old, old man, meeting his supposed victim of a generation before on the streets of Enid, Oklahoma, and falling dead from the shock, even as he reached for his gun to kill his man again."

There remains one final story to tell—a story, nothing more— which is odder even than that putting those elderly adversaries, Corbett and Booth, together in Enid, Oklahoma, after the turn of the century.

This story, like the others, pivots on a few known facts and coincidences and it begins with certain details of a man whose link with Corbett is at best tenuous if such a link existed at all. He was a very odd fish named "Dr." Francis Tumblety and in the War Department's search for suspects in the Lincoln assassination conspiracy, his name was listed and he was actually charged with complicity as a friend and confidant of David Herold, the young man caught with Booth in the Garrett barn on April 26, 1865.

Tumblety was described by authorities in St. Louis, where he was arrested on May 6, 1865, as an "imposter and quack" who had tramped the continent from Canada to New Orleans as an "Indian herb doctor." It was said that he "has been compelled to leave several towns and cities in Canada for his rascality and trickery, and is being continually importuned and threatened by those he has deluded and swindled."

In 1995 two British researchers found more about him than General Lafayette Baker's minions ever knew.

Tumblety, probably born in Canada in 1833, moved to Rochester, New York, at a young age, disappeared, then returned there at age twenty-seven representing himself as a "physician" and becoming a notorious figure in the city as he paraded the streets wearing a long fur overcoat and accompanied by a large greyhound.

He later turned up in Detroit, and at the outbreak of the Civil War, in Washington, wearing a military uniform and claiming to be a brigade surgeon on the staff of General George McClellan. In this period someone remembered that Tumblety had a private "anatomical museum" in his apartment in the capital that featured several glass jars containing what the "doctor" claimed were the "wombs of women from various social classes."

Tumblety, his acquaintances said, habitually denounced all women, especially "fallen" ones—meaning prostitutes.

After his arrest in St. Louis, newspapers reported the canard that he had been "appointed surgeon in a Union regiment," and said David Herold, the pharmacist's assistant subsequently hanged as an assassination conspirator, was "the agent and confident of the notorious quack."

The *Rochester Advertiser*, three days after his arrest, reported that Tumblety had been "charged with complicity with Herold" and reminded readers that the "doctor" had "lived in Rochester in his younger days and who, taking up the practice of medicine, went elsewhere to astonish the people." The paper described Tumblety as "a tall, dandified individual, sporting a heavy cane, and was followed by a hound which bore in appearance the same relation to the canine race as his master did to the human."

The story concluded that Tumblety "was a quack all over and nothing else."

Tumblety was held in prison in St. Louis three weeks in May 1865, questioned closely about his alleged relationship with David Herold, then released.

After that he disappeared for eighteen years—no doubt practicing his footloose trade as "Indian herb doctor."

Then, some time in 1888, he arrived in London, via Liverpool, and took lodging in a Barry Street boardinghouse in the East End ghetto. His residence lay close to the Whitechapel district where, beginning in August that year, a horrendous series of prostitute killings took place, the acts of mutilation and murder committed by a man who signed his teasing, tantalizing notes to authorities "Jack the Ripper."

There were five murders officially ascribed to the Ripper, the first occurring on August 31, the last and most sadistic on November 8, 1888. All took place in a half-mile area in Whitechapel, all the victims were prostitutes and all were mutilated with a knife, some with internal organs removed. All but one of the women were killed in the streets; the last victim was found in a small house, her head almost severed, her heart placed on a pillow beside her, her entrails draped over a picture frame, her liver, uterus, and breasts removed.

In the midst of the killings the London Central News Service received a note signed "Jack the Ripper" that said, "I am down on whores and shan't quit ripping them till I do get buckled."

The murders ceased abruptly after November 8 and while the Ripper was never caught or even identified, there were many "candidates" named as the possible Whitechapel fiend: a Harley Street surgeon whose son had died of syphilis contracted from a prostitute; a Russian doctor named Padachenko; Frank Miles, a homosexual artist and model for Oscar Wilde's *Dorian Gray;* a failed lawyer named Montague John Druitt who drowned himself in the Thames, his pockets filled with rocks, soon after the last killing. Even Prince Albert Victor, grandson of Queen Victoria and heir to the throne of England, has been investigated in modern times as "Prince Jack."

Then, twenty-five years after the crimes, Francis Tumblety, the American quack once considered a possible conspirator in

Lincoln's assassination, became a possible candidate as Jack the Ripper.

In September 1913, Chief Inspector John Littlefield, who at the time of the Whitechapel horrors headed Scotland Yard's Special Branch investigating the crimes, wrote to the British journalist George A. Sims reminiscing on the events of the summer of 1888. Littlefield said that among the Ripper suspects "and to my mind a very likely one" was "an American quack named Tumblety." The inspector continued, "He was at one time a frequent visitor to London and on those occasions constantly under the notice of police, there being a large dossier concerning him at Scotland Yard. He was not known as a sadist but his feelings toward women were remarkable and bitter in the extreme, a fact on record."

Littlefield said Tumblety was arrested at the time of the Ripper murders and "charged at Marlborough Street," then freed on bail, got away to Boulogne, and disappeared.

British authors Paul Gainey and Stewart Evans, in their 1995 book *The Lodger: The Arrest and Escape of Jack the Ripper*, say Tumblety returned to St. Louis and died there in a charity hospital in May 1903, age about seventy.

What connection is there between Francis Tumblety and Boston Corbett? If there is one it is as fragile as the connection between Corbett and John St. Helen and between both these men and Enid, Oklahoma.

Tumblety had a connection, at least circumstantial, to John Wilkes Booth through the conspirator David Herold. Corbett had a connection to Booth and Herold, killing the former and seeing the latter taken prisoner at the Garrett farm. (In fact, Corbett, under arrest for disobeying orders in killing Booth, may have returned to Washington on the tug and the ironclad with Herold.) Tumblety and Corbett were about the same age, both lived in upstate New York in their youth and in Boston in adulthood, and both had a London connection: Corbett was born there, Tumblety apparently frequently visited the city and was certainly there, as a high-level Scotland Yard official attested, in 1888.

This adds up to little—they were certainly not one and the same man and there is no real evidence they even knew one another. Tumblety, in fact, appears to have been a simple poseur and fraud, an unbalanced charletan who had the unfortunate distinction of being a suspect in two of the most notorious murder cases of the nineteenth century.

And while both had a connection to John Wilkes Booth, what possible connection could Corbett have had with the Jack the Ripper slayings?

Just as the U.S. War Department frenetically searched out suspects in the Lincoln assassination conspiracy, so did Scotland Yard, with a vengeance, line up Ripper suspects—especially *foreign* suspects, perhaps unable to believe that crimes so hideous could have been committed by an Englishman.

High on the list of possible Jack the Rippers were John Pizer and Aaron Kosminski, Polish Jews; Michael Ostrog and Alexander Pedachenko, Russians; George Chapman (Severin Klosowski), another Pole; and miscellaneous others, including Francis Tumblety, an American.

Did they, in questioning Tumblety, simply arrest the wrong man?

Corbett was London-born.

He was certifiably insane.

He escaped from a Topeka insane asylum in June 1888, almost three months before the first Ripper killing.

He was "down on whores."

He had killed—men, to be sure—before.

He was acquainted with sharp instruments in his hat-finishing trade.

He had motive, means, and opportunity.

There is a trace of him remaining. A few miles south of Concordia, Kansas, is a stone marker between two cedar trees in a pasture just off a county road. On the marker a plaque reads:

1878
Boston Corbett's Dugout
Sixty Yards South is the site of the
Dugout home of Boston Corbett, who as
a soldier shot John Wilkes Booth
the assassin of President Lincoln

Insofar as the facts on what became of him, we know that on
June 1, 1888, he was sighted in Neodesha, Kansas.
All else is mystery.

8

The Old Gringo's Last Laugh

Ambrose Bierce in Mexico

When his readers complained that he had gone too far in his daily vituperations, Ambrose Bierce answered them in his newspaper column suggesting they return to selling shoes or the law or the Gospel or whatever they were selling. "As for me," he wrote, "I sell abuse."

In the Gilded Age, no writer wielded a more abusive pen nor spattered his acidic ink on more varied targets—a bad poet one day, a robber baron the next—and he was certainly the only American journalist ever accused of aiding and abetting in the actual, not mere character, assassination of a president of the United States.

"November," he wrote in his glittering masterpiece The Devil's Dictionary, *"is the eleventh twelfth of a weariness," and*

in November, 1913, when he was eleven-twelfths weary, he crossed the border at El Paso into revolutionary Mexico.
The rest—an uncommon thing for Bierce—is silence.

Probably no mystery in American literature is so intriguing as the [1914?] notation that follows reference book entries on Ambrose Bierce, the only great writer produced by the Civil War and a name once mentioned in the same breath as Mark Twain, Bret Harte, and Jack London as among the greatest figures in Western American literature.

Some who have written of him maintain that Bierce's chief claim to fame today is that bracketed question mark after the supposed year of his death. Others have been kinder. H. L. Mencken, who recalled his acquaintanceship with Bierce a decade after the old man's last journey, eulogized the California newspaperman-satirist as the first writer, antedating even Émile Zola, to depict war realistically, in all its sordid horror and futility: "His war stories, even when they deal with the heroic, do not depict soldiers as heroes; they depict them as bewildered fools . . . dying at last like hogs in Chicago," Mencken said. And the Sage of Baltimore also called the epigrams contained in *The Devil's Dictionary* "some of the most gorgeous witticisms in the English language."

Mencken's assessment of his erstwhile friend's literary contributions seems to have been correct: Bierce's Civil War stories, contained in his *Tales of Soldiers and Civilians* (1891), and his *The Devil's Dictionary* (1906) remain in print to this day.

The verdicts on Bierce-as-author are endlessly varied but no more so than the theories on what happened to him in the upheaval of revolution-sundered Mexico.

Before getting to those eternal [1914?] brackets, there is the matter, for those who do not know, of who he was, beginning with that which he described as "the first and direst of all disasters"—his birth.

Ambrose Gwinett Bierce, born in the settlement of Horse Cave Creek, Meigs County, Ohio, on June 24, 1842, was the tenth of thirteen children of Laura Sherwood and Marcus Aurelius Bierce, all of whose progeny had names beginning with the letter "A": Abigail, Addison, Aurelius, Amelia, Ann, Augustus, Andrew, Almeda, Albert, Arthur, Adelia, and Aurelia. Ambrose thus began his life with a name he hated and when he later rose to fame as "The Wickedest Man in San Francisco," he signed his caustic newspaper work "A. G. Bierce" and showed no sign of annoyance when his critics translated this to "Almighty God" Bierce.

Judging from his frequent writings about parenticide, he loathed his parents, whom he described as "unwashed savages." They were stern and austere Calvinists who prayed, sang hymns, read the Bible aloud, and observed the Sabbath with puritanical fervor. His mother traced her lineage to the *Mayflower*'s Pilgrim father, William Bradford; his father, a failed farmer, seems to have been a brooding man with a rather daring love of literature (including the works of that infidel poet Lord Byron). Ambrose, who later recalled the hickory switches his father employed to instill discipline in his brood of children, also remembered his father's library, an unusual collection for a pioneer in the then-wilderness of the Western Reserve, and at the age of ten of having read Alexander Pope's translation of Homer.

When he was fifteen, and the family now farming in northern Indiana, Bierce left home for good. With the help of an influential uncle, he attended a military school in Kentucky for a semester, then found work as a printer's devil on a small newspaper in the town of Warsaw, Indiana.

In April 1861, when he was nineteen, he enlisted in Company C of the Ninth Indiana Infantry Regiment, first as a drummer-boy, later as a scout and topographical engineer. He fought in some of the bloodiest engagements of the war: Shiloh, in April 1862; Murfreesboro, in December 1862; Chickamauga, in September 1863; Franklin, in November 1864; and Nashville, in

December 1864. At Kenesaw Mountain, Georgia, on June 27, 1864, he suffered a severe wound—a rifle ball embedded among bone fragments in his skull—and while he eventually recovered, his brother Albert would later say of this incident, "He was never the same. . . . Some of the iron of the shell seemed to stick in his brain and he became bitter and suspicious."

He ended the war a first lieutenant and after a brief duty as custodian of captured and abandoned property in Selma, Alabama, joined an army mapping and inspecting expedition to California. In San Francisco, in November 1866, he resigned from the army, after learning he would not be promoted to a captaincy, and took a menial job at the U.S. Mint. He also began to write.

San Francisco in the late 1860s and early seventies was a notably literate and literary city. Writers such as Bret Harte, Mark Twain, Charles Warren Stoddard, Ina Coolbrith, Prentice Mulford, and Joaquin Miller were appearing in the city's newspapers and magazines and in an era of wide-open journalism there was room for a man of Bierce's undoubted talents.

His rise in San Francisco's literary circles to the title his later protégé George Sterling gave him—"Rhadamanthus of Letters" (after the Greek judge of the underworld)—began modestly with contributions of scraps of verse and snippets of news and satirical opinion to such journals as the *Californian,* the *Golden Era,* the *Alta California*, and the magazine launched by Bret Harte in 1868, *The Overland Monthly.* Editors recognized Bierce's aptitudes from the beginning: he wrote polished prose, had a knack for stinging little poems and an absolute genius for iconoclastic humor and invective—barbed observations on news and foibles of the day, deceptively cloaked character assassinations, and velvet-covered sledgehammer critiques of the literary efforts of major and minor authors.

In 1868 he began writing "The Town Crier," a weekly column of social commentary in the *San Francisco News Letter and Commercial Advertiser.* The column was a witty, venomous, and immensely popular collection of barbs and libels directed at local businessmen, politicians, religious leaders, lawyers, and literary dilettantes. His work was funny, at times hilarious, but Bierce made it clear that he was not a humorist but a purveyor of wit: "Humor is tolerant, tender; its ridicule caresses," he wrote. "Wit stabs, begs pardon—and turns the weapon in the wound."

The "Town Crier" and his other occasional writings put him in league with the best writers in the Bay Area, including Harte of the *Overland Monthly* and Sam Clemens—now writing as Mark Twain—who frequently visited the offices of the *News Letter.* His friendship with both men endured, although it was edgier with the prickly Twain. And his camaraderie did not prevent his writing in his column, after Twain moved to New York, "Mark Twain, who, whenever he has been long enough sober to permit an estimate, has been uniformly found to bear a spotless character, has got married. . . . For years he has felt this matrimony coming on. Ever since he left California there has been an undertone of despair running through all his letters like the subdued wail of a pig in a washtub."

Bierce himself, nearly thirty, was ready to marry. He had an established reputation as a journalist, satirist, and critic by now and was regarded as one of the city's most eligible bachelors. He was an extraordinarily handsome man: six feet tall, militarily erect in his carriage, with ice-blue eyes, pink complexion, curly reddish-blond hair, and meticulously trimmed mustache. He was so well groomed and scrubbed clean that one wag said of him, "Ambrose looks as if he shaved all over every day."

After a brief courtship, on Christmas Day, 1871, Bierce married Ellen "Mollie" Day, daughter of a mining engineer, in San Rafael, across the Bay in Marin County. The Day family had tried to talk Mollie out of her infatuation with a man whose profession—and perhaps whose character—they regarded as dubious if not lowly.

Bierce himself, who would later define marriage as "a community consisting of a master, a mistress, and two slaves, making in all, two," and who described a bride as "a woman with a fine prospect of happiness behind her," apparently had no such cynical thoughts at the time of his wedding and for a few years after. But the marriage was destined, for master, mistress, both slaves, and their offspring, to yield little but unhappiness.

"Here's to woman!" Bierce would later write in one of the most memorable toasts ever offered. "Would that we could fall into her arms without falling into her hands!"

He took Mollie with him on a sojourn to England, a venture that proved so successful it lasted nearly four years. Bierce's renown had preceded him and he was able to hobnob with British literati, be praised as a genius by Prime Minister Gladstone, and share a Fleet Street banquet table in 1873 with two other short-time expatriates, Mark Twain and the "Poet of the Sierras," Joaquin Miller. Now, too, he began selling poems, sketches, and stories to the magazine *Fun*, edited by the humorist and poet Tom Hood, and, using the gloomy pen name "Dod Grile," published three books in London: *The Fiend's Delight* and *Nuggets and Dust* in 1872 and another, with the ingenious title *Cobwebs From an Empty Skull*, in 1874.

On the basis of his growing reputation as a satirist he was also asked to edit a magazine called *The Lantern*, subsidized by the deposed Empress Eugénie of France, then in exile in England. But after presiding over two issues, Bierce was fired, legend has it because of a fatal faux pas: he disobeyed a royal command for an audience with Eugénie by not showing up.

In 1875 he returned home, a month behind Day and Leigh, his two children born in England, and Mollie, pregnant with their third child. Daughter Helen was born in October that year, shortly after the family resumed their residency in San Francisco.

Now he was treated as something of a celebrity—a book writer who had "conquered" England—and the *San Francisco Call*, the *Wasp*, and the *Argonaut* sought him out. "It is my intention," he said when he began writing a new column, titled "Prattle," in the *Argonaut*, "to purify journalism in this town by instructing such writers as it is worthwhile to instruct, and assassinating those it is not."

Butts of his invective included not only writers but railroad magnates, bankers, politicians, dog lovers, teetotalers, socialists, and practitioners of all organized religions. Of the latter he wrote, "No sane man of intelligence will plead for religion on the ground that it is better than nothing. It is not better than nothing if it is not true. Truth is better than anything or all things; the next best thing to truth is absence of error."

Except for a brief time in 1880 when he was involved in a gold-mining venture in the Black Hills wilderness of the Dakotas, he devoted his efforts to his newspaper and magazine work. His "Prattle" column ran weekly in the *Argonaut* and later in the *Wasp,* a satirical paper for which he composed the epigrams later collected in *The Devil's Dictionary.*

Bierce's relations with his editors and publishers were always stormy. He took no orders, insisted on a free hand, would permit no interference or emendation of what he wrote. (After a quarrel with the editor of the *Argonaut,* Bierce wrote an imagined epitaph for his former boss: "Here lies Frank Pixley—as usual.") And his imperious demands of his employers would never be better demonstrated than in his relations with his longest-suffering boss, William Randolph Hearst.

In 1887 Bierce was sought out by this son of George Hearst, one of San Francisco's richest Comstock Lode miners. William Randolph, a horse-faced youngster recently expelled from Harvard, came home with his head in the clouds after a brief stint working for Joseph Pulitzer's *New York World* and was asked by his father what he wanted to do with his life. William said he wanted a newspaper and so George Hearst gave him the one he had purchased in 1880 as an instrument to further his political ambitions, the failing *San Francisco Examiner.*

A reedy-voiced, outsized dynamo, Hearst had a knack for organization and in revamping the *Examiner* to suit his sensationalist ideas of journalism, he hired the best writers he could find and in some cases went so far as to personally seek out those he respected most. Bierce was one of these and in March 1887, Hearst found his writer in an Oakland apartment (Bierce was asthmatic and avoided the foggy dampness of San Francisco by living, alone, deep in the East Bay Area) and made an offer that could not be refused.

Bierce bit the hand that fed him for two decades. He resigned an average of once a year in the twenty years he worked for Hearst and was always lured back by the man he openly detested and distrusted. Hearst admired Bierce, loved the writer's scurrilous wit, linguistic pyrotechnics, and honesty. Above all Hearst knew Bierce sold newspapers.

His "Prattle" column became the rage of fin de siècle San Francisco as Bierce flailed and punished institution and individual without mercy. Big business, particularly the "railrogues," specifically the Southern Pacific Railroad and its president, Colis P. Huntington, were his principal targets.

In 1896, after nine years of work for the *Examiner,* Bierce was called to Washington as chief correspondent and Huntington watcher for the *Examiner* and Hearst's recently acquired *New York Journal.* The big story, which both papers were mobilizing to oppose, was the Southern Pacific Funding Bill, proposed by Huntington to delay the payment of his railroad's $75 million debt to the federal government. The bill was defeated.

Bierce's Washington sojourn, though the climate aggravated his asthma problems, gave him the opportunity to roam the Civil War battlefields and if he ever admitted to any happiness at the beginning of the new century it was in these quiet explorations of the places where he was first tested as a youth. Despite the horrors of war he described so eloquently in such stories as "An Occurrence at Owl Creek Bridge," "A Horseman in the Sky," "Chickamauga," and others, there is little doubt but that he longed for the excitement and turmoil of battle, of the hard camp life and of tests of valor (a word he mordantly defined as "a soldier's compound of vanity, duty and the gambler's hope").

But whatever satisfaction he had in recalling his soldiering days thirty-five years past, he differed with Hearst's strident militarism during the Spanish-American War (writing that Hearst's papers in the 1898 period were "indistinguishable from circus posters") and after a year's absence he returned to San Francisco to resume his work for the *Examiner.* From that point until the end of his life, the passing years piled on disappointment and disenchantment.

After his return to San Francisco Bierce managed to scuttle the political ambitions of his employer and cause Hearst and his newspapers to defend themselves against charges of contributing to the assassination of the president of the United States.

The occasion was the shooting, on January 30, 1900, of William Goebel, Democratic candidate for the governorship of Kentucky. Goebel was sworn into office on his deathbed and in the *New York Journal* on February 4, the day the governor died of his wounds, there appeared a malicious little quatrain by Bierce. The verse followed Hearst's editorial policy of attacking the incumbent president, William McKinley:

> The bullet that pierced Goebel's breast
> Can not be found in all the West;
> Good reason: it is speeding here
> To stretch McKinley on his bier.

After McKinley's assassination nineteen months later, Hearst (and to a lesser degree Bierce) was accused of helping plant the seed of murder in the mind of McKinley's murderer, Leon Czolgosz. Hearst's enemies, who were legion and included all the rival newspapers in New York and San Francisco, delighted in spreading the tale that Czolgosz carried a copy of the *Journal* with him when he left for Buffalo and the fatal rendezvous with the president on September 6, 1901. It mattered little that Czolgosz had done no such thing and that his insane inspiration derived from his readings of anarchist publications.

But while Bierce fomented newspaper controversies and kept in command of them, his personal life spun out of control.

His marriage to Mollie Day had been unhappy from the beginning and his two sons—Day and Leigh—provided proof of his failure as husband and father.

Day broke away from the family early, in 1889, at age sixteen, to try his hand at journalism on a small newspaper in Red Bluff, California. That same year he became involved in an adolescent love triangle that resulted in Day's killing the husband of the woman he professed to love, and then himself.

The tragedy deepened the alienation between Ambrose and Mollie.

Leigh Bierce accompanied his father to Washington in 1896, and after a time as a reporter on Hearst's *Journal*, he went to work for the *New York Morning Telegraph* (its sports section was then edited by the retired Western lawman William Barclay "Bat" Masterson). Leigh, like his father, developed into an "eminent tankardman," but whereas Ambrose never seemed to lose his self-control despite the quantity of alcohol he consumed, his son's uproarious binges became legendary even on booze-soaked Park Row. After one such bout with the bottle, Leigh developed pneumonia and, on March 31, 1901, died. He was twenty-seven.

Walter Neale, Bierce's close friend, publisher, and later biographer, claimed the writer's hair turned white a few weeks after Leigh's death.

Then, in April 1905, just before their divorce decree was to be granted, Mollie Day Bierce died of heart failure.

For three more years, Bierce carried on his work for Hearst despite his frequently stated disgust for his employer's favorite journalistic hue—bright yellow—then, in 1908, he resigned and this time Hearst did not try to woo him back.

The following year he began compiling his *Collected Works* for Walter Neale, the Washington, D.C., publisher, a twelve-volume, million-word publishing venture. It proved to be a paste-pot-and-scissors failure despite the occasional glimmer of gold (his *Tales of Soldiers and Civilians*, the stories in *In the Midst of Life*, the priceless wit of *The Devil's Dictionary*) to be found among the vast amount of ephemeral dross.

The last volumes of the *Collected Works* appeared in 1912, and Bierce, now seventy, still imposing with his ramrod-straight carriage and meticulous dress but with his curly copper-blond hair now snow-white and his handsome face lined, began thinking of an appropriate final chapter to another, and last, work— his own life story.

He had no precise plan; he let his mind wander. He spoke of making a journey on foot and mule-back across the southern Andes, starting out from Santiago, Chile, entering western Argentina, and ending up in Buenos Aires. It was a fantastic notion for a man of his age, but as late as September 1913, he wrote about beginning the South American trek via Mexico, then in the grip of revolution (which he defined as "An abrupt change in the form of misgovernment"), ". . . if I can get through without being stood up against a wall and shot as a gringo. But this is better than dying in bed, is it not?"

To Neale he wrote almost longingly of finding death in some remote place—the Grand Canyon, perhaps, or the Yosemite Valley. He did not fear the end. He viewed life as "A spiritual pickle preserving the body from decay. We live in daily apprehension of its loss; yet when lost it is not missed."

He wanted to make one final, valedictory visit to the Civil War battlefields.

The word "Mexico" recurred often in his final correspondence and conversations.

In September 1913, he returned east, stopping off in Bloomington, Illinois, to visit his daughter Helen and to leave some papers with her for safekeeping. On September 13 he wrote his niece Lora, "Yes, I shall go into Mexico with a pretty definite purpose, not at present disclosable. . . . You must forgive me my obstinacy in not perishing where I am."

Then he moved on to Washington. On October 2 he traveled southward to Tennessee to walk among the battlefield tombstones and monuments of the Union and Confederate armies. He stopped and wandered alone in Chattanooga, Chickamauga, Murfreesboro, Franklin, and Nashville, and spent the most time at Pittsburg Landing visiting the Shiloh battlefield. By the twentieth he was in Corinth, Mississippi, and on October 23 he arrived in New Orleans where an enterprising reporter for the *New Orleans States* found him. The reporter described Bierce as "dressed in black. From head to foot he was attired in this color, except where the white cuffs and collar and shirt front showed through. He even carried a walking stick, black as ebony and unrelieved by gold or silver. But his eyes, blue and piercing as when they strove to see through the smoke at Chickamauga, retained all the fire of the indomitable fighter."

"I'm on my way to Mexico because I like the game," Bierce told the reporter, ". . . there are many things that might happen between now and when I come back. My trip might take several years, and I'm an old man now."

To Helen he wrote:

Why should I remain in a country that is on the eve of prohibition and women's suffrage? In America you can't go east or west any more, or north; the only avenue is south. . . . I'll take some letters of introduction with me and strike the border near El Paso. It will be easy enough to get along. I'm going to buy a donkey and hire a peon. I can see what's doing; perhaps write a few articles about the situation; and then pass to the West Coast of Mexico. From there I can go to South America; cross the Andes and ship to England. This fighting in Mexico interests me. I want to go down and see if these Mexicans can shoot straight.

By late October he had pushed on to San Antonio where he was greeted at Fort Sam Houston by an old army friend. On November 6 he arrived in Laredo, jumping-off place for the revolution south of the border. In a hotel in Laredo he is believed to have left a trunk, probably with instructions that it be forwarded to his daughter if he did not reclaim it within a few months. Inside the trunk, some Bierce investigators believe, was an unfinished book, a scathing biography of William Randolph Hearst. The trunk, if it ever existed, never surfaced.

In another letter to a family member, he wrote: "If you should hear of my being stood up against a Mexican stone wall and shot to rags please know that I think it's a pretty good way to depart this life. It beats old age, disease or falling down the cellar stairs. To be a Gringo in Mexico—ah, that is euthanasia!"

In early December 1913, he crossed the border at El Paso into Juárez and journeyed by rail to Ciudad Chihuahua, arriving there on December 16, just a few days after the town was occupied by the revolutionary army of Francisco "Pancho" Villa.

On Christmas Eve Bierce wrote a friend, "Pray for me—real loud."

The last word anyone received from him was a letter, dated December 26, that he sent to his former secretary Carrie Christiansen in Washington. On orders from Bierce she destroyed the letter—along with a considerable amount of his other correspondence—but she remembered the essence of it: "Trainloads of troops leaving Chihuahua every day. Expect next day to go to Ojinaga . . ."

Whether or not he sought death in Mexico, or if he found it there, is unknown. Everything, after his purported December 26, 1913, message, is a blank while the theories on what happened to him range from the reasoned to the inane, with the latter most in abundance.

Among the farthest-fetched stories appeared in the *New York Sun* in the spring of 1915. It reported that Bierce's daughter Helen, in Illinois, had received a letter from her father saying that he was a member of the staff of Lord H. H. Kitchener, then England's war minister, and that Bierce had seen front-line duty in France. The only particle of "evidence" connecting Bierce and Kitchener is that the two apparently had a brief correspondence in 1899 when Kitchener was commanding troops in South Africa in the Boer War.

Helen Bierce's "letter," of course, was never produced but her father had mentioned England in his "cross the Andes" letter and so *The Bookman,* in August 1925, placed Bierce in Lincolnshire in 1914, and said he was training with British soldiers and that he died later in battle on the French front.

Neither the *Sun* nor *The Bookman* apparently thought it remarkable that a seventy-two-year-old asthmatic American, whose battle experience had occurred fifty years earlier, would be working on Kitchener's staff, training with British soldiers, and falling in battle, but similar bizarre stories abounded in the decade following his disappearance.

Just as his recorded mention of England generated a number of grotesque notions, so did his mention of South America. In Buenos Aires in April 1932, a story circulated quoting an explorer named Johnson as alleging to have met in the unexplored jungles of Brazil's Matto Grosso a strange white man "who has long-flowing white hair, and who is clad in jaguar skins." The man, Johnson said, "is being held as a prisoner by a tribe of Indians who look on him as a god, and have mounted a guard to see that he does not escape." The explorer ended his report on the Tarzan-like apparition saying, "This strange man gave me letters which we lost in our wanderings in the forests. I think he is the lost American writer, Ambrose Bierce."

(Bierce, surviving the heat and humidity, fevers and disease of the western Brazilian rain forest, would have been an asthma-cured ninety-year-old at the time.)

He was also reported, without evidence, to have committed suicide in the Grand Canyon (his publisher Walter Neale believed this and Bierce's most recent biographer, Roy Morris, Jr., gives the notion renewed support) and to have died in a Napa, California, insane asylum. And in 1932, Charles Fort, the eccentric journalist and collector of the "unexplained," noted in his book *Wild Talents* that a man named Ambrose Small disappeared at about the same time as Bierce and that perhaps "some demonic force was collecting Ambroses."

Another fantastic story, elaborately told in 1972 in a small book privately published by a San Francisco writer named Sibley S. Morrill, is that Bierce (1) went to Mexico as a spy for the United States (giving his offhand remark "I shall go into Mexico with a pretty definite purpose, not at present disclosable" a weighty meaning); and (2) he became involved with a British explorer, also a spy, named F. A. Mitchell-Hedges, and had a role in the discovery of the relic known as the Crystal Skull of the Maya.

In this weird scenario we learn that Mitchell-Hedges came to the U.S. in 1912 ostensibly to find employment with an American oil or shipping firm in Mexico. With his cash running low, he took a job as a waiter in New Orleans the summer of 1913, then made his way into Mexico. There he was taken captive by Villistas at about the same time Bierce is alleged to have joined Villa's *revolucionarios* near Chihuahua City as an "observer."

Morrill's story is that both Mitchell-Hedges and Bierce were spies for their respective countries, that Bierce had $2,000 in gold with him, and that the two men spent about ten months with Villa's army, then made their way to British Honduras in the fall of 1914. In the fever jungles of Central America, Morrill states in a breathtaking leap of speculation for which there is not a crumb of evidence, the two men purchased, perhaps with some of Bierce's spy money, the sacred crystal skull of the Maya. This eleven-pound artifact, an exquisite objet d'art carved from a chunk of crystal, is, Morrill states, at least 3,600 years old, and took 150 years to fashion using sand and water to abrade and polish the stone.

What Bierce gained from his association with the skull is not explained. Morrill, indeed, cannot say and has Bierce either going on to England after the Honduran adventure or finding death in some other "mysterious place."

(F. A. Mitchell-Hedges, in his 1955 memoir, *Danger My Ally,* states that the crystal skull was discovered in 1924 by his seventeen-year-old daughter Anna during their exploration of the site of the great Mayan city of Lubaantún in British Honduras. Mitchell-Hedges also tells of his ten months with Villa during the Mexican revolution but he makes no reference whatever to Bierce.)

In the months following his last letter, of December 26, 1913, which his secretary destroyed, the only credible reports on Bierce's final days place him in Mexico at the time of his death, but even these localized theories are varied and, of course, all are unproven.

Journalist and bookman Vincent Starrett wrote in his Chicago newspaper column of a story told to him by an unnamed source that Bierce was alive and well in December 1918, living in San Luis Potosí, Mexico, where he was known as "Don Ambrosio."

In his last message to his daughter Helen, Bierce wrote, "Expect next day to go to Ojinaga . . ." The battle for Ojinaga (across the U.S. border from Presidio, Texas, 125 miles northeast of Chihuahua City) opened on January 1, 1915, with Villa's forces taking severe losses for the first six days. On January 7 Villa himself arrived on the scene and by the tenth the federal garrison of the tiny Mexican border town had slipped across the Rio Grande for internment in U.S. territory. Several writers have speculated that Bierce may have joined the Villistas as an observer during the Ojinaga battle and was killed or at least died there, his body, along with hundreds of soldiers on both sides, burned in open cremation in an attempt to halt a typhus epidemic. His presence at Ojinaga was confirmed some years after the battle when a Major Gastón de Pridu, an investigator working for Mexican president Carranza, showed Bierce's photograph to officers who took part in the Ojinaga battle. One man, Captain Salvador Ibarra, recognized Bierce and said the old man had accompanied Villa's force to Ojinaga but that he did not know what happened to the American after that.

And if he were indeed present at the Ojinaga battle, where was he for the entire *year* before it was fought?

Among the most tantalizing theories are those that have Villa directly responsible for Bierce's death. These conjectures involve Bierce's supposed "desertion" from Villa's camp to join that of another, anti-Villa, revolutionary group, the Constitutionalists under General (later President) Venustiano Carranza. The fullest of these accounts is that of Elias L. Torres, a Mexican mining engineer, writer, friend, and adviser of Villa's and brother of a governor of one of the Mexican states. Torres wrote of Bierce in his book *20 Vibrantes Episodios de la Vida de Villa* ("Twenty Vibrant Episodes in the Life of Villa"), published in Mexico City in 1934. The author, in the chapter titled "El Chiste de la Muerta" ("The Joke of Death"), claims he interviewed Villa at the rebel general's huge Canutilla ranch near Chihuahua City in the 1920s and that Villa admitted knowing Bierce well. Villa said the old man was a frequent visitor in his camp and at his own dinner table where he regaled all present with his stories and witticisms.

According to Torres, Villa claimed that Bierce, during a meal with staff officers, denounced Villa's rebel army as a band of thieves and assassins and declared he would soon be joining Carranza's Constitutionalists. Villa thereupon made a "sign" to one of his officers, General Faustino Borunda, who quietly left the room. Meantime, Villa said he told Bierce he was sorry for the decision he had made, gave the old man an *abrazo* (embrace), and Bierce departed. A few minutes later Bierce and his *mozo* (servant) were heard riding off in the direction of the mountains. Suddenly shots rang out. Villa said he smiled and turned to his bodyguard, Rodolfo Fierro, and said, "Let's see if that damned gringo tells his last joke to the buzzards on the mountain."

Biographer and historian Edward Laroque Tinker, who knew Villa during the revolution and traveled in the general's battle train, said after publication of Torres's account, "That this account is true, I have no doubt. . . . it comes from a trustworthy source and every detail is in complete accord with the characters of both Villa and Bierce. . . . What I saw and heard persuaded me that he [Villa] would think no more of killing a man than a housewife would of stepping on a cockroach."

Perhaps so, but Elias Torres's story is no more substantiated than any of the others and contains at least one notable flaw: Torres claimed that Bierce "spoke very good Spanish." If this was true it was news to those who knew him. Moreover, it is at least passing strange that if Bierce were ever in Villa's camp, his presence was never noted by such American war correspondents as Floyd Gibbons, Timothy Turner, and Frederick Palmer—who would have known Bierce and chronicled his every step—nor by the American consul in Chihuahua, George Carothers, the U.S. government's liaison with Villa.

A variation of Torres's account was proposed by Adolphe Danziger de Castro, a San Francisco dentist and Bierce syco-phant with whom the writer collaborated on a book, *The Monk and the Hangman's Daughter,* in 1893. De Castro was in Mex-ico in 1922 and said he talked with Villa at the general's ranch near Chihuahua City. Villa, de Castro said, became greatly an-noyed at the mention of Bierce's name but proceeded to tell this story: that Bierce was in Chihuahua when the town was cap-tured and the *viejo Americano* got drunk and criticized Villa and his men. Villa said he ordered Bierce expelled from Mexico and later arranged to have the old man ambushed, killed, and left to the vultures.

But the late Professor Haldeen Braddy of the University of Texas at El Paso, whose Bierce researches included extensive trav-els in Mexico and interviews with several of Villa's widows, for-mer Villa soldiers, and confidants, interviewed de Castro in 1929 and later wrote, "He [de Castro] was not at all certain that Bierce had actually been murdered at Villa's command."

De Castro, in his *Portrait of Ambrose Bierce,* implied only that Bierce's death was probably hastened by excessive drinking.

Braddy's conclusion: "My present thought is that Villa did not murder this *Americano,* whose disappearance must rank among the greatest of mysteries. I rather think that age and al-cohol together with likely privation and possible exposure to the elements account for his end."

There can be little doubt, however, that Villa could deal with bothersome foreigners in such a fashion as de Castro and others have suggested. In February 1914, just over a month from Bierce's last communication to the outside world, Villa arrested William S. Benton, an Englishman who operated a huge ranch-ing operation in Chihuahua and whose lands had been confis-cated by Villa. Benton had the temerity—or downright foolhardiness—to seek out Villa at the general's camp headquarters in Ciudad Juárez and demand the return of his property. When this was refused, Benton, it is said, pulled a six-shooter but was wrestled to the ground before he could kill his enemy. Villa had Benton taken out of Juárez at night and near the village of Samalayuca, forty miles south of the border, the Englishman was executed by Rodolfo Fierro and buried in the desert. Later, under increasing pressure from U.S. and British authorities, Villa admitted Benton had been executed, claiming the deed had been done after a formal court-martial found Benton guilty of an assassination attempt.

Perhaps the most tempting of the Bierce death stories is that told by the soldier of fortune Edward Synott "Tex" O'Reilly in his book *Born to Raise Hell*. O'Reilly, born in Texas in 1880, had an astonishing military-mercenary career. He served in Cuba in the Spanish-American War, in the Philippine Insurrection, the Boxer Rebellion in China in 1900, and in banana republic wars in Honduras, Nicaragua, and Venezuela. During the Mexican Revolution, he served five years as a soldier-for-hire, mostly with Villa's army, and in his memoir (told to Lowell Thomas and published in 1936) he recounted his Bierce story.

O'Reilly was in El Paso at an unnamed date (but probably early December 1913) and at his hotel front desk found a note awaiting him. It was from Bierce who said he was in town, wanted to visit Villa's army, and asked to meet with O'Reilly. The Texan apparently recognized the name and left a note for the author to meet him at 10:00 A.M. the next day. Bierce never showed up and O'Reilly took the train south to return to Villa's camp.

At the Foreign Club in Chihuahua City, Bierce once again tried to make contact but O'Reilly says he could not locate the celebrated author.

In fact, the Texan never did meet Bierce but clearly asked around. In El Paso, O'Reilly said, Bierce was recognized by reporters gathered there (the Sheldon Hotel was unofficial headquarters for journalists covering the revolution), "but he would have nothing to do with them. He was drinking heavily and was morose and bad-tempered, would not talk to anyone.

"It is always printed," O'Reilly said, "that Villa killed him, but Villa never heard of him till after he was dead. Bierce did not go near any of Villa's officers or talk to any of the Americans there. Evidently he wandered around quite alone. He could not speak Spanish."

Some months after the futile attempts to meet with Bierce, O'Reilly and a detachment of Villistas were in the town of Escalón, between Chihuahua City and Torreón, waiting for the railroad to be repaired. There he heard that an American had been killed in the nearby mountain mining camp of Sierra Mojada and, with time on his hands, took the rail spur line there to investigate. He learned from Mexican miners that an old man had come alone into the camp on horseback, that the gringo spoke only a little broken Spanish and did not explain who he was or what he wanted.

"He stayed there several days in the midst of the Federals," O'Reilly wrote, "but apparently he did not know they were Federals. It is wild, mountainous country all around there, deserted mining country with very few ranches. He asked questions about the trails and made notes and maps, and they thought he was a spy. When the Federals heard that he was asking how to reach Villa's army they decided to kill him."

O'Reilly pieced together this account of Bierce's last laugh:

One afternoon he was drinking in a cantina with three Federal volunteers, and they decided to kill him then. They borrowed his pistol, and when he left they walked out with him to the edge of town. I talked with two eyewitnesses who had seen the whole thing. Apparently he suspected nothing until the three men turned on him and began shooting.

The first shot must have struck him in the leg or belly, because he dropped down, squatting on his heels. And the two Mexicans were impressed by the strange way in which he died. He squatted there in the dust of the road and began to laugh heartily. The three men kept shooting at him, hitting him, but they could not kill him, and he did not stop laughing. He sat there and laughed till finally they shot him in the heart. The Mexicans were amazed because he was laughing as though it were a tremendous joke that he was being killed.

"He had been buried about a week or ten days before I arrived." O'Reilly said. "They showed me where he had been buried beside the adobe wall of the little cemetery. . . . I burned his name into a board with a hot iron and set up this little wooden headboard at the grave."

O'Reilly's story of Bierce's last laugh echoes, perhaps uncomfortably so, H. L. Mencken's remarks, made in 1927 (nine years before O'Reilly's "as told to Lowell Thomas" memoir). Mencken wrote in his *Prejudices, Sixth Series:*

Death to him was not something repulsive, but a sort of low comedy—the last act of a squalid and rib-rocking buffoonery. When, grown old and weary, he departed for Mexico, and there—if legend is to be believed—marched into the revolution then going on, and had himself shot, there was certainly nothing in the transaction to surprise his acquaintances. The whole thing was typically Biercian. He died happy, one may be sure, if his executioners made a botch of dispatching him—if there was a flash of the grotesque at the end.

Leon Day, an Oakland, California, Bierce authority, says the O'Reilly account is "persuasive by its modesty," that the Texan did not claim to have met Bierce, know him, or witness his death, only that he was looking into the death of an unknown American in a remote mining camp and discovered, by accident, that the American was Ambrose Bierce. Moreover, the testimony about making "notes and maps" in Sierra Mojada may be significant. Bierce was an experienced topographical officer in the Civil War.

Day concludes, "Sometimes I think that Bierce, failing to make contact with Villa's staff, decided to move ahead of Villa's Division of the North and show what he could do by mapping a large part of the approach to Torreón from the summit of Sierra Mojada. And sometimes I speculate that he may have had another customer. The U.S. Army was then sorely deficient in good maps of Mexico, and it stayed that way until Pershing's Punitive Expedition in 1916 when most of the northern part of the country was mapped by aerial photo. We can't tell right now if Bierce was a spy, or whose spy he was. But he was sure in the right place for one."

How did Ambrose Bierce die, and where, and when?

While there may never be answers to these questions, Mexico holds the secrets and may yet surrender them to some tenacious researcher. In the meantime, we can only sort through the theories and cling to such verities as that stated by Thomas Beer in his *The Mauve Decade* (1926): "If it is true that they shot him against a wall in Mexico, some literate member of the firing-party heard a last pungency as the old man buttoned his coat and faced the rifles, smiling."

CALAMITIES

9

"Do Your Duty!"

The Massacre at Mountain Meadows

In the province of Bengal, India, in 1857, native soldiers called "sepoys" rose in a great rebellion against their foreign masters. In June that year, a sepoy force besieged the town of Cawnpore, held by a small garrison of English officers and civilians and their families. After a heroic defense, and burdened with the wounded and dying, with thirst, sickness, and despair, the survivors of the garrison surrendered. They had been assured by an envoy from the native mob that they would be given safe conduct out of the war zone and into safe hands and so they turned over their arms to their captors and were marched away. But on the road outside the town a signal was given and within a few minutes they were killed—men, women, children, the wounded in their litters—by gunfire and club and the hacking of knives and swords.

It took a while for the news of the Cawnpore massacre to reach the United States where newspaper readers at their breakfast tables could cluck their tongues and mutter over their coffee cups, "Thank God such a thing couldn't happen here."

But history has that familiar perverse tendency to repeat itself and within two and a half months of the butchery in India occurred the American West's Cawnpore—an equal act of such consummate evil that 140 years of time has not erased its horror or solved its mysteries.

He sat forlornly on his coffin, his head bowed, a shapeless hat covering his graying blond hair, the lower half of his face buried in a wool muffler and the collar of his black overcoat. He had once been a big man, erect, barrel-chested, stern-faced with squinting gray eyes that saw everything and forgot nothing. He had once been feared, ever ready to do Joseph's or Brigham's work as their Sword of the Lord and Son of Dan—but now he seemed shrunken, deserted, pathetic.

Around him as the sun rose, the great meadow, once so lushly grassed the stirrups of horsemen were lost in it—this grand green meadow on the southmost rim of the Great Basin, 260 miles south of Salt Lake City—now lay trampled flat and ugly, yellowed by the sun's sear and endless rainless days. Some said the meadow was dying, fallowed by the blood of those who had been slaughtered there.

The event that had bloodied the meadow had occurred twenty years ago; the man sitting on his coffin had been a part of it, and within minutes would pay the great price, alone, for what he—and many others who did not pay the price—had done there.

The Mormon Church, more properly the Church of Jesus Christ of Latter-Day Saints, already had a turbulent quarter-century history when the Fancher wagon train rumbled into Utah Territory that summer of 1857. The church had been founded in Fayetteville, New York, in 1830 under the mesmerizing leadership of an amazing dreamer and born zealot whose flock made its progress over great, often cruel, obstacles.

Joseph Smith had but a rudimentary frontier education but a heavy steeping in the Bible, a familiar mixture in the era of backwoods revivalism in which he spent his boyhood. In about 1823, when he was eighteen, he said he was visited by an angel named Moroni who set for him the task of finding certain golden plates upon which were inscribed ancient religious texts. In 1827, he said, he found the plates on Cumorah Hill near Palmyra, New York, and with the plates some mysterious optical devices to enable him to translate the texts—written in what Smith said was "Reformed Egyptian"—which told of an ancient people, the Lost Israelites, who lived in North America hundreds of years before Christ.

With a few adherents serving as scribes, Smith, sitting behind a screen, dictated the texts of the golden plates, and the resulting Book of Mormon (Mormon being the father of Moroni and the historian of the Lost Israelites) was published in 1830, creating a local uproar—the first of many Smith and his followers would experience. He was accused as a liar, a false prophet, and a fanatic, but he and his handful of believers managed to organize their new church and begin a series of searches toward finding a home for it.

In the first nine years of their faith, Mormonism's founder and his steadily growing band of believers moved to Kirtland, Ohio, to Jackson County, Missouri, back to Kirtland (where Smith was tarred and feathered at least once), back to Missouri, then in 1839 to a boggy tract of land on the Mississippi in western Illinois near the Iowa-Missouri border. In this place they built the town they called Nauvoo and put the big river between them and their sworn enemies, whom they called Missouri "pukes."

(Missourians had twice expelled the Mormons; their truculent governor, Lilburn W. Boggs, waged a virtual civil war against Smith and his self-styled "Saints," declaring, "The Mormons must be treated as enemies and must be exterminated or driven from the state. . . ." In May 1842, Boggs was severely wounded by a shotgun blast through his parlor window as he sat reading his newspaper by lamplight. The attempted assassination was the work of Orrin Porter Rockwell, one of Joseph Smith's bodyguards and a leader of the Mormon vigilante group called the Danites.)

Now ending the first decade of their church, the Mormons had an established reputation as an arrogant, dogmatic, and self-righteous group of cultists. It was said that Smith and his people harbored a rabid hatred for all "Gentiles," non-Mormons, and believed all other faiths were works of Satan and their followers blaspheming infidels. In Nauvoo, where they cleared the swampy land and built a respectable village and church, Smith's theocratic rule was despised as antidemocratic. He had won a liberal charter for his town, established a militia, was granted his own courts and jurisdiction. The clannishness of Smith's flock generated fear among non-Mormons in the area that these strange interlopers would vote as a block and eventually control the county, perhaps even the state, government.

In those early years of mutual paranoia at Nauvoo, Joseph Smith revealed to his inner circle a matter that had been rumored among Mormons and their enemies for years, a matter that would cause his church more derision, division, and pain than it had ever suffered before. This was the doctine sanctioning polygamy that Smith said he received as a "Revelation Concerning Celestial Marriage." The idea that Prophet Smith said God had told him that a man might have as many wives as he could support quickly moved from rumor to open secret. The whispers about it further isolated the church and its followers, deepened the hatred and ridicule of non-Mormon to Mormon, and caused a schism even among Smith's own parishoners.

It is in Nauvoo in these turbulent times that we become aware of the sullen presence of a man named John Doyle Lee, born in 1812 in Kaskaskia, Illinois, a veteran of the Blackhawk War of 1832, baptized into the Mormon Church in 1838. In Nauvoo, no doubt because of his experience as a soldier, he became one of the Prophet Smith's bodyguards and soon a member of the secret society of vigilantes known as the Sons of Dan (from Genesis 49:17: "Dan shall be a serpent by the way, an adder in the path, that biteth the horse heels, so that his rider shall fall backward"). These "Danites," or "Avenging Angels" as some came to call them, were militant thugs who sought out church enemies, punishing apostates and other offenders in various ways, including murder. (Porter Rockwell, a church hero on the dodge for his attempt on the life of Governor Boggs, was a founding member of the Danites.)

Lee was on a church mission in Kentucky when the act occurred that set in stone the Mormon hatred of the Gentile and gave the Saints a thirst for revenge that found a slaking thirteen years later.

In 1844, with his church membership believed to be near 35,000, and with Joseph Smith announcing he would run for the U.S. presidency that year, the church's most persistent problem was a newspaper, the *Nauvoo Expositor*. The paper was produced by ex-Mormons and dedicated to "exposing" what its proprietors considered to be the "crimes" of the church, specifically the sanctioned practice of polygamy. Its customary fare were stories accusing the Prophet and other high church officials of seducing or attempting to seduce numerous women, and chronicling a catalog of other crimes condoned by Smith and his followers.

Whether upon official orders from Smith and his inner council, or an independent act of his followers, the *Expositor*'s office was raided and destroyed and soon after warrants were issued for the arrest of Smith and others for destruction of property. The Prophet, his brother Hyrum, and two other church associates were arrested and taken to the nearest jail, that at Carthage, the seat of Hancock County, a few miles southeast of Nauvoo.

The prisoners were placed in the stone jail's second-floor cell on June 27, 1844, and within hours a mob descended on the building and killed both Joseph and Hyrum Smith. The Prophet was attempting to jump from a window when he was shot. He fell to the ground, a mob member propped him against a well curbing, and four more bullets were fired into his body.

With Smith's death, church leadership devolved upon Brigham Young, a burly forty-three-year-old Vermonter and former carpenter and glazier who served as president of Smith's Quorum of Twelve Apostles. He was Mormonism's greatest proselytizer, journeying to Canada and England, baptizing over 7,000 new members, and setting up church branches and foreign missions.

Young was in the east promoting the Prophet's bid for the presidency when Smith and his brother were murdered but upon his return he began the planning to abandon Nauvoo and seek the church's "Zion" in the West.

In February 1846, he led 16,000 of his people across the ice-blocked Mississippi in sub-zero weather, taking five months to cover the first 400 miles of the journey across Iowa to Council Bluffs on the Missouri River. Six hundred Mormons died en route. Winter quarters were established at Florence, Nebraska, and in the spring of 1847, Young took a company of 143 men and pushed west, entering the valley of the Great Salt Lake in July. There, legend has it, he stuck his staff in the ground and proclaimed, "This is the place!"

With their renowned pioneering industry and selflessness, the Mormons established the thriving settlement and church headquarters of Salt Lake City and other towns and settlements throughout the valley and began farming and irrigation projects. Young organized the provisional State of Deseret, was elected its chief executive in March 1849, and when Congress organized the Territory of Utah in September 1850, he was named governor.

Brigham Young also became the law of Utah Territory and its theocratic ruler.

In 1852 a prominent Mormon elder named Orson Pratt made a speech in which he disclosed the church's doctrine of plural marriage. This first official confession of the illegal practice of polygamy came at a time when Young's "rule" in Utah was already under national scrutiny. Pratt's disclosure further separated the Mormons from the rest of the United States—something that many believed was precisely what Mormons desired. Young's xenophobic speeches, and those of his Apostles and other prominent church leaders, had made it clear from the beginning that Utah Territory was a commonwealth for Mormons only and that all others were trespassers.

In addition to the polygamy issue, an accumulation of other condemnations of Young's governorship became a topic of hot debate in Congress. He was accused of appointing only church officers to territorial government posts and of being responsible for the harassment of argonauts passing through Utah en route to the California goldfields. Other non-Mormon emigrants— many of whom were forming a growing permanent population in the Territory—were critical of their treatment by the Saints and traced the problem to Young. Non-Mormon territorial officials and judges said they were routinely insulted and intimidated, that court records against Mormons were destroyed, that the affairs of the Territory were in a "disgraceful, dangerous state," and that Governor Young and his inner council were guilty of outright treason.

With great anti-Mormon sentiment spreading and seeping into Washington and a clamor for action by the press and rival churches, early in 1857 the Buchanan administration declared Utah Territory to be in a state of insurrection. The president appointed a new, non-Mormon territorial governor, and ordered an infantry regiment under Colonel Albert Sidney Johnston to march from Fort Leavenworth, Kansas, into Utah to remove Brigham Young from office and stamp out the "rebellion."

Young reacted to the news, made public in May, by declaring martial law and ordering all Mormons to resist the oncoming army and defend Zion.

On September 17, 1857, Colonel Johnston, his staff and dragoon escort, led about 1,200 soldiers, two batteries of artillery with twelve howitzers and siege cannon, out of Fort Leavenworth, headed west to Utah.

In the midst of the hysteria of awaiting the invading Gentile army, just six days before it marched west, in a meadow in the sparsely settled southern rim of the Great Basin of Utah Territory, occurred a crime that culminated, more savagely than the "Utah War of 1857" ever did, the first twenty-seven years of Mormondom.

No timing could have been more perverse for the Fancher wagon train to roll into Utah Territory than that August of 1857, but the emigrants who accompanied him had every confidence in the man who had led them there.

He was Alexander Fancher, a tall, slim, dark-complexioned man who came out of Overton County, Tennessee, and married Eliza Ingram in Illinois in 1836. The Fanchers moved to farming lands around Illinois and Missouri in their early married life, then to Benton County, Arkansas, in the early 1850s. He may have led at least two wagon trains to California—and thus earned the trail title of "captain"—before the one he organized in the spring of 1857 at Fort Smith.

He and Eliza were parents of nine children in all; two of whom would survive past 1857.

Although all the Fancher train papers—sign-on lists, diaries, logs, expense rolls—were destroyed, the number of people in Captain Fancher's last wagon train is reasonably known: fifty men, forty women, and fifty children, representing between twenty to thirty families, with about a dozen of the men mounted on horseback, the others, with their wives and children, afoot.

The 140 people, including Fancher, his wife, and nine children, were accompanied by a rich assortment of stock: at least 600, perhaps 900, cows, oxen to pull forty to sixty wagons, a dozen to thirty horses and mules.

The emigrants also brought with them their life savings, totaling as much as $100,000 according to some estimates, and household belongings that were priceless to their owners, at least valuable to anyone else.

These families—mostly Arkansans with names like Baker, Huff, Beller, Mitchell, Prewitt, McIntyre, Dunlap, Wood, Wilson, Jones, Tackett, Eaton, Edwards, Miller, Scott, Rush, Deskazo, King, Morton, Hudson, Stevenson, Hamilton, Cameron, and Smith—set out under Fancher's command from the vicinity of Fort Smith on the eastern end of the Oregon Trail, in late March 1857. Their destination was the rich farmlands around San Bernardino, California.

Captain Fancher led his train to the Platte River around Fort Kerney, Nebraska Territory, west along the North Platte to Fort Laramie, thence across the Continental Divide to Fort Bridger and Salt Lake City, lying at the crossroads of the northern and southern routes to California.

The Fancher train reached the outskirts of the Utah capital on August 3, making camp in the eye of a hurricane of war and anti-Gentile hysteria.

The families had no sooner unharnessed their animals and started their campfires when visitors to their camp warned them of the dangers. The air was electric with suspicion. In town, many merchants refused to sell to them. They heard threats and rumors. It was being said that the Fancher party included a number of Missouri "pukes" who had participated in the murders of Joseph and Hyrum Smith. It was said that some of Fancher's people were bragging of involvement in the killing of the popular Mormon Apostle Parley Pratt, shot to death in Arkansas just three months earlier.

(In fact, there were some Missourians in the Fancher party, a few perhaps at the outset, others joining along the route to the Salt Lake Valley. Among them may have been some outspoken veterans of the Mormon "troubles" in their state twenty years ago. Nor were the Arkansans necessarily innocent of anti-Mormon sentiment, particularly after the difficulties in the capital.)

Captain Fancher, clearly concerned by what he heard and

saw, did not tarry his train long in the capital. Since his families were headed to San Bernardino and not the Sacramento area, he and the other emigrant leaders decided at some point to take the southern trail to California rather than the Oregon Trail route and so, on August 5, with all the people, wagons, and stock organized, they struck south out of the menacing capital.

The slow journey south to Iron County cannot have given Fancher and the families under his care much comfort. They were distancing from the hotbed of anti-Gentile hysteria in Salt Lake City, but it dogged them on the trail. Strange horsemen followed them at a distance and reports and rumors drifted in from non-Mormon settlers. Stories were spreading that the emigrants were fouling wells and springs, planting poison in slaughtered beef, harassing the normally placid Paiutes and other Indians in the area, ridiculing the faith by calling their oxen Brigham and Joseph and other names sacred to the church, letting their animals graze without permission on Mormon fields, and boasting that the advancing army would stamp out Mormonism forever.

At Cedar City, the last major settlement on the trail inside the Territory, storekeepers refused to sell supplies to Fancher and his families.

The train crawled on south and in the first week of September entered the narrow strip of grassland known as Mountain Meadows.

Much had happened to John D. Lee since the days in Nauvoo when he had been among Joseph Smith's Danite bodyguards. Throughout the exodus from Illinois in 1846 he had been a tireless aide to Brigham Young and always an ardent and loyal churchman. In the early years in the newfound Zion, he had been rewarded for his good works when, through religious rites, he became Young's adopted son and a member of the Mormon leader's family in this life and the next.

He had been among the first to put the doctrine of "Celestial Marriage" into practice; as early as 1845 he was "sealed" to a second wife and in his lifetime married at least nineteen women.

Lee had farmed for a time around Salt Lake City, became one of the founders of the city of Provo, then moved south to Iron County, there establishing the settlement of Parowan. In 1856 he began work as farmer-agent in charge of the Iron County Agency, one of five Indian agencies in the Territory. Over the years he served as probate judge, clerk, and tax assessor for neighboring Washington County.

He did his agency work well. The Paiutes, Pahvants, and other tribes of the region remained docile and Lee learned their languages and earned their trust and friendship.

He was a recognized pioneer of Utah Territory and an explorer of its southern reaches.

People who knew him remembered an imposing man with hooded gray eyes, narrowed either in perpetual suspicion or from living in the sun, or both; perfect white teeth, and a mane of straight blondish hair combed into a great swirl over his squarish face. He had an amiable smile. One observer said he resembled "a good-natured, kind-hearted, easy-going, pleasant-spoken old Pennsylvania farmer." And a later biographer described him as "a gifted and intelligent man, generous and kindly, but egotistical and apt to be dictatorial."

All agreed on his one unchanging feature: John Doyle Lee had an utter and unquestioning faith in his church and its leader, Brigham Young.

The meeting that would prove fatal to the Fancher party took place on Sunday, September 6, 1857, in Cedar City. Thanks to the assiduous work of the late Juanita Brooks, Lee's biographer, we know the names and histories of some of the conspirators in that gathering just thirty miles north of Mountain Meadows. Chief among these men were Isaac C. Haight, president of the Cedar City Stake of the church, age forty-four, a New Yorker and Nauvoo veteran; John M. Higbee, a major of the Iron County militia, a courier between Haight and William H. Dame, the militia commander; a Pennsylvania blacksmith named Philip Klingonsmith, a Mormon bishop in Cedar City; Charles Hopkins, a

Cedar City Mormon president; and John D. Lee, a key man because of his work among the Indians.

Precisely what this group of vengeful men, and the others
who were present, decided upon is not known. It seems clear
that they had convened before September 6, perhaps several
times as news of the approach of the Fancher party reached them
some weeks before. (Josiah Gibbs, who in 1910 wrote a scathing
book on the Mormon involvement in the Fancher train affair,
said, "The fate of the emigrants had been predetermined by Isaac
C. Haight, who was the direct agent of the 'holy' viceregents
who resided at Salt Lake. The 'council' was merely a ratification
meeting.")

The glimpses that Lee and others subsequently gave into the
proceeding show that it became a consensus among them that the
emigrant party would pay for its crimes and insults. And someone suggested that whatever would be done had to be done
quickly before the wagon train got too far away and the oncoming federal army too near.

It appears that the group of conspirators reached agreement
that the Fancher party "be done away with," this cynical resolution accompanied by another, to send an urgent message to
President Young in Salt Lake City asking his direction and orders.
To put the latter decision into motion, a rider named James
Haslam was sent north with the message and wore out horses
getting to the capital in under three days. He later testified that
Brigham Young told him to return quickly and, "spare no horse
flesh," and that Haight and his group were to be told "that the
emigrants are not to be meddled with."

But Haslam, despite his heroic effort, returned to Cedar City
too late to stop the crime. In fact, judging from the timing of the
events that followed, the conspirators had no intention of waiting for instructions from Brigham Young.

When the Cedar City meeting broke up, each man involved
seems to have had his orders.

Lee proceeded to the settlement of Harmony to seek the help

of his Indian friends. Apparently with the promise of an easy fight with little or no resistance, and of cattle and booty, he enlisted between 200 and 300 Paiutes and Pahvants to attack the emigrants in their camp.

Meantime, Haight, Higbee, Dame, and the others rounded up a gang of like-minded Mormon settlers, and all rendezvoused on the predawn hours of September 7 a mile or so from the Fancher camp in the grassy slopes of Mountain Meadows. Lee later testified that under the cover of night, he and his men managed to run off most of the emigrants' stock, grazing some distance from their camp, and to herd the animals into a makeshift corral. This was done, he said, without disturbing the sleeping camp.

It appears that among Captain Fancher's fatal mistakes was his failure to post guards with the stock or at the camp. This matter, and the careless positioning of the camp, are among the mysteries of the fate of the emigrant train. Given the climate of hatred of outsiders the emigrants had experienced for over a month, it is inexplicable that Fancher, with his experience on wagon trains in hostile territory, would not have armed men assigned as outriders and sentries, especially during the night.

But it appears he did not and at dawn Lee and the other white men daubed their faces with paint, some even donning feathered headdresses, and urged their Indian confederates into making the first attack on the emigrant camp. The Fancher party was caught off guard as they rebuilt their cooking fires, the sudden yelping and rifle fire creating an instant panic. Several of the emigrants fell dead or wounded from the first enfilade and there was a scurrying for cover, shouted orders, the screaming of women and children, the spang and thump of bullets, and the crisp pop-pop-pop of rifle fire from some invisible adversary.

The confusion in the camp lasted only minutes. Fancher left orders to trusted lieutenants, gathered a number of men, and led them to a rocky outcropping near the camp where they lay down a concerted answering fire in the general direction of what by now was judged to be an Indian attack. In the camp, men and women managed to drag the dead and wounded to cover and fetch their weapons. Under sporadic and largely ineffective fire they pulled their wagons in a circle, tongues inward, and dug holes for the wheels so that the beds lay near flat on the ground. A rifle pit was dug, four feet deep and twenty long, and an earth barricade thrown up in front of it. In a brief time the emigrants had established a crude siege works.

They also had a serious problem other than what appeared to be an Indian attack: they had made their camp forty yards from their only source of water, a spring that now lay outside their defensive perimeter and across bald ground.

During the first few minutes of the attack six or seven of the Fancher party were killed outright, another fifteen wounded. The return fire also did some damage. John D. Lee later wrote that several of the Indians were killed and many wounded. The return fire from Fancher's sharpshooters became so effective, Lee said, that couriers were dispatched to Cedar City to ask for reinforcements from the local Mormon militia.

A stalemate now in effect, the emigrants had time to assess their damage and survival potential. The captain and his men had no good news. They knew the "Indian attack" would renew at any moment and the first firing had occurred before the morning's water supply had been carried in from the spring. The water barrels were almost empty and as the sun rose that morning attempts were made to reach the spring, each water party driven back by heavy rifle fire. The wounded were suffering; the women and small children panicky.

As the day drew on, and during the next day, Mormon reinforcements arrived from the settlements in Iron County. Isaac Haight, Colonel Dame, Major Higbee, John D. Lee, and other leaders of the attack held councils to decide how to handle the unexpected resistance.

By Wednesday, September 9, the third day of the stalemate, the water supply in the emigrant camp had dwindled to cupfuls and a desperate attempt was made to dig a well within the camp confines. The well produced no water.

But Fancher had hope of rescue—from the Mormons. He believed his party was under attack from Indians and that if he could send messengers through the lines to Cedar City, militiamen and others would ride to his aid. Three men volunteered for this mission, two of whose names are lost to history. The other was William A. Aiden, a Tennessean and a landscape painter who had joined the Fancher party at Provo.

Aiden and his companions left the camp on the night of September 9, leading their horses several miles before feeling safe enough to ride. About fifteen miles from Mountain Meadows they stopped to water their horses and during this brief rest, several riders approached—white men. Aiden excitedly explained his mission. He was shot dead by one William C. Stewart, a Mormon priest and member of the Cedar City council. It is not clear if the other two emigrant riders were present at Aiden's murder, but both were later killed attempting to return to their camp.

Most of what is known of the events at Mountain Meadows on Friday, September 11, 1857, derives from the testimony of John D. Lee, in court records and in his own memoirs. Other Mormons testified and historical investigators have added considerably to the record, but it is Lee who is the principal source of information. While he denied personally killing any of the emigrants, his account is straightforward and passionless.

By September 10, Lee said, reinforcements from Cedar City, Parowan, Harmony, and other settlements had arrived. Fifty-four Mormons and 300 Indians, mostly Paiutes, now lay in wait.

In the councils held during the stalemate, the Mormons decided that Lee would lead the effort to bring the emigrants out from their camp.

It was predetermined that once out of the camp and on the trail, ostensibly to Cedar City, each militiaman would be responsible for killing one adult male, Lee would "supervise" killing the wounded, the Indians would kill the women and older children.

This bloodcurdling plan, made by a handful of pious fanatics, was put into motion on the morning of September 11.

John D. Lee and William Bateman, son of an English-born bricklayer and Mormon convert, washed the paint from their faces and, carrying a white flag, descended from the cover of a copse of trees and rode up to the besieged camp. Two young men came out to greet them—white men, rescuers, at last, these two must have thought—and led them into the crude wagon-redoubt.

Lee wrote later:

> As I entered the fortifications, men, women and children gathered around me in wild consternation. Some felt that the time of their happy deliverance had come, while others, although in deep distress, and all in tears, looked upon me with doubt, distrust and terror. . . . My position was painful, trying and awful; my brain seemed to be on fire; my nerves were for a moment unstrung; humanity was overpowered, as I thought of the cruel, unmanly part I was acting. . . . I knew that I was acting a cruel part and doing a damnable deed.

Lee introduced himself to Fancher and his lieutenants as the Mormon agent to the Indians and said the attack on their party had come to his attention at Parowan and that he and a number of other Saints in the area had sped to the Meadows, calmed the attackers, and persuaded them to a truce. He told Fancher he appreciated their distress, knew of their water shortage, but could not help them further unless they gave up their arms. He suggested a "ceremonial surrender" to placate the Indians surrounding the camp and promised the Fancher party safe, escorted passage to Cedar City where they could reorganize and proceed.

The emigrant leaders had little choice but to put their faith in the Mormons' hands. Their stock had been run off, the water supply nearly dry, ammunition running out, the wounded lying in agony in their bloody dressings, people becoming hysterical and losing hope.

Fancher and his leaders agreed to Lee's plan. At about noon two big wagons were driven into the camp. The youngest children were loaded into the first together with bedding, guns, and other goods; the second held the wounded men. These wagons pulled out with Lee walking between them.

The procession that set out on the trail toward Cedar City was cunningly organized. Lee and the horse-drawn wagons led the way. At some distance behind walked a long line of women, some pregnant, some carrying babies, and the older children. A quarter mile behind these trudged the men, husbands, fathers, and sons of the women ahead, in single file, each with an armed Mormon militiaman alongside. Major Higbee rode on horseback up and down between the wagons and rear guard, and about a half mile to the north, hidden in roadside brush, the Indians waited.

The sun blazed directly overhead as the two lead wagons disappeared over a knoll and creaked past the place where the mixed band of Paiutes and Pahvants crouched.

Then the line of women and older children reached the dense scrub along the trail and there was a sudden shouted order—believed to have come from Higbee—"Halt! Do your duty!"

What followed was quickly and efficiently done. Each Saint in the rear column raised his weapon and shot the unarmed emigrant closest to him at point-blank range. Those who ran or tried to crawl away had their throats cut, were shot, or clubbed to death with rifle butts. This few seconds of sudden mass murder occurred simultaneously with the Indians pouring from the brush ahead along the trail and falling on the women and older children. All these innocents were shot, hacked to death with knives, or brained with war clubs. As the rear massacres were taking place, Lee and his wagon party killed the wounded in the wagons, then dumped the bodies out along the trail.

In as little as fifteen minutes about 120 of the emigrant party, were slaughtered, including Alexander Fancher, his wife, and seven of his nine children.

Eighteen small children—too young to testify on what had happened to their parents and friends—survived and were taken in the wagons to the ranch of Mormon elder Jacob Hamblin whose property was closest to the Meadows. Later these children were distributed among various Mormon families.

The emigrants' 300 head of cattle were turned over to Lee to rebrand and sell.

There is varied testimony as to Lee's participation in the massacre. He denied in his confession that he killed anyone but few believed him. He wrote of his experience with the wounded in the wagons:

> I drew my pistol, cocked it, but somehow it went off prematurely and I shot McMurdy [Samuel McMurdy, a Mormon militiaman] across the thigh, my pistol ball cutting his buckskin pants. McMurdy turned to me and said, "Brother Lee, keep cool, you are excited . . . You came very near killing me." Knight [Samuel Knight, one of the Mormons who participated in the massacre] then shot a man in the head. Knight also brained a boy that was about fourteen years old. . . . all of the sick and wounded were killed almost immediately. I fully intended to do my part of the killing, but by the time I got over the excitement of coming so near killing McMurdy, the whole of the killing was done.

He gave the number killed at 121, counting Aiden and his two companions who had tried to ride to Cedar City for help.

While the Indians were looting the wagons at the Fancher camp—"throwing out dishes, scattering feathers from pillows, ransacking like gleeful, mischievous children," in Juanita Brooks's description—many of the dead were buried in the rifle pit that had been dug by the victims, others in shallow graves scratched in the ground along the trail.

When this was done, the murderers rendezvoused at the Hamblin ranch, got something to eat, and, exhausted from the day's work, found places to sleep. Lee said he "lay down on the saddle blanket, using my saddle for a pillow, and slept soundly until the next morning."

The massacre came close to being the only recorded instance of a perfect crime of mass murder. The only white witnesses were the perpetrators and they were not talking, nor were the Indians, who, for a long time, were accused as the sole culprits.

On November 20 Lee wrote to President Brigham Young an official lie on the "incident" in his role as farmer-agent to the southern territorial tribes. He said the Fancher party had poisoned a slaughtered ox and gave it to the Paiutes, four of whom died from eating the meat. The emigrants, he said, also poisoned water on Paiute lands and these acts "raised the ire of the Indians" and "Capt. Fancher and Co. fell victims to their wrath near Mountain Meadows."

Lee's own papers, supported by testimony of others, show he had a personal meeting with Brigham Young about two weeks after the massacre. Whether Lee told the truth to his adoptive father then is not known, nor is it known when Young learned of Mormon complicity in the crime. He certainly learned of it before 1870, the year his associates later claimed.

Notice of the massacre began appearing in the press within two months of it. In November 1857, a man named John Aiken passed through Mountain Meadows only a few weeks after the bloodshed and told a California newspaper, "I saw about twenty wolves feasting upon the carcasses of the murdered."

The pact of silence among the Mormon killers seems to have lasted only a few months. By early 1858 persistent rumors were abroad in the Territory that white men had taken part in the "incident." Certain names even kept cropping up—Haight, Dame, Klingonsmith, Hopkins, Higbee, Lee, among them—and questions were being asked about the complicity of the highest officers of the church in Salt Lake City, including especially Brigham Young.

Within a year, with the "Mormon War" ended, public clamor for an investigation into the massacre resulted in two military parties, one from California, the other from Camp Floyd, Utah Territory, setting out to gather information. And in March 1859, a tough customer named John Cradlebaugh, U.S. associate justice for the district of Utah, began his own investigation of various alleged Mormon crimes including the Fancher party murders. At Cedar City and elsewhere he gathered damaging information and asked embarrassing questions. He wanted to know why the emigrants' cattle had received Mormon brands and had been sold along with jewelry and other valuables from their camp, the proceeds given to the church. He asked why the surviving children, contrary to reports that they had been taken by Indians, were in fact living with Mormon families.

Judge Cradlebaugh even gathered some confessions from a number of high-ranking Mormons present during the massacre and issued arrest warrants on several of these men. But when he found they could not be served—those named had fled from the Territory—and that other potential witnesses seemed to have evaporated, lost their memories, or refused to testify in court, he had to abandon his efforts.

In the course of his investigations, however, the judge told a Mormon-controlled grand jury, "You are the tools, the dupes, the instruments of a tyrannical Church despotism. The heads of your Church order and direct you. You are taught to obey their orders and commit these horrid murders. Deprived of your liberty, you have lost your manhood, and become the willing instruments of evil men."

The Civil War distracted attention from the massacre for a decade and a half.

John D. Lee and Isaac Haight were excommunicated from the church in 1870—after Brigham Young said he first learned of the complicity of certain Mormons in the massacre—and both men were indicted for the crime of thirteen years past. But by then, both men had fled into exile in Arizona Territory.

A year or so before his excommunication, Lee, whose name was by then so closely associated with the Fancher train murders many believed him the sole instigator of it, moved across the southern Utah border into Arizona. He built a small house at the mouth of the Paria River, cleared a garden there, and called the place "Lonely Dell." In 1872 he opened a ferry across the Colorado River that would remain in operation until 1928, fifty-one years after his death.

In June 1872, a newspaperman named J. H. Beadle visited Lonely Dell. Lee seemed anxious to talk and maintained his innocence in the Mountain Meadows affair, saying he had been made a scapegoat on "the most infamous charges ever cooked up on a man." He repeated his story that the Fancher party had intimidated the Indians, that the Indians were responsible for the bloodshed, and he stood steadfast in his loyalty to Brigham Young.

Passage of federal legislation in 1874 outlawed polygamous marriage and ended Utah's theocratic governance and Mormon control of the territorial courts. With the new federal laws came U.S. attorneys granted rights to prosecute, U.S. marshals to serve and execute writs, and various other federal law officers to make arrests—even for such distant crimes as the Mountain Meadows murders.

Lee periodically traveled from the relative safety of his home and ferry on the Arizona side of the Colorado to visit wives, children, and other family members in the town of Panguitch, northeast of Cedar City, in territory in which he was a wanted man. He made this journey once too often and on November 7, 1874, was arrested in Panguitch by William Stokes, a deputy U.S. marshal.

The case against John D. Lee for complicity and murder at Mountain Meadows opened on July 23, 1875, in the town of Beaver, thirty miles north of Cedar City, with a jury of eight Mormons, three Gentiles, and one "Jack Mormon" (an apostate) hearing the evidence. The chief witness against him was Philip Klingonsmith, the former bishop of Cedar City and confessed participant in the massacre who had turned state's evidence in exchange for immunity from prosecution. Despite his condemning account of the crime and Lee's role in it, the jury could reach no decision. The eight Mormons voted for acquittal, the others for conviction.

(Klingonsmith was found dead in a prospector's hole in Sonora, Mexico, in August 1888, apparently murdered.)

On August 5 Lee was taken back to jail in Salt Lake City to await a second trial. The following May he was released on $15,000 bail and his promise he would return for trial.

A year passed before the second trial opened. It was now nineteen years since the massacre and yet none of the others involved in the murders—Haight, Higbee, Hopkins, Dame—had been brought to justice although named in indictments. Haight, in fact, had been welcomed back into the church in 1874 after having succeeded in placing full responsiblity for the massacre on Lee and others. Hopkins was dead. Higbee would return to Utah shortly, never to be prosecuted, nor would William H. Dame, the militia commander, who once said that if brought to trial he would "put the saddle on the right horse," which was interpreted as meaning he would indict the whole Mormon leadership.

Lee, however, like a faithful dog trailing a cruel master, returned from his Lonely Dell on the Colorado to face a second trial, and this time, in the passage of but a year, things were entirely different. Now there were witnesses where none, other than Klingonsmith, could be found before; the district attorney now claimed that Lee was in collusion with the Indians and drew other Mormons in the affair under false pretenses and that the others merely helped bury the dead.

Lee's lame defense was that he never denied being present at the massacre but that he was a mere subordinate in a military operation and that he did not kill any of the emigrants.

If the first trial was a farce, the second was little better than a star chamber. It opened on September 14, 1876, and the case was turned over to an all-Mormon jury on the twentieth. After deliberating three and a half hours, a unanimous guilty verdict was returned.

The presiding judge gave Lee his choice of execution. "I prefer to be shot," Lee said.

In prison he wrote, "I have been treacherously betrayed and sacrificed in a most cowardly manner by those who should have been my friends."

❧

His execution date was set for March 23, 1877, and the place—apparently decided upon by a judge with a poignant sense of justice—Mountain Meadows.

He was taken, shackled and under close guard, by wagon from Salt Lake City to the Meadows with stopovers along the long route. The morning of the twenty-third was chilly and he wore a long overcoat and muffler. He sat on his coffin waiting for the sun to rise and provide adequate light for his executioners. Near where he sat lay a stone cairn built around a cedar cross, placed there by soldiers to mark the Fancher campsite.

He had some last words: "I feel resigned to my fate," he said. "I feel as calm as a summer morn. . . . My conscience is clear before God and man. I am ready to meet my Redeemer and those who have gone before me, behind the vale. . . ."

When the firing squad lined up, he shook hands with each man, saying to them, "Center my heart, boys. Don't mangle my body." Then he took off his hat and coat and was escorted to the place where he would die. He accepted a blindfold but asked that his hands be free.

The volley quickly followed, crashing into the still morning air, echoing out across the rich pastureland.

John Doyle Lee, explorer, farmer, ferryman, friend of the Indian, Son of Dan, Joseph Smith's bodyguard, Brigham Young's adopted son, Mormon zealot, conspirator and participant in mass murder, fell dead without so much as a groan.

He was buried by relatives in Panguitch.

Brigham Young survived him by only five months.

❧

On September 11, 1857, the day of the Fancher party massacre, a Pennsylvanian named Jacob Forney was appointed by President James Buchanan as superintendent of Indian Affairs in Utah Territory. Forney assisted Colonel Albert Sidney Johnston during the "Mormon War" and devoted much of his time away from his regular work locating the eighteen missing children from the emigrant party.

He found seventeen of them living with various Mormon families, including the two surviving Fancher children, Kit Carson, age five at the time of the murder of his parents, and Trifina, age two. Forney took all the children to Salt Lake City and eventually saw them returned to their Arkansas relatives.

Kit Carson Fancher died unmarried in Arkansas in 1873.

Trifina married James C. Wilson in Carroll County, Arkansas, and became the mother of nine children—the same as her mother. She died in 1897.

In 1932 the Utah Pioneer Trails and Landmarks Association placed a bronze tablet on a rock wall around the mass grave of the Fancher party at Mountain Meadows. The tablet referred to the massacre as "one of the most lamentable tragedies in the history annals of the West" and said, "John D. Lee, who confessed participation as a leader, was legally executed here March 23rd, 1877."

In 1988, over 130 years after the massacre, descendants of Mormon pioneers and those of Fancher train emigrants came together at Mountain Meadows in a spirit of reconciliation.

The countless questions and lingering doubts about what had happened there, and why, went unasked and unstated.

Most of it is a mystery, after all, and by definition is unsolved.

10

An Afternoon on the Greasy Grass

Custer and the Little Bighorn

The place lies off Interstate 90, sixty-five miles southeast of Billings and about fifteen miles south of Hardin, Montana, on Crow Agency lands. Until 1991 it was called the Custer Battlefield but while his name has today vanished from the official National Park Service title—the Little Bighorn Battlefield National Monument—his presence is everywhere in this 765-acre killing ground.

Stand at the monument on Custer Hill (he died close by so it is still called Custer Hill) and look out at the wrinkled, sun-ochered slopes and the dry, puckered-edged ravines resembling badly sutured wounds on an old brown hide. If the place didn't have a name, if there were no monument, no signs, no graveyard, you would know something awful happened here.

What did happen here on Sunday, June 25, 1876, was awful beyond description, and almost all of it is a mystery.

Colorado became the thirty-eighth state in that Centennial year and Jack London was born in San Francisco. Alexander Graham Bell uttered the first sentences ever transmitted over a telephone wire that year and Queen Victoria became Empress of India. That year the Tilden-Hayes presidential election ended in an electoral college snarl, James Butler "Wild Bill" Hickok was murdered in Deadwood, Dakota Territory, and the James and Younger brothers ended their outlaw careers in a hail of bullets outside a bank in Northfield, Minnesota. That year people were singing such new songs as "I'll Take You Home Again, Kathleen" and "What a Friend We Have in Jesus," were reading *The Adventures of Tom Sawyer,* and were buying such new products as player pianos, Remington typewriters, Heinz tomato ketchup, Budweiser beer, canned boneless hams, and B.V.D. underwear.

Midway through that mighty, muscle-flexing year, thirty-seven foreign nations and twenty-six states set up exhibits at Fairmount Park in Philadelphia and President U. S. Grant opened the official celebration marking the Centennial of American independence.

And then, by a perverse turn of fate, amid the gaiety, in the finest moment of a joyous, optimistic year, smiles vanished and brows furrowed as the news reached Centennial revelers of an awful event out on the Western frontier.

On July 6, 1876, the New York *Herald* carried the story, based on a dispatch from the Bismarck, Dakota Territory, *Tribune.* The chilling laddered headline ran:

A BLOODY BATTLE
An Attack on Sitting Bull on the
Little Horn River.
GENERAL CUSTER KILLED.
The Entire Detachment Under His
Command Slaughtered.

SEVENTEEN OFFICERS SLAIN.
Narrow Escape of Colonel
Reno's Command.
A HORRIBLE SLAUGHTER PEN.
Over Three Hundred of the
Troops Killed.

The dispatch told of a fight eleven days earlier in Montana Territory "between General Custer's force and about 5,000 Indians, near the Little Bighorn River, in which Custer and all the men of five companies of soldiers, about 300 in number, were killed."

Reporters found General Philip H. Sheridan, commander of the Division of the Missouri, among the Philadelphia celebrants and he said flatly that the report from Montana was preposterous. General William T. Sherman, commander-in-chief of the army, said more circumspectly that the reports "lacked official confirmation."

But the story didn't lack confirmation for long and by July 10, with new, horrific details appearing daily, the *New York Tribune* ran a poem by Walt Whitman titled "A Death Song for Custer" containing these lines:

Thou of the tawny flowing hair in battle,
I erewhile saw, with erect head, pressing ever in front,
  bearing a bright sword in thy hand,
Now ending well in death the splendid fever of thy deeds.

There were errors in those early reports and in Whitman's poem—Custer was a lieutenant colonel, his hair had been cut short, he carried no sword, there were fewer than 5,000 Indians in the battle, fewer than 300 troopers killed—but the essentials were correct and clear. On June 25, 1876, on a windswept ridge overlooking the Little Bighorn River in Montana Territory, five companies of the U.S. Seventh Cavalry, including the regiment's commander, had been annihilated.

Long before his name became synonymous with the worst debacle in American military annals, George Armstrong Custer had made a place in history. Fifteen years of his thirty-six-year life were spent in the army and by the time he led his regiment out of Fort Abraham Lincoln on May 17, 1876, to his—and its— bloody destiny, everyone knew his name. He was the controversial personification of the U.S. Cavalry, an author, explorer, plainsman, Indian fighter, crusader against political corruption, a hero and "Boy General" of the Civil War.

The son of a blacksmith and born in the hamlet of New Rumley, Ohio, in 1839, Custer entered West Point in 1857 and even at the earliest stages of his military career managed to make his name known. He was a lazy, lackadaisical prankster with a penchant for insubordination who graduated last in his class of '61. But plunged into battle, a different George Custer emerged. War, as he had suspected as a boy when he hid novels of battle behind his schoolbooks, was his true métier and he would never be quite so fulfilled as when bullets were flying and he could ride to glory, sword upraised, against an enemy.

He became the *beau sabreur* of the army, the George Patton of his era.

In the Civil War, he served with Generals Irwin McDowell, George B. McClellan, and Alfred Pleasonton, and in 1863, at the age of twenty-three, he earned a promotion to brigadier general of volunteers, the youngest in the Union Army. He commanded a brigade at Gettysburg and fought in all the cavalry actions of the Army of the Potomac—the Shenandoah Valley, Yellow Tavern, Winchester, Fisher's Hill, and Appomattox, among them—and a year later was given a second star and command of the Third Cavalry Regiment.

In 1864 he married Elizabeth Bacon, daughter of a Monroe, Michigan, judge. He called her "Libbie." To her, he was "Autie."

After the war, and reduced in rank to lieutenant colonel in the Regular Army, Custer's orders sent him west. He served in General Winfield Scott Hancock's Cheyenne campaign in 1867 and

the following year led the Seventh Cavalry in its attack against a
Cheyenne village on the Washita River in Oklahoma south of
Fort Hays.

In the spring of 1876 he traveled to Washington and gave
testimony before congressional committees, elaborating on
charges against the Grant administration for illegal post trader-
ships and various other Indian Bureau frauds and peculations
that had appeared in his newly published memoir, *My Life on the
Plains*.

He dawdled and fretted in the capital and as his regiment
outfitted for a campaign to round up "renegade" Sioux and
Cheyenne in the Yellowstone River country, he finally appealed
to General Alfred Terry, commander of his department, to be
permitted to rejoin the Seventh for the forthcoming summer
march. Grant, meantime, furious over Custer's charges against
his Indian policies, was determined to punish his accuser by keeping him kicking his heels in the capital. Custer wrote to Grant,
"I appeal to you as a soldier to spare me the humiliation of seeing my regiment march to meet the enemy & I to not share its
dangers."

After the intervention of Terry and Sheridan, both of whom
wanted Custer in the forthcoming campaign, Grant relented.

He was utterly fearless in battle and utterly unpredictable in
every other circumstance. He demanded unquestioning obedi-
ence to his own orders yet flouted or ignored orders from his superiors. He imposed rigid discipline among his officers and men
yet had little self-discipline. He passionately loved Libbie yet
was unfaithful to her and took childish pride in being a "lady's
man." He had an egoist's intolerance for the flaws of his peers,
a blindness to his own shortcomings, and a penchant for flam-
boyance he could not abide in others. His regiment was torn by
factionalism and included two important officers who despised
him and others, including his brother Tom, who were blindly
loyal to him.

Now in his thirty-sixth year, his curly reddish-blond hair,
once worn shoulder length, thinning and cut short, his blue eyes
surrounded with crow's-feet, his face lined and freckled, he re-

mained the hyperactive, fast-talking, war-loving, glory-seeking, ever-dashing figure, whether in cavalry blue, buckskins, or mufti, as he returned, in May, 1876, to Dakota Territory, to Libbie, to his regiment, and to his fate.

The army's Sioux-Cheyenne campaign of 1876 was the culmination of a struggle for the ancestral homelands of the nomadic tribes in today's Dakotas, Wyoming, and Montana. Following the Civil War, these lands were invaded by white traders and settlers and the U.S. government seemed to sanction this invasion. The government, after all, had a partnership in the Northern Pacific Railroad that sought to push its transcontinental line through the northern plains oblivious to the sanctity of the lands to the Indians.

In 1868, in a treaty signed at Fort Laramie, the government set aside much of present-day South Dakota as a permanent, supposedly inviolate, Sioux reservation. The peace lasted six years, until 1874, when gold was discovered in the Dakotas and thousands of prospectors invaded the Territory.

The man who blazed the trail through the Black Hills used by the treaty-breaking argonauts—the trail the Indians called the "Thieves' Road"—was George Armstrong Custer at the head of his Seventh U.S. Cavalry.

The government tried to buy the Black Hills but failed and thousands of Cheyennes and Sioux—the most renowned being the Hunkpapa medicine man Sitting Bull and the Oglala war chief Crazy Horse (see Chapter 12)—deserted their reservations and fled into the grasslands of Wyoming and Montana. These Indians were called "non-treaties" and the Commissioner of Indian Affairs issued an ultimatum for them to return to the reservation by January 1876, or be considered "hostile."

They did not return.

Sheridan's plan called for three columns to converge on the Wyoming-Montana border where most of the "non-treaties"

were said to be located. Brigadier General Alfred H. Terry, commanding the Department of Dakota, would march west from Fort Abraham Lincoln (across the Missouri from present-day Bismarck, N.D.) on May 17; Colonel John Gibbon, a veteran of the Mexican, Seminole, and Civil Wars, would move east with his 500-man Montana column from Fort Ellis (near Bozeman) on April 1; and Brigadier General George Crook, commander of the Department of the Platte and a seasoned Indian fighter, would push north with 1,300 men from Fort Fetterman, Wyoming, on May 29.

Terry's force, which marched out of Fort Lincoln with the regimental band playing "The Girl I Left Behind Me," consisted of about 1,000 men—3 infantry companies, 718 officers and men of the Seventh Cavalry Regiment, 35 Arikara scouts, a battery of Gatling guns, 150 supply wagons, and a beef herd.

On June 17 Crook suffered a serious setback in his march north. On Rosebud Creek his force fell under attack by Sioux and Cheyenne warriors led by Crazy Horse. The six-hour battle ended with the Indians leaving the field and Crook compelled to take his wounded and fall back to his base camp. There he determined not to proceed without support and took no part in the events that followed.

Meantime, Terry and Gibbon linked up on the banks of the Yellowstone River in southeastern Montana and on June 21, on the river steamer *Far West,* tied up on the Yellowstone at the mouth of Rosebud Creek, Terry gathered his officers to work out final details of the plan to find and, if necessary, fight the hostiles.

The general's orders to Custer were ambiguous. Scouts had found an Indian trail leading up Rosebud Creek and Custer was ordered to take the Seventh and follow the creek, then swing north along the Little Bighorn River. He was to cross into the Little Bighorn Valley while Terry and Gibbon took their more cumbersome forces west along the Yellowstone to the mouth of the Bighorn, thence up to the Little Bighorn. These maneuvers were to put the Indians in a vise.

Terry believed there were no more than 800 hostiles in the

area and that these would run rather than stand and fight. In fact, there were as many as 7,000 Indians, among them perhaps 2,000 fighting men, in the loose coalition of tribes on the lower reaches of the Little Bighorn. Their village, a half-mile wide and strung out along the west bank of the river a distance of four miles, contained a pony herd of from 25,000 to 30,000 animals, as many as 1,000 lodges, and formed the largest confederation of Indians ever known to have gathered in one place in North America. All seven tribes of the Teton Lakota were represented— Hunkpapa, Oglala, Minneconjou, Sans Arc, Brulé, Blackfeet, and Two Kettle. There were also 120 Northern Cheyenne lodges and a scattering of Yanktonnais and Santee Sioux and even a few Arapahos. Prominent among the chiefs and warriors were Sitting Bull, Gall, Rain-in-the-Face, and Crow King of the Hunkpapas, Red Horse of the Minneconjous, Crazy Horse and Low Dog of the Oglalas, Lame White Man and Two Moon of the Cheyennes.

Many of the Indians were armed with .44 caliber, sixteen-shot Henry and Winchester rifles. They had unlimited ammunition and they were not going to run.

On June 22 Custer led his troopers up Rosebud Creek, following the Indian trail. His force consisted of 31 officers and 566 men in 12 companies. Their average age was twenty-seven; a large percentage had at least a year's service on the Western frontier; thirty-two percent were of Irish extraction. Thirty-five Arikara—"Ree"—and Crow scouts, a number of civilian packers, and a train of mules carrying rations, forage, and 24,000 rounds of ammunition completed Custer's column. He had been offered, but refused, a Gatling gun battery, figuring the guns would slow his march over rough terrain.

The Seventh was armed with the .45-70 caliber Model 1873 Springfield single-shot trapdoor carbine. This weapon had a tendency to foul when hot and, even more deadly, had a defective shell ejector in which the heads of brass cartridge casings would break off, leaving the body of the casing stuck in the breech.

There was a "broken-shell extractor"—a three-piece rod that had to be screwed together—in a compartment in the the butt-stock, useful only in target practice but certainly not in the heat of battle. The side arm of issue was a Model 1872 Colt six-shot revolver. Each man carried fifty rifle cartridges (another fifty in his saddlebags) and twenty-four for the pistol.

Custer, dressed in a dark blue shirt, buckskin trousers, high boots, and a white, wide-brimmed hat, carried a brace of British-made Webley revolvers.

In his Seventh were his two brothers, Thomas W., captain of C Company, and Boston, a civilian forage master, and two other family members: brother-in-law James Calhoun, first lieutenant of L Company, and nephew Harry Armstrong "Autie" Reed, who had joined his uncle for a summer excursion to see an Indian fight.

The colonel's scouts included the Illinoisian Charles Alexander "Lonesome Charley" Reynolds, a veteran of the Black Hills Expedition; the half-breed Minton "Mitch" Bouyer, a protégé of mountain man Jim Bridger; the Crows White-Man-Runs-Him, Curly, Goes Ahead, and Hairy Moccasin, and the Arikaras Young Hawk and Strikes Two. Bloody Knife, son of a Hunkpapa Sioux father and Arikara mother, was Custer's particular favorite.

Besides Tom Custer and James Calhoun, among Custer's most important officers were Major Marcus A. Reno, Captains Thomas Weir, Myles Keogh, George Yates, and Frederick W. Benteen, and Custer's adjutant, Lieutenant William W. Cooke, a giant Canadian soldier of fortune.

Both Reno, described by Custer biographer Robert Utley as "a besotted, socially inept mediocrity," and Benteen, "a fearless combat commander and able but crotchety company commander," loathed Custer and made little secret of it.

On June 24, after a grueling march, Custer's scouts reported with growing alarm that the Indian trail up the Rosebud was growing larger and that the signs indicated a much larger force than had been anticipated. Custer brushed aside these concerns and continued to the summit of the divide separating the Rosebud and the "Greasy Grass"—the Sioux name for the Little Bighorn Valley.

On the morning of the twenty-fifth a huge pony herd came into view fifteen miles distant in the valley, and shortly thereafter, when scouts reported that several Indians had been found near the Seventh's bivouac, Custer believed he needed to march quickly to find and engage the enemy and not wait for Terry and Gibbon's arrival. His vague orders gave him the flexibility to make quick battle-born decisions.

Now, he divided his command for the first time. His most experienced officer, Captain Benteen, and three companies of 125 men were sent to the southwest with orders to block any Indians from escaping and to "pitch into" any found. With Benteen he sent the pack train, including the mules and reserve ammunition, with a company of men under Captain Thomas McDougall.

Major Reno and 140 men, and Custer with 225, marched west to the Little Bighorn to approach the enemy lodges.

At about 2:30 P.M. a cloud of dust was spotted rising up from the immense Indian village in the valley and Custer, apparently intending to attack the camp from two directions, sent Reno and his three companies to ford the river and strike the southern end of the village. "Move forward at as rapid a gait as you think prudent," he told Reno, "charge the village and you will be supported by the whole outfit."

Custer himself, with troops C, E, F, I, and L, turned northward to ford the river, attack the Indians three miles downstream, and cut off any retreat.

Reno's companies splashed across the Little Bighorn, the shallow stream no more than four feet deep and fifty to seventy-five feet wide, and rode down the valley toward the distant line of tipis. The Indians, at first surprised at the impending attack, rallied and poured out to meet the troopers who, now dismounted, had formed up in a skirmish line. The fight began at 3:30 P.M. and within ten minutes the Sioux and Cheyennes so outnumbered Reno's command he was forced to withdraw his men into a stand of timber beside the river. After forty-five minutes of fighting from this sparse cover, Reno withdrew farther, making a dash for the high bluffs on the east side of the river, the retreat disintegrating into a rout as the Indians pursued the panicky troopers, inflicting many casualties.

Bloody Knife, among the scouts accompanying Reno, was shot through the head as he stood with the major, his brains spattering Reno's face and coat and, some said, so unnerving Reno that the incident marked the end of his effective command of his detachment. (Soon Bloody Knife's head was paraded on a pole through the village. He was regarded as a traitor by Sitting Bull.)

Reno lost twenty-nine men killed and thirteen wounded in fleeing to the bluffs. After a brief continuation of the fight, the Sioux and Cheyennes abandoned the field and rode off to the north where the sound of gunfire signaled an engagement at the north end of the great village, a bit over four miles away.

Benteen, meantime, led his three companies to join the battered remnant of Reno's command, arriving there at about 4:20 P.M. The regimental pack train later joined and the combined force on the bluffs now numbered about 350 men. The troopers dug in and held off attacks until the late morning of the twenty-sixth when Terry and Gibbon approached from the north. Soon after, the Indians struck their lodges, set fire to the dry grass above the river, and withdrew to the south.

"Where is Custer?" the generals asked Reno. Neither he nor Benteen knew.

The question plagued everybody that afternoon of the twenty-sixth: Where was Custer?

After separating from Reno, Custer and the combined troops under Captains Keogh and Yates—about 225 men in five companies—rode north along the high ground above the Little Bighorn. The vastness of the enemy camp and the enormity of the enemy numbers were now evident to all and at about 3:20 P.M., Custer instructed his adjutant to send a message to Benteen to join him with the ammunition pack animals. The scrawled message—"Benteen—Come on. Big village. Be quick. Bring packs. P.S. Bring pack. W.W. Cooke"—was carried by a young Italian-born trumpeter, John Martin.

It was the last message from Custer's command and Martin became the last man to see Custer and his troopers alive.

The colonel now continued northward, leading his men across a deep coulee (dry ravine) to the final battlefield.

From this point on, all is speculation.

At about 4:00 P.M. Custer's remnant of the Seventh clashed with a huge force of Sioux and Cheyennes led by Sitting Bull's war chief, Gall. (Called Pizi by his Hunkpapa brethren, Gall was a menacing thirty-six-year-old with a huge body and a head like a nail keg. He had lost two wives and three children in the firing on the village by Reno's Ree scouts and later told a newspaper-man, "It made my heart bad. After that I killed all my enemies with the hatchet.") Badly outnumbered, the troopers at first held off the attackers with well-directed volley fire, then fell back to the north toward what was later named Greasy Grass Ridge and Custer Ridge. There the retreat was met by another large enemy force under the Oglala mystic Crazy Horse.

Now, along what later was called Battle Ridge, Custer's companies became separated and fought a number of individual actions until they were engulfed.

The final stand occurred on Custer Hill at the north end of the high ridge when about fifty troopers clotted around their commanding officer, shooting their horses to make a breastwork. Contrary to countless fictional treatments in novels and films, the Indians apparently did not overwhelm this last fragment of the five companies in a massive charge, nor did they encircle them and tighten the circle. A few men who broke and ran for the river were cut down in their tracks; Custer and the rest of his men died in a rain of arrows and bullets.

The battle lasted two hours, perhaps less (Benteen, after examining the battlefield, thought no more than ninety minutes) from the moment Reno was first engaged to the death of the last man in Custer's remnant. On Battle Ridge the wounded died hideously, skewered with lances, cut with knives, brained by war clubs, cleaved by axes. Some bodies were apparently used for target practice: one was found quilled with thirty arrows.

The dead, including the sole newspaper correspondent with Custer, Mark Kellogg of the Bismarck *Tribune* and New York *Herald,* were stripped naked and savagely mutilated, many by the Indian women and children who came to plunder the battlefield. Tom Custer's head was smashed flat to the ground and had to be identified by a tattoo on his arm. Some were beheaded; many had arms and genitals hacked off.

Custer himself died of gunshot wounds in his temple and chest but was otherwise unmarked. He was found naked except for his socks and left among the corpses of forty-one of his men and thirty-nine horses.

The sole survivor on the battleground was Myles Keogh's claybank gelding, Comanche, found wandering about with seven gunshot and arrow wounds. (The horse, carried on the *Far West* river steamer to Bismarck with the wounded, was never put to work again. He lived to age twenty-eight, the pet and pride of the regiment, and died in the winter of 1891–1892.)

Altogether, the Little Bighorn battle, Reno's casualties included, cost 263 killed and 60 wounded. Indian casualties were probably under 100 killed. Some estimates place the number as low as thirty.

At about 11:00 A.M. on the twenty-sixth, the Indians besieging Reno's and Benteen's combined force on the bluffs above the river began riding off, alerted to the approach of Terry's force and Gibbon's Montana column, setting the tinderlike prairie grass on fire as a smoke screen to cover their departure.

On the twenty-seventh, the surviving Seventh Cavalrymen set about the grim task of burying and marking the graves of Custer and his men and those of Reno's command. The naked and mutilated corpses, bristling with arrows, bloated and baked black in the searing summer sun, were placed in shallow, hastily dug graves. The experience was so unnerving that no man who participated in it ever forgot it. Captain Thomas B. Weir, one of Benteen's battalion commanders who had a bitter fight with Reno, trying to persuade his senior officer to move out to Custer's relief, was so seared by what he saw on Battle Ridge that he fell into alcoholism and died less than six months after the battle.

❦

In December, the month Thomas Weir died in New York City, the first book-length biography of Custer appeared: Frederick Whittaker's *Life of Custer*, a hagiography based mostly on newspaper sources.

Libbie Custer survived her husband by almost fifty-seven years. Widowed at age thirty-four, she wrote three lively and still-readable books—*Boots and Saddles* (1885), *Following the Guidon* (1890), and *Tenting on the Plains* (1893)—about her life with her saintly "Autie," and died on April 6, 1933, two days before her ninety-first birthday.

She is buried with her beloved husband at the West Point cemetery on the heights above the Hudson River.

❦

From about 3:20 on the afternoon of June 25, 1876, when Custer's adjutant, Lieutenant William Winer Cooke, a big Canadian with flowing Dundreary whiskers, sent a message to Benteen to "Come on. Big village. Be quick. Bring packs," the "Last Stand" is a massive mystery within which lie dozens of other mysteries. The main questions involve what went wrong and associated matters involving Custer's sole culpability or his ruination by his subordinate officers. Among the countless lesser mysteries are the questions: Who killed Custer? How many died? Were there survivors?

❦

In the 120 years since the battle the debate has continued unabated on the matter of who was to blame for the disaster.

Custer's critics insist he led his regiment into the lion's mouth because he was an ambitious, self-serving glory-hunter dooming himself and his men by his pathological hubris. He disobeyed orders, had no battle plan, did not know the lay of the land, was deaf to warnings of even trusted scouts on the magnitude of the Indian camp and the dangers of precipitating a fight a full day before the Terry-Gibbon force arrived in the valley, had no respect for the fighting ability of the Indians. And perhaps the most consistently cited flaw in his plan, assuming he had one, is the splitting up of his command into three battalions, none of them in supporting distance of one another, a fourth segment created by sending his pack train and reserve ammunition a fatal distance behind the main force then still fifteen or more miles from the enemy camp.

"Inasmuch as their [the enemy's] numbers and exact placement remained unknown to Custer," wrote the eminent military historian S.L.A. Marshall in 1972, "the problem required that he keep the regiment together and under tight control until he could measure the danger. Common sense and tactical logic demanded nothing else."

Frederick Van de Water, among the first and still the deadliest of the Custer critics, said in 1934:

Custer with less than six hundred men moves forward against an enemy which he himself believes outnumbers him almost three to one; which his scouts insist is far more numerous than that. Almost his first act violates a cardinal military principal. He divides his inferior force into four fractions. . . . With the remaining five troops, he rides away. Custer confides no complete plan of battle to his officers. He makes no arrangement for communication between the scattered subdivisions. When committed to conflict, he, the commander, has less than half his outnumbered force under his control and only a vague idea where the remaining seven troops are.

Then, Van de Water says in a memorable denouement in his book-length beholding of Custer as anti-hero: "Even in the battle rapture that filled him, the Glory-Hunter, when he first looked down upon that ominously still village, must have experienced the chill recognition of fortune's desertion. By then, he had doomed himself past all possible reprieve."

As to disobeying the orders of his superiors—a familiar tendency in Custer's history—there remains some question as to what those orders were and whether these orders, or the absence of them, sewed the seeds of the coming tragedy.

On June 21–22, when General Terry gathered his officers aboard the *Far West* at the mouth of the Rosebud, fatal assumptions formed part of the discussion: that the enemy probably numbered less than a thousand fighting men, and that when attacked, the warriors would scatter and flee into the mountains. Terry expressed the hope that the Indians would not be engaged before June 26, at which time Gibbon's infantrymen would arrive in the expected battle zone of the Little Bighorn Valley. Even more critically, Terry's written orders to Custer—and presumably his oral ones as well—carried a lethal imprecision. Terry expressed confidence in Custer's "zeal, energy, and ability" and said he could not provide overly defined orders that might "hamper your action when nearly in contact with the enemy." In general terms, Terry said Custer should conform to his commander's battle plan unless he determined "sufficient reason for departing from them." Writing in third person, the instructions—they were not "orders"—were framed in terms of what "He [Terry] thinks" and "The Department Commander desires" Custer should do.

Custer critics maintain that these instructions, intended to give an experienced, energetic, eager, and confident commanding officer the latitude needed to win a battle, were transformed by that officer, through his rashness, blind ambition, and military inaptitude, into a blueprint for losing it.

Apologists have speculated that Custer may have been mortally wounded early in the fight, his command devolving upon other senior officers, and that had he lived longer he might have found a way to inspire a day's survival until the Gibbon-Terry forces arrived on the scene.

And, the Custerphiles say, he was brought down ultimately through a combination of bad luck and the timidity, if not outright cowardice, of his senior subordinate officers—specifically Captain Frederick W. Benteen and Major Marcus A. Reno.

The Virginian Benteen, age forty-two and a white-haired, bug-eyed, boozy, crotchety but courageous "old hand" at the time of the Little Bighorn, was by all accounts the best soldier and most vociferous of Custer's antagonists. He was a capable officer who served notably in the Civil War in engagements west of the Mississippi and at the siege of Vicksburg, rising to a brevet rank of brigadier general of Missouri volunteers. In Custer's Seventh Cavalry Regiment he was a cool and effective fighter at the Battle of the Washita, in northwestern Oklahoma in November 1868, but during this engagement he developed an enmity toward Custer that festered for thirty years, continuing long after Custer's death.

In that campaign, against peaceable Cheyennes under their chief Black Kettle, Custer dispatched Major Joel H. Elliott, a zealous and popular officer, to lead a force of sixteen troopers to search out hostiles behind the main Cheyenne village on the Washita River. Elliott and his force were cut off from Custer's regiment, drawn into an ambush, and slain to a man by Cheyennes and Kiowas. Custer's search for Elliott and his party was widely considered to be at best cursory and he was censured by many for abandoning the young officer and his men before learning of their fate.

Elliott had served as a captain in Benteen's brigade in the Civil War and Benteen, who admitted later he disliked Custer the first time he met him, was furious over what he considered to be the colonel's lack of concern in finding the officer and his men before leaving the battleground. In a long and acidic letter written anonymously to the *Missouri Democrat,* Benteen, who freely admitted authorship of it, railed about Elliott's being left to his fate while his commander "occupies himself in taking an inventory of the captured property" and shooting captured Indian ponies— "Our chief exhibits his close marksmanship and terrifies the crowd of frightened, captured squaws and papooses by drop-

ping the struggling ponies in death near them." At the end of his
screed, Benteen wrote, "But surely a search will be made for our
missing comrades! No, they are forgotten. Over them, and the
poor ponies, the wolves will hold high carnival, and their howl-
ings will be their only requiem."

Custer originally threatened to thrash the "Participant in the
Capture of Black Kettle's Camp" who signed the damning letter,
but when Benteen acknowledged authorship, the colonel brushed
the matter aside.

In the Little Bighorn Valley, because he had been ordered by
Custer to take his troopers to explore a range of hills four of five
miles away and to "pitch into" any hostiles encountered, Benteen
was some distance from the Custer fight and rejoined Reno only
after that action had settled into a intermittent siege. Later he
would be accused of disobeying Custer's order to "come on . . .
be quick" and of consciously returning to the main command in
a laggardly fashion.

In his testimony at the Reno court of inquiry in 1879, Benteen
praised Reno's tactics of survival on the bluffs above the river but
had no kind words for Custer, characterizing the "last stand,"
after examining the battlefield, as "a rout, a panic, till the last
man was killed." He said, "In General Custer's mind there was
a belief that there were no Indians, nor any village," and that
Custer had sent him off to find some Indians and "pitch into"
them, orders he considered "rather senseless."

"The fact is," Benteen said as his last word on the subject,
"all the talk about Reno's being able to reinforce Custer is simply absurd. Custer himself was responsible for the Little Big Horn
action, and it is an injustice to attribute the blame to anyone
else."

The irascible captain went on to fight the Nez Perce in Montana and was promoted to major of the Ninth Cavalry in 1882.
His command of Fort Duchesne, in Utah, was marred by his
drunkenness and he was subsequently court-martialed for drunk-
on-duty offenses. He was found guilty and would have been dismissed from the army but for the intervention of President

Grover Cleveland. Instead, he received a suspension from duty for a year.

He retired in 1888 on a disability pension and died in 1898 in Atlanta.

Beginning with Frederick Whittaker's biography of Custer, published six months after the battle, a legion of Last Stand investigators have pointed a finger at Marcus Reno as a major culprit, accusing him of timidity—this was his first Indian battle—if not outright cowardice, characterizing him as a drunken, dithering, panicky officer incapable of making a decision. His orders were to "charge the village" and if he had done so, his critics say, the outcome of the battle would have changed. And why did he not come to Custer's relief after Benteen and his three companies had joined him on the bluffs upstream?

But, others insist, wasn't it Reno who had been promised support by Custer—"you will be supported by the whole outfit"? And should Reno have led his paltry 175 men into a certain Valley of Death after he discovered the overwhelming number of Indians in the vast village along the river? He held out as long as he could, the Ree scouts on his left under attack and the Sioux-Cheyenne force maneuvering toward his rear and firing down on him from the heights across the river. He gave the order to retreat to save his command, his defenders say, and lost twenty-nine men before reaching the bluffs, four miles from Custer's position.

"No object was defined for the Reno battalion," S.L.A. Marshall was to write on the matter, "no limit was fixed on the depth to which it might involve the regiment. Reno was simply to run after Indians. Here was military operation being conducted in the spirit of the paper chase or the huntsman bawling, 'Tally Ho! There goes the fox!' "

As to the combined Reno-Benteen force coming to Custer's relief, Marshall says, "It is a thought for simpletons. Any observer of the impact of combat stress on men's powers must hoot at the idea. . . . Reno was incapable of doing other than he did, and so were his people."

There is, moreover, some question as to whether or not Reno knew the magnitude of the attack on Custer's remnant. Reno's force, "a fair slice already *hors de combat* from death, wounds, malingering, and stark fear," as Marshall puts it, was four miles upstream, under a withering fire, the pack train still several miles to the rear. After Benteen and the pack animals arrived, Reno did advance a mile or so to a point where he could overlook Battle Ridge. But by then most of the shooting had ceased and while he saw Indians milling around, Custer and his men were not in sight and Reno thought they had retreated to join Terry's and Gibbon's advancing forces.

The defense on the bluffs occupied Reno and Benteen all day on June 25–26, a heroic stand against overwhelming odds.

Because of continuing criticism of his role in the battle, Reno requested an official army court of inquiry be convened and in Chicago, in January 1879, the court found nothing improper in Reno's behavior at the Little Bighorn and he was exonerated of any misconduct. Captain Benteen was among those who testified in Reno's behalf.

After the inquiry, a petition, signed by 235 members of the Seventh Cavalry, was sent to General Sherman in Washington asking that Reno be promoted to lieutenant colonel and Benteen to major for their "skillful conduct" in the battle.

Reno's subsequent career, tainted by accusations of drunkenness, "improper advances" toward the wife of a fellow officer, striking a fellow officer, and other charges, reached its nadir in 1880 when he was charged as a Peeping Tom, for striking a junior officer, and being drunk on duty at Fort Meade, Dakota Territory. He was dismissed from the army in April that year for "conduct unbecoming an officer and gentleman" and behavior "prejudicial to good order and military discipline."

He died nine years later of cancer, age fifty-five, in a Washington hospital and was buried in an unmarked grave near the capital.

In 1967, after a relative asked the army to reexamine the charges against him, the U.S. Army Board for Correction of Military Records cleared Major Marcus Albert Reno of Carrollton, Illinois, West Point '57, brevet Brigadier General of Volunteers, Army of the Potomac, second-in-command of the Seventh U.S. Cavalry Regiment at the Battle of the Little Bighorn, of all charges. His remains were disinterred and buried with full military honors in the cemetery at the Little Bighorn Battlefield National Monument.

Still, the debate over Reno's conduct continues. A modern student of the battle, Robert Nightengale, in his book *Little Big Horn,* posits a theory that Custer actually crossed the river and penetrated and attacked the Indian village in a flanking maneuver to drive the enemy toward the oncoming column of General Terry. But, the author says, Custer was overwhelmed when Reno abandoned his part of the attack to the south, causing the remnant of the Seventh to retreat to what became Battle Ridge and Custer Hill and the annihilation of its commander and his five companies of men.

Nightengale contends that Reno and Benteen were chief players in a cover-up to place the blame for the battle on Custer.

The first man to see the the Custer battlefield was Lieutenant James H. Bradley of the Seventh Infantry, chief of scouts for Colonel John Gibbon's Montana column out of Fort Ellis. Early on the morning of June 27, two days after the battle, Bradley and his Crow scouts reached the east bank of the Little Bighorn and saw something, dottings of white against the brown backdrop, on a high knoll in the distance. He rode up and found a field littered with ghastly white corpses, all stripped, most mutilated, lying in piles of two or three, and everywhere dead horses bearing the brand "7USC." Bradley's first hasty count was 197 bodies; he subsequently said 206 were hastily buried on the field. (Benteen, who rode up with the Terry and Gibbon force soon after, counted 203; Terry 204; Lieutenant Edward S. Godfrey, one of Benteen's officers, counted 212. The best modern authority on the battle, Robert S. Utley, gives an estimate ranging from 210 to 225.)

Lieutenant Bradley (who was killed the next year in fighting the Nez Perce in Montana), in a report published in the Helena *Herald* on July 25, spared the families of the dead the horrors he saw. He reported seeing little mutilation beyond scalping and said Reno's dead suffered more postmortem atrocities since these fell closer to the village and were subject to the fiendishness of the Indian women and children. There was truth in that. Among the dead in the Reno battle was the civilian interpreter Isaiah Dorman, called "Teat" by the Sioux, a black man who was married to a Hunkpapa woman. After the Reno fight and the departure of Gall's warriors, Dorman lay badly wounded when Sitting Bull rode up. "Don't kill that man," the great medicine man said to those gathered around. "He is a friend of mine." But Dorman was killed, nonetheless. It is said that he was shot by a Hunkpapa woman and if so, the atrocities that followed were perhaps performed on a dead man. In any event, his body, bristling with arrows, was found nailed to the ground with an iron picket pin through his testicles. He had been slashed with knives and his penis had been cut off and stuffed in his mouth.

Bradley's report on Custer was a bit closer to the truth when he said, "Probably never did a hero who had fallen upon the field of battle appear so much to have died a natural death." He said the colonel had the appearance of falling asleep, his "features wholly without the ghastliness of any impress of fear, horror or despair."

Lieutenant Godfrey of K Company, who also viewed Custer's corpse on the twenty-seventh, later wrote, "He laid on his back, his upper arms on the ground, the hands folded or so placed as to cross the body above the stomach; his position was natural and one that we had seen hundreds of times while he was taking cat naps during halts on the march. One hit was in the front of the left temple, and one in the left breast at or near the heart."

There were, however, other wounds. His left thigh had been cut to the bone and he was probably missing a joint of a finger.

Also, a fact Godfrey later told a friend and that was not revealed until after Libbie Custer's death, an arrow had been shoved into Custer's penis.

In 1927 a Southern Cheyenne woman, Kate Bighead, told her story of observing the battle from a distance. Among her revelations she claimed to have seen several of the soldiers on Battle Ridge kill themselves with their revolvers, some shooting their comrades and then themselves. But her most startling statement had to do with what she learned from two other Cheyenne women. These women, who said they recognized Custer after being taken prisoner after the Washita battle in 1867, told Kate Bighead that they came upon Custer's body on the battlefield and prevented some warriors from mutilating the corpse by saying he was a "relative." The women, Bighead reported, then proceeded to cut off a joint of Custer's finger and to insert an awl in each of his ears and into his brain "to improve his hearing." The reason for this latter act, Bighead said, was that Custer "had not heard what our chiefs in the South said when he smoked the pipe with them. They told him that if ever afterward he should break that peace promise and should fight the Cheyennes the Everywhere Spirit surely would cause him to be killed."

While the public seemed satisfied that the five companies of the Seventh, and others in Reno's command—by and large faceless and nameless soldiers to the newspaper reader—had been killed by a "horde of Sioux and Cheyenne savages," there was a great public craving to know more about the fate of the one celebrity in the fight.

Who killed Custer?

Six months after the Little Bighorn, the hack writer Frederick Whittaker cobbled together a massive, worshipful book, *The Complete Life of Gen. George A. Custer,* and in it launched a campaign against Marcus Reno as the chief miscreant in the Custer disaster, and even more important to those sharing the author's view ("as a soldier there is no spot on his armor") of Custer as demigod, Whittaker named Custer's killer.

This was the Hunkpapa warrior Rain-in-the-Face, and Whittaker was not the first to select him as Custer's killer or to recall the reason for Rain's savage "revenge."

In the summer of 1873, Rain-in-the-Face (whose name derived from an incident when, as a youth, he took part in a fight against the Gros Ventres and emerged with his face streaked with blood and war paint) was accused of killing a civilian veterinarian attached to the Seventh Cavalry and a post sutler, in the Yellowstone River country. Captain Tom Custer and Lieutenant George Yates of the Seventh (both subsequently killed at the Little Bighorn) were sent to the Standing Rock Agency, on the Grand River south of Bismarck, Dakota Territory, to arrest Rain and bring him to Fort Abraham Lincoln. After being interrogated by Custer, Rain escaped but was later rearrested, arraigned in federal court on the murder charges, and released after the case against him was dismissed.

Whittaker and numerous other writers insisted that Rain-in-the-Face held a grudge against Custer, killed "Long Hair" in the Little Bighorn battle, and cut out his heart.

In 1880 Henry Wadsworth Longfellow got into the act with publication of his poem "The Revenge of Rain-in-the-Face," with such lines as:

> *"Revenge!" cried Rain-in-the-Face.*
> *"Revenge upon all the race*
> *Of the white chief with yellow hair!"*
> *And the mountains dark and high*
> *From their crags echoed the cry*
> *Of his anger and despair.*

In 1894, in an interview with newspapermen, Rain said it was Tom Custer's heart he had cut out. "I leaped from my pony," he said, "and cut out his heart and bit a piece of it and spit it in his face."

But, in September, 1905, a few days before his death at Standing Rock, Rain-in-the-Face told Dr. Charles A. Eastman, a full-blooded Oglala physician, that he had done none of the deeds attributed to him (and presumably none he had himself created). "Many lies have been told about me," he said.

In the 1930s Walter S. Campbell, who was best known by his pen name "Stanley Vestal," was preparing a biography of Sitting Bull. In the course of his research Vestal interviewed a Sitting Bull nephew named White Bull and became convinced, in recounting the warrior's story of his participation in the Little Bighorn battle, that he was Custer's slayer. In the fighting, White Bull said he engaged in hand-to-hand combat with "a tall, well-built soldier" and struck the man in the face with his quirt. The soldier grabbed White Bull by his hair and tried to bite the Indian's nose off. White Bull yelled for help and two warriors, Bear Lice and Crow Boy, came to aid him, raining blows on the soldier. White Bull said he pistol-whipped the white man and took his side arm and cartridge belt.

After the battle ended, White Bull said that he and Bad Soup, a warrior who had been at Fort Lincoln and knew Long Hair on sight, found Custer dead, lying on his back, and did not scalp him "for his hair was cut short."

White Bull died in 1947 and Vestal, in a new edition of his *Sitting Bull* biography, expanded on the Oglala's story, saying that White Bull had counted six coup during the Little Bighorn fight, had killed two soldiers in hand-to-hand combat, captured two guns and twelve horses, and suffered a wound in the fight.

"There are those who believe that White Bull is the man who shot General Custer," Vestal wrote. "Certainly he was among those Indians who fired into the group around Custer, and when asked to point out the place where he saw the body of the General lying, he indicated the exact spot where the body of General Custer was found by his comrades after the battle."

But, as subsequent research into Vestal's papers showed, White Bull never claimed to have actually killed Custer, only to have grappled with him, and the theory seems to have been that of the writer alone. Campbell/Vestal, a Kansan raised near a Cheyenne reservation who became a Rhodes Scholar at Oxford and a professor at the University of Oklahoma, was a romantic and a man of literature first, an historian a distant second.

In fact, there were others who claimed to have killed Custer. The Minneconjou Red Horse said a Santee warrior, name unknown, did it; a Hunkpapa named Flat Hip was credited by some. Brave Bear, a Cheyenne considered by many of his Indian contemporaries to have been the bravest warrior in the Reno fight, was another candidate. He had fought Custer at the Washita in '69 and against white soldiers in the Red River War in the Texas Panhandle in 1874. After leaving the Reno engagement to join the action downstream, Brave Bear killed a soldier riding a sorrel horse who might have been Custer. Whether it was or not, he was selected by the Southern Cheyennes as the Warrior Who Killed Long Hair.

In truth, few of the Indians knew they were fighting Custer. Low Dog, an Oglala war leader who took part in both the Reno and Custer battles, later said, "We did not know till the fighting was over that he was the white chief."

Not only has Custer's slayer never been identified, so too is there a question as to who is buried next to Libbie in the Custer tomb at West Point.

The original burials were crude in the extreme. On June 27, 1876, the day Colonel John Gibbon's Montana column relieved the Reno-Benteen companies, Lieutenant James H. Bradley of the Seventh Infantry and his Crow scouts, first to see the carnage of the battlefield, were soon joined by Benteen and other officers and troopers to identify the slain and see to their temporary burial.

But the burial detail lacked the picks and spades necessary to dig proper graves deep into the hard, dry Montana hillside and as a result the bodies, black and bloating in the sun, were hastily covered with dirt and brush. The makeshift graves became feasting places for wolves and other predators.

In May 1877, the War Department authorized recovering the remains of the officers slain in the battle and delegated Captain Michael V. Sheridan (General Philip Sheridan's brother) to take charge of the operation. Sheridan traveled from Chicago to Bismarck that summer, and embarked on the steamer *John Fletcher* to a cantonment on the Tongue River where he was joined by a company of men and two officers from the Seventh Cavalry. Pine coffins were knocked together and a party of teamsters with four ox wagons proceeded overland, followed by Sheridan's troopers, all arriving at the Little Bighorn on July 2, a year and a week after the battle.

The Custer battlefield, carpeted with dust and scrub in 1876, now lay covered by deep grass, the spot where Custer had been originally found now strewn with ivory-colored horse bones. A Sioux warrior named Pretty Shield said the heights above the Little Bighorn held the stink of the dead all that summer of 1876, but now the odor of corruption had been displaced by the scent of wildflowers.

Beginning at the Reno battlefield, a skirmish line of fifty men slowly marked graves with willow sticks, later cutting cedar headboards and stakes to mark the graves. On Battle Ridge and Custer Hill, as in the Reno field four miles distant, the bones were scattered, gnawed clean by predators, and bleached white in the sun. Sets of bones, many mixed from several bodies, were reinterred in trenches under three feet of earth and marked with stakes or a cairn of rocks topped by a horse skull.

Bones supposed to be those of Custer were placed in a pine box and, with coffins containing the remains of ten other officers, conveyed by ox team to the mouth of the Little Bighorn and loaded on the *Fletcher* for a journey that would end in Fort Leavenworth. The remains of Autie Reed and Boston Custer were exhumed that summer by Reed's father and reburied in Monroe, Michigan. W. W. Cooke's bones were shipped for reburial in Hamilton, Ontario; the family of Lieutenant John Crittenden asked that he remain buried in the battlefield. Three other officers who fell in the battle were never found—or at least never identified.

In 1991 speculation arose again on the Custer remains when Clyde Snow, a forensic scientist who had examined newly found bones during an anthropological dig on the battlefield in 1985, said he doubted the bones in Custer's grave in West Point were actually Custer's. Snow said Libbie Custer (buried alongside her husband in 1933) may be lying next to a rubble of unidentifiable remains.

Chances are that at least some of the bones are Custer's. When his remains were uncovered in 1877 a lock of hair was cut from his skull and sent to his wife. Libbie positively identified it as her husband's.

彩

The matter of survivors of the "Last Stand"—apart from Captain Keogh's horse "Comanche"—cropped up regularly for seventy years after the fighting above the Little Bighorn ended.

One of the more detailed survivor stories was told by the battle historian Dr. Charles Kuhlman and involved a private named Frank Finkel, who enlisted in 1874 as Frank Hall, of Company C, Seventh Cavalry, the company commanded by Captain Tom Custer. At the height of the battle on a ridge south of where Custer was engaged, a bullet struck the stock of Finkel's Springfield and a splinter of wood gashed his forehead, splashing blood in his eyes. Then, he said, a bullet grazed his horse's flank and it bolted through the line of advancing Sioux with Finkel flattened against its neck. On a wild ride, Finkel said he was struck twice by bullets, in the side and foot, but made it through the melee of fighting to safety. He halted and used his saddle blanket to stanch the blood seeping from his wounds, then began a search for water for himself and his horse. He found a settler on a remote ranch, he said, who helped him and he subsequently made his way to Fort Benton (some 300 miles to the northwest). There, Finkel said, he told his story of escaping the Custer battle to a post officer who refused to believe him, telling the private he would need at least two corroborating witnesses. Finkel, in effect, said to hell with it, rode out, and headed west where, during the next fifty-four years he became a respected citizen of Dayton, Washington, married, and raised a family.

In 1930, while playing horseshoes with friends, Finkel told his story to those outside his family for the first time.

Dr. Kuhlman went over the Finkel account and found it held

up, writing years later, "The Finkel story does not contain any of the earmarks of a fraud. There is nothing in it that cannot be either verified or explained in a plausible manner."

Perhaps so, but the Finkel-as-survivor story gained few adherents and soon died away.

Custer authority Lawrence Frost at one time counted 200 "sole survivors" of Custer's five companies and speculated that the number would eventually be larger than the actual participants in the fight.

The real last survivor of the fight on the Greasy Grass was Private Charles Windolph of H Company in Reno's detachment, who was awarded the Medal of Honor for his repeated forays under heavy fire to bring water to the wounded on the bluffs.

Windolph died in Lead, South Dakota, on March 11, 1950, at the age of ninety-nine. With him died the last human link to the Little Bighorn battle.

What remains is the debate on what happened there, questions that are unanswerable and therefore eternal.

THE BURIED TREASURE

II

A Waltz in the Superstitions

The Lost Dutchman Mine

No book of Western American mysteries can avoid a lost mine or buried treasure story and the Lost Dutchman, which is both, has everything: a pillar of gold in the midst of an island of volcanic rock; a setting as primeval and forbidding as any spot on the continent; a chance encounter, a map, a cave, burros burdened with rich ore; Apaches, Zunis, mountain gods, superstitions—even an earthquake.

What you do is drive south from Phoenix on I-17 to the Tempe junction of I-10, then east on Route 360 through Mesa to Apache Junction. Just to the north lay the Superstition Mountains, in which lay many mysteries including the one about the old Dutchman and his gold.

Stand anywhere in the United States and look in any direction: there is buried treasure out there.

Look north. Oak Island, off the coast of Nova Scotia, has a "money pit" where for 200 years people have been digging for something—a treasure variously reported as Inca gold from Peru, Captain Kidd's pirate booty, and, after a strange fragment of old paper was brought up from the excavation, holograph copies of Shakespeare's plays.

Look south. Somewhere between the Yucatán jungles and a *kiva* (an underground chamber for religious and ceremonial purposes) in a Pueblo Indian village in New Mexico is said to be buried a literal king's ransom. This treasure is believed to be an incalculable mass of gold, precious stones, and priceless artifacts from Tenochtitlán, removed from the old Mexican capital on order of Montezuma II just as the Spaniard Hernan Cortés and his army of conquistadores were approaching the city in 1520.

Look east. Off Cape Hatteras, North Carolina, the steamship *Merida*, chartered by the soon-to-be-deposed Mexican dictator Porfirio Díaz, was rammed and cut in two on May 11, 1911, by the American steamer *Admiral Farragut*. All crew and passengers on the *Merida* were saved, but the vessel sank to the bottom of the Atlantic with the fortune Díaz hoped to take with him into exile, at least $6 million in gold, silver, and jewels, the treasure of the House of Hapsburg's puppet Emperor Maximilian of Mexico.

Look west—look *especially* west. Here there are legendary treasures at every point of the compass, so many it is difficult to select among them. To name just two: on Victorio Peak, in the San Andres Mountains north of Las Cruces, New Mexico, there are said to be gold bars, an astronomical fortune in Spanish bullion, hidden in a cave; another, reportedly buried by Jesse James and his gang, is supposed to be located in the Wichita Mountains of southern Oklahoma—raw gold ambushed from a twenty-mule pack train near El Paso, Texas, in 1876.

And then there are the lost *mines,* most intriguing (and, some experts say, more likely real) of all the hidden riches of the West.

In the Guadalupe Mountains of West Texas, for example, awaiting the lucky prospector, rock hound, or hiker, is Ben Sublett's lost gold mine; in the *malpais* (badlands) south of Grants, New Mexico, is the Lost Adams Diggings—a cache of pure gold nuggets the size of hen's eggs; elsewhere in the West there are lost mines with such fetching names as "Two Suns East," "Lost Nugget," "Tayopa," "Six-Shooter," "Glory Hole," and "The Peg-Leg."

But none of these have lit the fires of the actual or armchair treasure-dreamer's imagination so brightly, or produced a more amazing, complex, and frustrating legendry, as has the Lost Dutchman Mine of Arizona.

A good part of the enchantment the Dutchman poses has to do with where (approximately, of course) it is located.

It would be difficult to find a more stunningly primitive place for a treasure trove than the Superstition Mountains, that grandly ugly jumble of jagged lava peaks that rise starkly 6,000 feet from the floor of the desert thirty-five miles east of Phoenix. Everything about the 240 square miles of that ancient, thrusted-up volcanic detritus of the Superstitions is human-forbidding. The gray igneous rock of the sharp cliffs and treacherous canyons of these mountains seem to proclaim that there is nothing here for mortal man or woman and precious little for any other kind of life.

Most of what does manage to live there either bites, claws, snags, stings, poisons, gores, or at least annoys the human visitor. Finding home among the pitiless rocks, in temperatures rising to 120 degrees in the summer and falling to bone-piercing cold at night, are diamondback rattlesnakes, lizards, bobcats, mountain lions, kangaroo rats, javelinas (tusked wild pigs), coyotes, foxes, hawks, turkey buzzards, Gila monsters, centipedes, tarantulas, scorpions, fire ants, and wasps. Among the few non-sinister creatures are jackrabbits and mule deer, prey for the others, and, winging in and out, cactus wrens, flickers, woodpeckers, doves, and quails. The plant life that is permitted a bare root-hold on the rocks and in the arroyos of the Superstitions also tears and argues with the unwary human: thorny chaparral, cat-claw (called the "wait-a-minute"—graze against this shrub and you find out why the name is appropriate), locoweed, creosote bush, burrobush, manzanita, scrub oak, and—in special abundance and variety—cactus: great saguaros, some of them twenty feet high, their pleated hides dimpled with pockmarks from woodpeckers and other birds on their ceaseless bug hunts; hedgehog and pincushion cactus, ocotillo (fittingly called "the devil's coachwhip" for its barbed branches), yucca with its bayonetlike leaves, the nopal or prickly pear, the barrel cactus (so often in desert history a source of life-sustaining water for the unprepared journeyer), and, among the most insidious of all desert plants, the cholla, a dense mass of tentaclelike branches on which are thousands of fish-hooked spines that can pierce a leather boot.

From before recorded history, the Superstitions were in the homelands, the territory between the Gila River on the south and the Salt on the north, of the Pima Indians and later of the Maricopa tribe that had emigrated from the east. Beginning in the 1400s, Apaches of the Tonto and San Carlos bands arrived and soon dominated the region, swooping out of the mountain crags to attack the normally peaceful Pimas and Maricopas plus Mexican wayfarers and, after the early 1800s, white travelers making their way across the Arizona desert.

(The Superstitions probably got their name as a result of a misunderstanding. The friendly Pimas tried to warn white sojourners to stay clear of the mountains to avoid the Apaches who infested them; the whites interpreted the admonition as meaning the mountains were taboo, the home of various of the Pima's heathen gods.)

California historian Hubert Howe Bancroft, in his 1889 history, *Arizona and New Mexico,* told of a huge land grant given in 1748 by King Fernando VI of Spain to Don Miguel Peralta of Cordova. This tract included much of the southern portion of today's New Mexico and Arizona, the latter including the Superstition Mountains. The Peralta clan, from its estates in Chihuahua, grew prosperous in its cattle raising and mining enterprises and around 1800 the family is said to have explored northward into the Peralta Land Grant, finding placer (surface gravel) gold in streambeds of tributaries of certain rivers far to the north, in present-day Arizona—including, presumably, the Gila and Salt rivers.

More significantly (but unfortunately more fabulously since the historical record dips to near zero at this point) the Peraltas are said to have found a large lode of gold-bearing quartz in the area known today as Weaver's Needle in the Superstition Mountains.

The Peralta family may have established as many as eighteen mines in and in the vicinity of the Superstitions, bringing out pack trains of gold and silver-bearing ore under constant threat by marauding Apaches. This enterprise, lasting nearly a half century, was doomed to end in 1848, about the same time the goldfields around Sutter's Mill in northern California were drawing argonauts from all over the nation. For the Peraltas, 1848 marked the end of the war between the United States and Mexico and the stipulations of the Treaty of Guadalupe Hidalgo. This paper ceded part of Arizona and New Mexico to the U.S., the ceded lands including much of the Peralta Grant.

Now, according to the meager evidence, the Peraltas hastened to make a final foray for ore in their lost lands, especially those in and around the Superstitions. In the late 1840s an expedition of 400 Peralta men was mounted, together with a pack train of mules carrying arms, explosives, equipment, and ore bags. This miniature army of miners and Apache fighters spent months in the mountains extracting and loading up the rich ore, hiding what couldn't be carried, and sealing up mine entrances and caches. Then, with its mule convoy laden with gold-bearing rocks, the expedition departed south for Mexico.

Not long out of the mountains, so the story goes, Peralta's expedition was attacked by Apaches and massacred almost to a man. Since the Indians cared nothing for the rocks the Mexicans were transporting, the cargos were scattered as the pack animals were slaughtered by the Apaches for food.

As the presumptive historical origin of the legendary gold of the Superstitions, the Peralta story has lost some credibility in modern times. Bancroft's account of the Peralta Land Grant seems to have been based, at least in part, on spurious documents, for example. But the Peralta name occurs over and over again in southwestern U.S. history (Pedro de Peralta was the founder, in 1610, of Santa Fe, New Mexico), and the name crops up again in connection with the man who inspired the name "Lost Dutchman."

Everything about him, like everything about the Peraltas and the mine in the Superstition Mountains they are said to have discovered, is opaqued by conflicting evidence or no evidence at all. It seems certain he was not Dutch but a Prussian (in the patois of Western mining camps, *deutsch* translated to "Dutch") and that his name was Jacob Waltz (or perhaps Walsz, Walzer, or von Walzer). He may have studied mining engineering at Heidelberg University, he may have come to the United States in 1848 as one of the immigrant miners attracted by the Sutter's Mill gold strike in California, and he may have served briefly with the Confederates in the Civil War. He appears to have become a U.S. citizen in 1861 and appears to have settled in Prescott, Arizona Territory, in about 1863. There he and Jacob Weiser, a German-born carpenter who came to the Territory about the same time as Waltz, are said to have prospected in the mountains of the northern part of the Territory.

Enters now a Peralta.

In 1870, the legend goes, Waltz saved the life of one Miguel Peralta II in a cantina brawl in the northern Mexican town of Arizpe, Sonora. As a reward for this courageous act, Waltz received from Peralta a map of a gold mine, discovered by his grandfather, the original Miguel Peralta, in 1847. The map gave the location of the mine in former Peralta Land Grant territory in the Supersitition Mountains of Arizona. Waltz and his partner

Jacob Weiser were told by Peralta that his grandfather, Miguel I, and his father, Enrico, were killed by Apaches in 1848 together with a great number of other miners and workmen. Miguel II's brother, Ramón Peralta, discovered the site of the massacre several years later and made a map of it and of the mine from which the ore, scattered with the bodies of the dead and the bones of the pack mules, had been taken. This, apparently, was the map he gave to Waltz in gratitude.

(It does seem unnaturally coincidental that the Peralta map was of a mine so close to Waltz's stamping grounds of Prescott. And, it is at least an amazing example of propinquity that Waltz happened to be in Arizpe, Sonora, at the precisely correct moment in time and history to save the life of a man who had a map of a mine so close to Waltz's stamping grounds of Prescott. And, at first glance, it seems absurd to think Miguel Peralta would give away anything so potentially rich as a gold mine as a reward to the man who came to his aid in a saloon fight. On the other hand, Peralta may have believed the map worthless and in any event he appears to have made a sort of partnership with Waltz and Weiser to share in the proceeds if the Americans actually found the mine.)

Chances are the two Jacobs were familiar with the area depicted on the map and may have panned the streams off the Gila and Salt rivers, but had not wasted time prospecting the Superstitions. (If Waltz was a trained mining engineer or even an experienced prospector, he knew that igneous rock—lava rock—is normally devoid of metal-bearing ore.) But the two men hurried back to Arizona and, we are told, not only found the Peralta mine in the Superstitions but brought out $60,000 in gold ore to an assayer in Tucson, giving half the sum to their benefactor, Miguel Peralta.

Upon returning to the site, Waltz later claimed, he and Weiser found two Mexican men mucking ore from their mine and killed them on the spot. Later (we do not know how much later, not even the year; dates are always vague or nonexistent in the Dutchman story), Waltz went off to a Gila River town to buy supplies, returned, and found Weiser dead, slain by Apaches. He buried his partner near where he fell, then covered the mine entrance and, perhaps fearful of working the mine alone and not trustful enough to take on another partner, abandoned the Superstitions.

He said he lived with the Pimas for a time and in 1875 bought land in Phoenix and settled there, living with a mulatto woman named Julia Thomas, a divorcée who owned an ice cream parlor in the town. Periodically, he said, he returned to the mountains, taking circuitous routes and covering his trail, returning to Phoenix, living a high life and buying supplies with the profits from the ore he removed.

The record seems to show a different story: Waltz appears to have been perpetually broke, forever looking for a grubstake, living the dreamer-prospector's shabby, down-and-out life. There are only fugitive references to him in Arizona's territorial newspapers in the 1870–1890 period. For example, in a June 1884, story in the Phoenix-based *Arizona Gazette,* there is a story of the murder of a man named Pedro Ortega by one Selso Grajalva "at the house of Jacob Waltz." Ortega, the story says, was killed with Waltz's shotgun and that Waltz was questioned but cleared of any complicity in the murder.

Toward the end of his life, Waltz (who died in Phoenix on October 25, 1891, one of the few nailed-down dates in his story) told a purposefully confusing number of stories about the mine. He confided mostly to his mistress, Julia Thomas, who apparently took care of the ill and impoverished prospector in his final years. But even she does not seem to have spared his colored, clouded, and contradictory tales.

He told of killing up to eight men who had followed him into the mountains at various times, told of caching gold ore in secret locations, told varying accounts of the murder of his partner (always stoutly denying doing the killing himself), told of squandering dust and nuggets in drunken sprees in nearby towns where he bragged about his bonanza.

And he told miscellaneous stories about the location of his gold, among them his description of the mine as a chimney formation of rose quartz in a cone-shaped pit in a ravine located in the vicinity of an old stone house in a north-south canyon of the Superstitions. The mouth of the mine, he said, faced west where the setting sun shone on it.

Virtually nothing of what Waltz said, or is alleged to have said, can be documented. One thing is certain: he did no favors in describing the whereabouts of the mine. There are numerous north-south canyons in the Superstitions, many ravines, several stone structures, an estimated 125 miles of trails. Waltz's mine was a needle in a mountain haystack in savagely rugged country.

To make matters worse, an earthquake that struck the area in May 1887, may have collapsed and erased any mine entrance or cave where Waltz hid his ore.

(Actually, it has never been clear if the "treasure" in the Superstitions is gold or silver, or both; or if it is a mine or a cache of high-grade ore in a cave. Nor did Waltz ever explain if he found the pack train of ore supposed to have been scattered by the Apaches who attacked the Peralta expedition in 1848.)

And not least among the confusing legends of the treasure is a story that predates Jacob Waltz.

This tale involves a very real frontier character, Dr. Abraham Thorne, a New Yorker born in 1826 who graduated from a medical school in Philadelphia and became an army surgeon. Thorne arrived in New Mexico shortly after the outbreak of the Civil War, settling at Lemitar, a farming community north of Socorro. In the mid-1860s he was stationed at Fort McDowell, a new military post located above the junction of the Salt and Verde rivers. The fort was built in a strategic spot for the army's campaigns against plundering Apache bands who periodically poured out of the mountains to raid among communities in the area, then fled into their sanctuaries in the Salt River canyon and the Sierra Ancha, Mazatzal, and Superstition Mountains.

As a contract surgeon, Thorne treated and befriended captive Apaches, curing some, it is said, of a mysterious eye disease. As a reward for his work among them, some Apaches took Thorne, blindfolded, into the Superstitions, and led him to a great cache of gold at a spot he estimated to be in a canyon about five miles from Weaver's Needle. It is not clear if Thorne brought any of the gold ore back to Fort McDowell, but he is believed to have returned to the mountains at some later time and failed to find the cache.

Thorne practiced medicine at Lemitar and Belen, New Mexico, to the end of his life, regularly returning to the mountains with others who heard and had faith in his story.

He died in 1895 without ever locating the hidden ore.

But it was Jacob Waltz who gave the lost mine its name and its perpetual legendry.

Even before he died, rumors of the "Dutchman's" mine had drawn searchers to the mountains, Julia Thomas among them, and the number increased dramatically after his death. In the century that has passed, the number who have tried to find it—from expensively mounted expeditions to lone prospectors with a day's grub and water on their back—is beyond calculating.

In the 1920s a Lost Dutchman Mining Corporation was set up in a storefront office in Phoenix, the proprietors claiming to have found Waltz's mine, vaguely identifying it as an immense gold ledge near Weaver's Needle in the Superstitions. Many bought stock and ventured out to the mountains to check on their investment. There they quickly discovered they had been bilked, that the Lost Dutchman Corporation was a sophisticated version of the gold-brick scam and that the corporate con men had skipped town with the proceeds from the phony stock.

In 1949 a Los Angeles man named Henry H. Bruderlin was reported in the *Denver Post* to have found the Dutchman using an old map and that he had filed mining claims. Bruderlin, the newspaper story said, had found seven abandoned and caved-in mine shafts in the Superstitions. The shafts turned out to be the worthless leftovers of a modern, failed Mexican mining operation.

In the 1960s an Oklahoma man and his partners said they found the Lost Dutchman on Bluff Spring Mountain in the Superstitions and in the 1970s a Florida treasure hunter and his syndicate claimed to have found it. Neither operation found anything of value.

In 1964 one of the most ludicrous "searches" for the Lost Dutchman was mounted by detective novelist and Perry Mason creator Erle Stanley Gardner. Using four-wheel-drive vehicles and helicopters, the Gardner expedition, which included secretaries to take down the author's dictation, spent a few days in the Superstitions making desultory aerial surveys, then left. Gardner included the venture of hunting but not finding the Dutchman in his book *Hunting Lost Mines by Helicopter.*

Since 1940, most of the Superstition Mountains have been part of the Tonto National Forest and designated a National Wilderness Area. In 1990 the Superstition Mountains Historical Society opened a museum in the newly designated Lost Dutchman State Park.

Now, the treasure-minded visitor can find the answer to questions about the mine and its legends, hike trails that might have been trod by Pimas, Maricopas, and Apaches, by the hooves of pack mules and burros and the boots of the Peraltas or even of Jacob Waltz himself.

It is a memorable place, filled with history, some recorded, most not, and with lore and fable. Of all the lore there, the Lost Dutchman Mine story is easily the most compelling. No matter the empty historical record, the absence of any real evidence that a single chunk of gold- or silver-bearing ore was ever removed from the vicinity, the legend of the Lost Dutchman has a tenacious grip on the imagination.

A LEGEND

The Fall of Tashunke Witko

Crazy Horse Betrayed

Mystic warriors! Rodrigo Díaz de Bivar—"El Cid"—fighting the Moors for Christian Spain in the eleventh century; St. Jeanne d'Arc, leading an army against the English at Orléans in 1428, dying at the stake at age nineteen; Shaka of the Zulus, his terrible regiments washing their spears in the blood of his foes across the South African veldt; Tecumseh, the war-loving, charismatic visionary of the Shawnees; others, from David and Samson of the Old Testament to Gordon of Khartoum and George Patton . . .

Of all these strange immortals—all driven by spiritual forces no other could understand, many dying as martyrs, many dying for lost causes—of them all, none had a more poignant history or was truer to his faith than Crazy Horse, that young paladin of the Oglala Sioux of the Western Plains of America.

When he died, surrounded by many enemies and a few

friends, on the floor of the adjutant's office at Fort Robinson, Nebraska, at twenty minutes before midnight on September 7, 1877, the white physician who attended him said, "The lights went out, and the last sleep came. It was an Indian epic."

All of Crazy Horse's brief, epic life is a mystery—all of it— and so it is fitting that the circumstances of his death have left lingering doubts.

He was a warrior and a war chief but lived a reclusive and silent life. He rarely attended the councils of tribal leaders, never counted coup or spoke of his victories, never wore a warbonnet, never tied his horse's tail in a knot in the Sioux custom. He sometimes wore a single feather in his hair but he wore no war paint except for white spots, signifying hail, on his chest and on his horse's rump. Before battle, he dusted himself and his horse with dirt thrown up by a burrowing mole so that he would be rendered invisible to his enemies. He is said to have carried an eagle-bone whistle and to have worn a medicine bag around his neck containing the dried heart and brain of an eagle mixed with aster seeds. He also wore a flat black stone, the size of his palm—a talisman called Tunkan (grandfather)—on a rawhide thong around his neck and positioned over his heart. He would rub the stone over his body, and touch others with it, keeping them invulnerable to enemy weapons, before suspending it over his heart. And he would permit none of his band to ride ahead of him into battle.

The Strange Man of the Oglalas they called him, with good reason.

His charms and talismans, his courage, and his closeness to Wakan Tanka, the father-creator of his Lakota people, protected him in war but had no effect warding off the white man's wiles or, for that matter, the treachery of his rivals among his own people.

The life and death of Crazy Horse has been likened to classic tragedy and certainly the elements are present. Dr. Valentine

T. McGillycuddy, the post surgeon at Fort Robinson, Nebraska, in 1877, said of this Silent Petrel of the Great Plains. "In him everything was made secondary to patriotism and love of his people. . . . His early death was preordained."

He was born in 1840 or 1841 near Bear Butte, close to present-day Sturgis, South Dakota. His father, named Crazy Horse—more correctly His Crazy Horse—was a holy man of the Oglalas, one of the seven council fires of the Teton Dakota tribe (commonly called the Sioux). In his teens he was called His Horse on Sight and later Curly, for his wavy, sand-colored hair.

When he was about fourteen he witnessed for the first time the work of white men. In August 1854, near Fort Laramie, Wyoming Territory, when he was living with his uncle, Spotted Tail, chief of the Brulé Sioux, he saw another Brulé chief, named Conquering Bear, killed by soldiers. This tragic opéra bouffe affair, known to Western history as the "Mormon Cow Incident" and the "Grattan Massacre," resulted when a Brulé man shot an arrow into the hindquarters of an ox belonging to a Mormon who was traveling through the North Platte Valley. The ox owner complained at Fort Laramie and an eager young lieutenant, John L. Grattan, was dispatched to the Indian village to investigate, taking with him an interpreter, twenty-nine men, a howitzer, and a mountain cannon. Grattan parleyed with the chief, who offered to pay for the ox with a more valuable horse, but would not surrender himself or the warrior who shot the animal. Grattan would have none of this and ordered his men to open fire on the village. Conquering Bear was killed and the Brulés, joined by some Oglalas, fought back and overwhelmed the soldiers.

Grattan and all his men died in the counterattack.

The farcical battle, which Crazy Horse witnessed (and in which he may have been a participant), opened forty years of warfare between the army and the tribes of the central and northern plains.

By age sixteen he had fought against the Gros Ventres and at eighteen against a band of Arapahos, returning home wounded from this battle. When others reported that Curly had repeatedly charged the enemy alone, his father bestowed on his son the name Crazy Horse, taking the lowly name "Worm" for himself.

When yet a young man the Oglalas were divided into bands led by two formidable chiefs, Red Cloud and Man-Afraid-of-His-Horses. Crazy Horse and his boyhood friend He Dog were with Man-Afraid's band and some years later, after this band was again divided, He Dog, Red Cloud, and others became "shirt wearers"—grand councillors—of the northern Oglalas while Crazy Horse became a shirt wearer, together with American Horse, Sword, and Young-Man-Afraid-of-His-Horses, of the southern quarter of his tribe, its village near the Bighorn Mountains.

In this period, young Crazy Horse fought Crows, Shoshonis, Flatheads, and other enemies of his tribe. He would be in his mid-twenties before he again encountered the white man in battle.

He Dog, who lived to be 100 years old and the last surviving grand councillor of his tribe, told how Crazy Horse had to give up his shirt for failure to keep the oath he pledged before its conferral. It seems that the unmarried Crazy Horse began paying attention to the wife of a man called No Water and took the woman on a war expedition. No Water followed them, borrowed a revolver from another warrior, and found his wife and Crazy Horse sitting before a campfire. The cuckolded husband walked up and shot Crazy Horse in the face, the bullet entering just below the left nostril and fracturing the jaw.

Crazy Horse had to surrender his shirt, but the incident was soon forgotten and he is said to have married twice, fathered a child who died at the age of two, and rose again to become war chief of all his Oglalas.

While the country dom
larger, the region of Cr
of his fights against
scribed. His was th
lowstone River wi
on the west (with
ning south from the
Paha Sapa hunting ground
Oregon Trail on the south. In th
portant in Crazy Horse's history as
man, on the Oregon Trail, the latter close
Forts Reno and Phil Kearny, north of Fetterm
Fort) Robinson, in Nebraska, a short distance east o.
and on the White River just south of the Black Hills; Camp
dan on the lower fork of the White, east of Robinson and belo
the Black Hills; and the Red Cloud and Spotted Tail Agencies, Indian camps on the White River between Camps Robinson and
Sheridan.

Twelve years after his first encounter with white soldiers in the
Grattan fight, Crazy Horse had some role, probably as a decoy,
in the "Fetterman Massacre" near Fort Phil Kearny, a fight considered the worst army debacle west of the Mississippi before the
Custer battle a decade later.

Captain William J. Fetterman, a brilliant Civil War infantry
soldier twice breveted for gallantry under fire, reported to the
Eighteenth Infantry at Fort Phil Kearny in the fall of 1866 and
soon became a popular officer at the remote outpost in Dakota
Territory. He had no experience among them but had a fatal dis-
regard for the Indians in whose lands he had been assigned.
"Give me eighty men," he once said, "and I'll ride roughshod
through the whole Sioux nation."

Like Grattan before him, Fetterman was eager for a fight and

en, with Kearney virtually besieged by the
oud, he was placed in command of a cavalry
ieve a wood-gathering party that was under In-
December 6, 1866, he had his first skirmish with
which he lost an officer and a sergeant, but man-
a few losses among the Indians. On December 21,
again rode out, with precisely his foreordained eighty
ursue the "hostiles." He led his force north over the
n Trail to a point beyond which his commanding officer
rbidden him to move. He proceeded nonetheless, was lured
razy Horse and his warriors into a trap, and in under an
ur was killed along with his entire command.

A decade of goading followed the Fetterman fight, a time when the United States became less concerned with abiding by its treaties and more truculent toward the Plains tribes. The government, in brief, became a sort of national embodiment of the hubris of Grattan or Fetterman, disdaining the Indians' fighting ability and general worth and overrunning the Indians' lands while uttering and writing down lofty but intrinsically worthless words to lull the tribes into an uneasy peace.

In 1868 a treaty signed at Fort Laramie gave to Red Cloud of the Oglalas most of what he sought from the white man, stating that "The country north of the North Platte and east of the summits of the Big Horn Mountains shall be held and considered to be unceded Indian territory. . . . No white person or persons shall be permitted to settle upon or occupy any portion of the same; or without the consent of the Indians, first had and obtained, to pass through the same." The treaty also provided for the abandonment of the army forts along the Bozeman Trail and established a great Sioux reservation west of the Missouri River in present-day South Dakota, with buffalo hunting privileges outside the reservation.

The treaty, shaky from the start (the Missouri River reservation area was desolate, the buffalo virtually nonexistent) was in effect thrown into the wind in the spring of 1875 when gold was

discovered in the Black Hills, bringing a tide of prospectors to en-
croach on the Lakota treaty lands. Red Cloud of the Oglalas and
Spotted Tale of the Brulés protested the incursion and commis-
sions were sent out from Washington to study the problem—in
effect, to arrive at ways for the Sioux to relinquish the Paha Sapa.
At one point in these negotiations, Sitting Bull, the great
Hunkpapa medicine man, told the commissioners, "I want you
to go and tell the Great Father that I do not want to sell any land
to the government." He picked up a pinch of dust and added,
"Not even as much as this."

And an Oglala warrior named Little Big Man, close to Crazy
Horse in those days, threatened to kill any chief who favored selling the Black Hills.

Crazy Horse himself was not a party to the Fort Laramie
treaty signing or to any of the subsequent negotiations. He had
no intention of being exiled to the Missouri River reservation and
agreed with Sitting Bull's opposition to any sale of the Black
Hills. He had, since the Fetterman fight, studied the white man's
way of fighting, had gone many times into the Paha Sapa to seek
inspiration and power from Wakan Tanka, and while he probably knew the ultimate futility of it, he was ready to go to war.

In June 1876, the signal month of General Philip Sheridan's great
summer campaign against the Plains tribes, Crazy Horse fought
his last two battles.

In mid-month, Brigadier General George Crook, commander of the Department of the Platte, came north from Fort Fetterman, crossed the Tongue, turned northwest, and camped on
the headwaters of Rosebud Creek, thirty miles east of the Little
Bighorn River. Crook's force of 1,300 men consisted of over 800
cavalry troopers, 200 infantry, plus a large contingent of Crow
and Shoshoni scouts. On the morning of the seventeenth, after
his scouts spotted a large number of Sitting Bull's combined
Sioux and Cheyenne force descending toward them, Crook
halted his army in an enormous natural amphitheater encircled
by hills and bisected by the creek.

Crazy Horse's precise role in the Rosebud and Little Bighorn battles is unknown but that it was significant in both seems clear. At the Rosebud he appears to have led his warriors—as many as 1,500—against Crook's advance pickets and flanks while keeping another large number of fighters in reserve, concealed in the surrounding hills. The surprise attack gave Crook no time to form skirmish lines and his command was soon split into many small clots of men while the Indians created confusion by advancing, drawing away, closing again, and allowing no respite in the fight.

In the daylong battle, Crook's force expended 25,000 rounds of ammunition. His casualties were twenty-eight men dead, fifty-six wounded. Thirteen Sioux and Cheyennes died on the field.

At dawn, the bluecoats retreated to Crook's camp on Goose Creek, a tributary of the Tongue, to await reinforcements.

❦

Eight days later, along the Little Bighorn, the Hunkpapa war chief Gall turned Major Marcus Reno's flank and drove him and his force into the bluffs above the river, thereby diverting hundreds of warriors to the five companies of the Seventh Cavalry commanded by Lieutenant Colonel George A. Custer.

Horseback fighters led by Crazy Horse and the Northern Cheyenne chief Two Moon struck Custer's flank and rear, "like a hurricane . . . like bees swarming out of a hive," said Kill Eagle, a Blackfoot Sioux chief who witnessed it.

❦

The battle had been won, the war lost. Less than a month after the Little Bighorn, General of the Army William T. Sherman received authority to assume military control of all reservations in Sioux country and to treat the Indians as prisoners of war. In August 1876, orders were issued that the tribes were to surrender the Paha Sapa and their Powder River hunting grounds between the Black Hills and the Bighorn Mountains. The orders also stipulated that the Sioux would be moved to the Missouri River reservation, a region already ruined by white interlopers, its buffalo slaughtered, its plains denuded of timber.

Red Cloud and his subchiefs signed the paper, then Spotted Tail, then the other Teton Lakota leaders, and that fall they surrendered their arms and ponies. The horses were used to transport their goods to Fort Robinson, the chiefs and their people traveling on foot to the camps there.

In the spring of 1877 Sitting Bull took his people north into Canada. He sought to have Crazy Horse join him but the Oglala fighter and his band could not be found. General Crook and a huge force supported by 168 wagons and 400 pack mules scoured the Powder River region for the "non-treaty" Oglalas, soon followed by a column led by General Nelson A. "Bear Coat" Miles. But Crazy Horse had taken his band into the region along the Tongue, north of Fort Phil Kearny, there to face the bitter winter.

Miles and his soldiers caught up with the "renegades" on January 8, 1877, at a place called Battle Butte, but Crazy Horse and his followers, short on ammunition, long on imagination, escaped through the Wolf Mountains toward the Bighorns while his Oglala ally Little Big Man, with Hump, the Minneconjou, and the Cheyenne Two Moon, drew Miles's force into a canyon and kept them busy until a blizzard drove the troopers off.

During that winter, while Crazy Horse and his other "wild Indian" (the government term for them) followers were starving on the Little Powder River, Crook, at Fort Fetterman, promised Spotted Tail that if he would bring his nephew in, his people would not have to move to the Missouri River reservation. Subsequently Red Cloud was told the same thing: persuade Crazy Horse to surrender and be rewarded with a reservation on the game-rich Powder.

If Crazy Horse's death is seen as a Western classical tragedy, the staging area where the final scenes were to be enacted and the players participating were in place at the dawning of 1877.

At center stage was Fort Robinson, located in northwestern Nebraska east of the North Platte and between Forts Laramie and Fetterman. The post was commanded by Lieutenant Colonel Luther P. Bradley of New Haven, Connecticut, a fifty-five-year-old professional soldier and Civil War veteran who had served with Crook throughout the 1876 campaign.

Another important officer at Robinson was Lieutenant William Philo Clark, known as "Nobby" to his friends, "White Hat" to the Indians. He was a New Yorker, a West Pointer, and, by most accounts, an exceptional officer. Among his duties, Clark commanded the Indian scouts on the post and was the liaison officer to General Crook, headquartered in Omaha.

The Indian agent at Robinson was James Irwin, who referred to Crazy Horse as "an unreconstructed Indian."

The post surgeon was Valentine T. McGillycuddy. He was twenty-eight, a Michigan native who in 1875 became the first white man to ascend Harney Peak in the Black Hills (his ashes are buried there) and later the first mayor of Rapid City, Dakota Territory. He had served with Crook on the Rosebud and practiced medicine in Sioux country (with Martha "Calamity Jane" Cannary his occasional nurse). He came to know Crazy Horse as well as any white man ever did.

An interpreter at the post, Frank Grouard, had an especially exotic history. A six-footer weighing over 200 pounds, he is believed to have been born in the Society Islands in the South Pacific in 1850, the son of a Mormon missionary and a native woman. In 1869, roaming in the West, he was captured by Sioux near the Milk River in Montana and for six years lived among them, coming to know Crazy Horse and being adopted as a son by Sitting Bull. He was a veteran of the Rosebud and Crook once said he would rather lose a third of his command than be deprived of Grouard's services. The Indians called him "The Grabber," reflecting the image of a standing bear clawing at an opponent.

Among the common soldiers on the post was a red-bearded, heavyset private named William Gentles, born in County Tyrone, Ireland, in 1830. Except for a single forthcoming act, his name would not appear in Crazy Horse's or any other story.

Adjacent to Fort Robinson lay the Red Cloud Agency (an "agency" being the headquarters of a U.S. government Indian agent). In the summer of 1877 it was populated by an estimated 9,000 Oglalas, 2,000 Northern Cheyennes, and 1,500 Northern Arapahos.

Forty miles downstream from Robinson on the White River was situated Camp Sheridan and the Spotted Tail Agency—in mid-1877 having 8,000 Brulés, 1,200 Minneconjous, and some Oglalas. Sheridan's commanding officer was Captain Daniel W. Burke, another of Crook's officers, as was the Indian agent, Jesse Matlock Lee, a friend of Spotted Tail and one who might have become, given the chance, Crazy Horse's friend.

In the spring of 1877 Crazy Horse surrendered at Fort Robinson. His people were starving and he had been promised an agency of his own in the north.

The officers who rode out to meet him and who saw him for the first time were amazed at the spectacle of the long train of his followers—a concourse two and a half miles long that strung out back to a series of bluffs and out upon the highlands, men, women, children, horses, dogs, countless travois loaded with the bundles of their possessions and their packed deerskin lodges. But the officers were more fascinated with the Strange Man and his biographer, Mari Sandoz, tells what they saw:

> He was a small man for a fighter, less than six of the white man's feet, and slim as a young warrior. But they knew it was Crazy Horse for he wore no paint and nothing to show his greatness. One feather stood alone at the back of his head, and his brown, fur-wrapped braids hung low over a plain buckskin shirt, his Winchester in a scabbard at his knee. Beside him, making a straight row, in paint, war bonnets, and fringed buckskin, rode his headmen,

Little Hawk, Big Road, He Dog, and Little Big Man strong among them.

At Fort Robinson, all came out to watch the brilliant procession advancing toward the Red Cloud Agency and, as Sandoz wrote, "to see this wild war leader who had scared the whites for so many years, who whipped two of their big soldier chiefs, Crook and Custer, in eight days—to see him give up his gun and his horse and become a coffee-cooler like the rest."

(Sandoz tells of one of the soldier chiefs, perhaps Colonel Bradley, watching through field glasses and exclaiming, "By God! This is a triumphal march, not a surrender!")

Crazy Horse and his people were assigned a campsite near Cottonwood Creek between the Red Cloud and Spotted Tail Agencies and there they set up their lodges—145 of them—the openings facing the sun. He had brought in 217 fighting men (not counting some who drifted off to other camps, such as his friend Touch-the-Clouds, and his father, Worm, who moved their lodges to the Spotted Tail Agency), 889 women, children, and elderly, and 1,700 horses. He also surrendered 117 guns—old muzzle-loaders, rifles, cavalry carbines, and a few revolvers.

Soon after his surrender, Crazy Horse's wife, Black Shawl, fell ill, probably with tuberculosis, and Dr. McGillycuddy rode out to the Oglala's camp on several occasions to deliver medicines and attend to the woman. The physician developed a great admiration for Crazy Horse.

Another who came to know him was the Spotted Tail agent Jesse Lee. To Lee, who met him for the first time upon his surrender at Fort Robinson, Crazy Horse "seemed like a frightened, trembling wild animal brought to bay."

Crazy Horse *was* troubled. He fretted over his decision to surrender and learned from friends among both Red Cloud's and Spotted Tail's people things that distressed him even more: the Cheyennes had been marched south to Indian Territory; the Nez Perce under Chief Joseph had rebelled against forced removal from their ancestral homelands in the Wallowa Valley of Oregon; rumors were rampant that the Sioux would be taken to the hated Missouri River reservation.

If there was a plot to kill Crazy Horse, or at least the creation of an atmosphere in which he could be killed with impunity, it began soon after his surrender that spring of 1877 and gained momentum by summer. It seems clear that Red Cloud and his followers had a role in the discrediting of the famed fighter. This willingness to betray one of their own may have been the result of Red Cloud's, perhaps even Spotted Tail's, alarm over Crazy Horse's charismatic character, his "born leader" attributes. In her biography of him, Mari Sandoz says that not long after Crazy Horse's surrender, "Like the smell of a dead dog spreading through the village on a warm afternoon, and as hard to find and drag away, came a whispering of plans to make a big chief of Crazy Horse over everybody."

In August, the Red Cloud and Spotted Tail Agencies were notified by General Crook that eighteen Indian leaders would journey to Washington to make their grievances known about the plan to remove them to the Missouri River reservation. Crook, in what appears to have been a gesture to improve the attitude of the Indians departing for the capital, announced that the leaders could go on a buffalo hunt provided they agreed to return to the agencies at a specified time.

Crazy Horse was not interested in the journey to visit the Great Father: he saw nothing to be gained by discussing the Missouri River reservation with the white chiefs and he did not admire the changes such visits had made in Red Cloud and Spotted Tail. They had returned with too many of the white man's ideas, too few of those of their people. He probably voiced these objections and the effect did not help his standing with the two principal Sioux leaders.

Now, Young-Man-Afraid-of-His-Horses, formerly of Crazy Horse's band and subsequently one of Red Cloud's subchiefs, suggested a feast and celebration of the buffalo hunt at Crazy

Horse's camp. This idea, however, was not agreeable to Agent Irwin. He explained to his superiors at Fort Robinson and to those at the Bureau of Indian Affairs that Crazy Horse had only recently joined the agency, said Red Cloud's people considered the Oglala war chief an "unreconstructed Indian." Irwin proceeded to say that Crazy Horse "had constantly evinced feelings of unfriendliness toward the others," was "sullen, morose and discontented at all times." The agent, who seems to have had a genuine fear of Crazy Horse, warned that "Once away on a hunt, he with his band of at least 240 braves, well armed and equipped, would go on the warpath and cause the government infinite trouble and disaster."

These alarmist views, most reflections of what Irwin learned from Red Cloud and his followers, were larded with such words as "silent," "sullen," "cruel," "lordly and dictatorial," and with observations that Crazy Horse was "tricky and unfaithful to others and very selfish as to the personal interests of his own tribe"—words that cannot have been born of Irwin's personal observation. He warned that it would be a mistake to issue ammunition to Crazy Horse and his followers for the hunt as it "would be used for the destruction of the whites against whom they seemed to entertain the utmost animosity."

The buffalo hunt never took place.

At the end of August occurred an incident that further deepened the fear and distrust of Crazy Horse held by the army as well as by certain leaders among his own people.

That month, with his friend, the splendidly named seven-foot-tall Minneconjou, Touch-the-Clouds, and other Indian leaders, Crazy Horse traveled to the Red Cloud Agency in answer to a request for a meeting with Lieutenant William P. Clark. "White Hat," his words translated by Frank Grouard and a man named Louis Bordeaux, had orders to recruit Indian scouts to aid General Miles in his campaign to capture Chief Joseph and his Nez Perce, now on the run in Idaho.

At one point Clark posed the question of joining the cam-

paign as a scout directly to Crazy Horse. Grouard translated
Clark's words and *mis*translated Crazy Horse's reply—many
thought purposefully.

Crazy Horse said, as to the matter of helping fight the Nez
Perce, that he thought the white man wanted his people to be
done with war but that if the white man wanted him to fight he
would fight until there were no Nez Perce left. Grouard translated the final words as "until there were no *white men* left," a
critical alteration that Louis Bordeaux caught instantly and chal-
lenged. Grouard walked out of the meeting and William Garnett,
the son of the commander at Fort Laramie and a Sioux woman,
took Grouard's place.

Later, in the office of Captain Daniel W. Burke at Camp Sheridan, the meeting with Clark was recounted in the presence of
Burke, Captain Jesse Lee of the Spotted Tail Agency, Touch-the-
Clouds, Grouard, Bordeaux, and several agency chiefs. It became clear that Grouard had mistranslated Crazy Horse's words
and at one point Touch-the-Clouds called Grouard a liar while
Grouard insisted that he and Crazy Horse were "closer than
brothers." (Some years later, Dr. McGillycuddy was questioned
about this incident and replied, "I never had any use for
Grouard.")

In any event, the damage had been done and could not be reversed. Captain Clark relayed his fears to Colonel Bradley who
in turn relayed them to General Sheridan: "There is a good
chance for trouble here . . ."

Sheridan ordered Bradley to delay on the Nez Perce volunteer
plan, then contacted General George Crook and ordered him to
Fort Robinson.

In this period of the summer of 1877, a keen observer named
John Gregory Bourke, Crook's aide-de-camp, met Crazy Horse
and left one of the best of all white-perspective descriptions of the
war leader. Bourke, a Philadelphian who had earned a Medal of
Honor for heroic conduct at Stone River, Tennessee, in
1862–1863, and who served in all of Crook's campaigns, in-

cluding fights on the Powder and Tongue rivers and at Rosebud Creek, was a prolific diarist and able ethnologist. In his book *On the Border With Crook,* he wrote:

> I saw before me a man who looked quite young, not over thirty years old, five feet eight inches high, lithe and sinewy, with a scar in the face. The expression of his countenance was one of quiet dignity, but morose, fogged, tenacious, and melancholy. He behaved with stolidity, like a man who realized he had to give in to fate, but would do so as sullenly as possible. . . . All Indians gave him a high reputation for courage and generosity. In advancing upon an enemy, none of his warriors were allowed to pass him. He had made hundreds of friends by his charity toward the poor, as it was a point of honor with him never to keep anything for himself, excepting weapons of war. I never heard an Indian mention his name save in terms of respect.

Crook, known by the Indians as "Three Stars," came out to Robinson and lost no time in calling together a council with certain chiefs and subchiefs. It appears that the first meeting was to be held on White Clay Creek just west of the Red Cloud Agency, but was called off after an experience William Garnett had en route to the gathering to act as interpreter. Garnett said he was met by an Indian scout called Woman's Dress who told him a story he had gotten thirdhand: "Crazy Horse is going to come there with sixty Indians and catch General Crook by the hand, like he was going to shake hands, and he is going to hold on to him, and those sixty Indians are going to kill Crook and whoever is with him."

When Crook and Captain Clark arrived on the scene shortly thereafter, Garnett reported what he had been told. Crook was skeptical but Baptiste Pournier, a scout, translator, and friend of Garnett's, vouched for the honesty of Woman's Dress. Clark urged Crook not to proceed to the council and put himself at risk so the general turned back to Robinson while Garnett proceeded to White Clay Creek with a message informing the chiefs that the council was postponed.

Garnett discovered that neither Crazy Horse nor any of his band were present at the council.

(Three months after Crazy Horse's death, Garnett and Baptiste Pournier caught up with Woman's Dress. Pournier told the Indian, "You are a liar and you are the cause of a good man's death." Of course, Woman's Dress was responsible only for agitating an already overmixed brew of distrust and fear toward the Strange Man.)

The council was rearranged a short time later and the meeting held in the commanding officer's office at Fort Robinson. Colonel Bradley was away from the post, Crazy Horse was invited but, as was his custom, did not attend. Red Cloud, the Cheyenne American Horse, and an old nemesis, No Water, all from the Red Cloud Agency, were there together with Crook and Clark and translators Frank Grouard, William Garnett, and Baptiste Pournier.

The precise time and details of this meeting are not known but Crook was apparently furious over the absence of Crazy Horse and told Red Cloud and the others that it was their duty to "control" the troublesome Oglala. Someone in the Indian delegation said bluntly that Crazy Horse could not be controlled and would have to be killed. Others agreed but Crook said this would be murder and he would not be a party to such thinking.

(Crook's biographer, Dan Thrapp, says, "Crook had no compunction about slaying hostiles in action, but he had little taste for executions, impromptu or planned, and treachery was not part of his makeup." This seems incontrovertible. The forty-eight-year-old Ohioan had a long history of Indian fighting—against tribes as far-flung as the Klamaths of the California-Oregon border, the Yakimas of Washington, the Snakes in Idaho, Paiutes, Sioux, Cheyennes, Arapahos, and later the Apaches and Navajos in the Southwest—and he had a well-known sentiment toward these foes. But he was a tough, pragmatic general of the U.S. Army and his personal sentiments did not stand in the way of practical military thinking: he mirrored the views of his superiors, Sherman and Sheridan, that Crazy Horse was at the very least an irritant and a nuisance, possibly a threat, and he shared the view that if the Oglala were to be "removed" from the vicinity of his people, they would submit meekly to removal to the Missouri River reservation.)

The talk about killing Crazy Horse appears to have continued after Crook's disavowal. William Garnett later said that each chief present at the meeting agreed to select four dependable men to go to Crazy Horse's village and kill him there. Ammunition was actually issued, Garnett claimed, and someone said that the man who succeeded in the assassination would receive $300 and a horse Captain Clark was offering for the deed.

This plot—and it seems likely that it, or something similar to it, was actually formulated among the Red Cloud group at or directly following the meeting with Crook—came to the attention of Colonel Bradley. While no ally of Crazy Horse, he sanely put a stop to it. Garnett says he was called into Bradley's office and questioned; later Clark said to Garnett, "Bradley has got hold of that council we had with the Indians today, so you go down to the Indian village right away, and stop the Indians from approaching Crazy Horse."

Garnett said he did so.

While Crook would hear no talk of the plot, and while Bradley (probably acting on Crook's orders) put a stop to any plan by Red Cloud's people to murder Crazy Horse, orders were issued to Fort Robinson that the Oglala war leader was to be taken prisoner, spirited from the post at night, and transported by rail to the Dry Tortugas. (This was the atoll seventy miles off Key West in the Gulf of Mexico where the army had a fort and prison, the cells dug deep into the coral reefs with bars across the top.)

At about the time the council was held in Bradley's command post, Crazy Horse and a number of his warriors left their camp. They were reported to be heading for the Powder River country but in fact did not ride far. The Oglala, who knew that the Indian police had orders to bring him back to Fort Robinson, seems to have been buying time to decide what to do. He sought advice from his friends Touch-the-Clouds and Fast Thunder at the Spotted Tail Agency—the latter, although a member of the Indian police, was still trusted by Crazy Horse. As a result of their meeting, Fast Thunder and Touch-the-Clouds rode with their brother to Camp Sheridan where they were joined by the post commander Major Daniel W. Burke and the agent Jesse M. Lee.

Burke and Lee told Crazy Horse that he must ride with them to Fort Robinson and surrender and that there he would have the opportunity to talk to Colonel Bradley and put on the record whatever complaints he had—among them the promise made to him when he first led his band to the fort, that he would have his own agency.

Early on September 7, 1877, Crazy Horse began his last journey, riding forty miles to the west, with Burke, Lee, and others from Camp Sheridan and the Spotted Tail Agency escorting him. The entourage grew en route as Indian scouts, police, friends and foes, Indian and white, joined the procession.

In the summer of 1930, Eleanor Hinman, a thirty-year-old former newspaper feature writer and stenographer at the University of Nebraska, drove out in a Model T coupe to the Pine Ridge reservation in South Dakota to interview certain Oglalas and others who had known Crazy Horse. Riding with Hinman on the jolting road was a former country schoolteacher and now a University of Nebraska student named Maria Susetta Sandoz, who, as Mari Sandoz, would write a poetic book about Crazy Horse twelve years later.

The most important man Hinman and Sandoz met at the reservation was Sunka Bloka, He Dog, age ninety-two, last of the "shirt wearers" of the Oglala, nephew of Red Cloud, veteran of the Little Bighorn and countless other battles, and lifelong friend of Crazy Horse. He Dog had an extraordinary memory, filled with detail, and when the interviewers found him, living with his great-niece near the town of Oglala, he spoke with great melancholy of the events of that September day, fifty-three years past.

He said that when he learned that Crazy Horse was being escorted to Fort Robinson, he put on his warbonnet, got on his horse, and found his friend in the midst of the procession nearing the fort. He rode up, clasped Crazy Horse's hand. "I saw that he did not look right," He Dog recalled. "I said, 'Look out—watch your step—you are going into a dangerous place.' "

The swelling entourage now rode through the Red Cloud Agency and a message was sent over to Fort Robinson: "Crazy Horse has been taken. A large body of Indian soldiers have just passed this agency on the way to the post having him in custody. All quiet."

The procession entered the fort and at that moment, according to Sandoz, occurred a bizarre incident. Crazy Horse, on foot, was confronted by an old friend, now "a self-important member of the Indian Police," Little Big Man, the warrior who had decoyed General Miles's troops into a canyon at Battle Butte just nine months earlier. Sandoz says Little Big Man (others say it was a warrior named Buffalo Chips) grabbed Crazy Horse's arm and said, perhaps in a crude attempt to ingratiate himself to his white masters, "Come along, you man-of-no-fight. You are a coward."

Crazy Horse did not respond to this shocking affront and was escorted into Colonel Bradley's office while the crowd surged impatiently and noisily on the parade ground, on one side the Strange Man's adherents, on the other Red Cloud, American Horse, and other agency Indians. Others continued to pour in, in wagons, on horseback, and on foot, to witness Crazy Horse's surrender.

In the commander's office he waited patiently while Major Lee pleaded with Bradley to meet with the Oglala and hear him out. The colonel demurred, said nothing could be accomplished by such a hearing, that Crazy Horse would not be harmed but must be turned over to the officer-of-the-day, Captain James Kennington.

In the anteroom, Lee reported that Bradley had said it was too late in the day to talk. At this, Crazy Horse rose, his blanket folded over his arm, and walked to the door followed by the few Oglalas who had waited with him. He shook hands with Lee and stepped outside. There Kennington and Little Big Man took up positions on each side of him and, with two soldiers walking behind, some agency Indians ahead, the prisoner, his captors, and his friends headed for the adjutant's office.

Crazy Horse had no idea where he was being taken. He may have thought he would be meeting with another white chief—perhaps Three Star Crook. He may have thought, or been told, that he would spent the night with his people at the fort and meet Colonel Bradley the next day.

Whatever he thought, he did not think of jail.

It was a short walk to the adjutant's office, adjoining the post jail, where a sentry, bayoneted rifle on his shoulder, walked a path in front of the small building. When his escort led him across the threshold, Crazy Horse stopped abruptly—he saw the bars on the windows and, inside, men with chains on their legs.

He jumped back and from his buckskin shirt drew a hidden knife. There was a warning shout, a scramble, and Crazy Horse's arms were suddenly pinned behind him by Little Big Man. The great Oglala flailed and struggled, dragging Little Big Man with him. "Let me go!" he shouted. Now Red Cloud and American Horse's people, who had followed the escort, yelled, "Kill him!" and Kennington, sword drawn, had to knock aside the guns that were raised.

For an instant, Crazy Horse broke loose, slashing Little Big Man's arm. Then some Indians in the crowd—Swift Bear and Black Crow of Spotted Tail's Brulés, and, reluctantly, Fast Thunder, the erstwhile friend with whom Crazy Horse had sought advice the day before—held him down as voices shouted, "Stab him! Kill the son-of-a-bitch!"

Kennington rushed forward but before he could reach Crazy Horse, the sentry, William Gentles, lunged with his bayonet, driving it deep into Crazy Horse's body, pulling it free, and lunging again.

Fast Thunder's wife heard the Oglala chief say to her husband, "Cousin, you killed me. You are with the white people." Then, still pinned to the ground, his shirt and leggings reddening, he said, "Let me go, my friends. You have got me hurt enough."

Dr. McGillycuddy made his way through the throng and knelt beside his friend. He said later that he "found Crazy Horse on his back, grinding his teeth and frothing at the mouth, blood trickling from a bayonet wound above the hip, and the pulse weak and missing beats. I saw that he was done for."

He Dog, close by when the incident occurred, asked permission of Captain Clark to go to his friend's side. He knelt beside the great Oglala and placed an agency blanket over him. "See where I am hurt," Crazy Horse said, and He Dog pulled the buckskin shirt up and saw the wounds, a lump rising under the skin along the ribs on the right side of his back, the second wound through the small of the back.

Crazy Horse was carried into the adjutant's office, a room barely big enough for a desk and cot. The stricken warrior refused the bed and so was placed on the board floor, a red blanket covering him. In the kerosene lamplight, armed guards, Kennington, "White Hat" Clark, Crazy Horse's father, and a few friends—Touch-the-Clouds and He Dog among them—watched as McGillycuddy continued his examination. One of the wounds was deep through the kidneys. The physician administered a hypodermic of morphine.

Touch-the-Clouds asked if he could take Crazy Horse to his lodge so that he might die among his own people but this request was denied.

McGillycuddy recalled that at about eleven that night "Taps" echoed out mournfully from the bugler on the parade ground and Crazy Horse struggled to rise. "A good day to fight, a good day to die," he said.

His pain was quieted by the morphine but he remained alert. Outside were the sounds of women keening, men talking, sentries walking, their boots crunching on the gravel. Worm bent over his son and said, "I am here." Crazy Horse stirred and whispered, "Ahh, my father. I am bad hurt. Tell the people it is no use to depend on me anymore now . . ."

At twenty minutes to midnight, September 7, 1877, Crazy Horse settled back, eyes open, and died.

Touch-the-Clouds placed his hand on his friend's stilled breast and said, "It is good. He has looked for death and it has come."

Many years later McGillycuddy thought back on the moment and said, "The lights went out and the last sleep came. It was a scene never to be forgotten, an Indian epic."

Just hours after Crazy Horse breathed his last, accounts of his death were being muddied. Colonel Bradley and his officers at Fort Robinson were clearly horrified at what had happened to their prisoner and attempts were made to mollify angry superiors. Captain Clark's report was a classic example of clasping a protective hand over the army's backside. He wrote that it was "impossible to ascertain" how Crazy Horse died, "as the Doctors from the appearance of the wound thought it might have been done with his own knife."

This patent lie was quickly answered by surgeon McGillycuddy who said flatly, "I saw him enter the guardroom next door, out of which he sprang without delay, with a drawn knife, to regain his freedom, and I was standing forty feet from him when one of the guards, a private of the Ninth Infantry, lunged his bayonet into the chief's abdomen, and he fell to the ground."

Lieutenant Jesse Lee said, ". . . just then an infantry soldier of the guard made a successful lunge, and Crazy Horse fell, mortally wounded, with a deep bayonet thrust in his right side."

Lee's wife Lucy, an onlooker, gave a similar account.

The method of his death was never in question, the factors leading up to it have been a source of mystery for 120 years.

To some contemporaries—Dr. McGillycuddy, He Dog, Red

Feather, Touch-the-Clouds, William Garnett, and others—and to some later historians (most notably Mari Sandoz and Robert A. Clark), Crazy Horse was the victim of the fear, jealousy, and betrayal of both his Lakota brethren and his white captors.

Red Feather, the younger brother of Crazy Horse's first wife and a member of the Oglala's band throughout the 1876 fighting, was among those interviewed by Eleanor Hinman in 1930. He recalled that Crazy Horse's fame as a fighter and magnetic leader of his people captivated the whites at Fort Robinson. "All the white people came to see Crazy Horse," he said, "and gave him presents and money. The other Indians at the agency got very jealous."

Dr. McGillycuddy (who died in Berkeley, California, in 1939) often spoke and wrote to friends of this harbored jealousy and resentment. He said that after the Custer battle and Sitting Bull's retreat into Canada, the leaders of the Sioux, including Red Cloud and Spotted Tail, were forced to make a final peace with the white man and afterward assisted the whites in bringing Crazy Horse to bay.

The physician said, "Spotted Tail and Red Cloud, however, did not realize or anticipate the 'hero worship' that always follows the return to his people of a successful military leader, which Crazy Horse had developed into. Hence, the jealousy. Spotted Tail, more of a diplomat, did not show it so much." He added that General Crook did, in fact, contemplate having Crazy Horse "made head chief of the Oglalas," replacing Red Cloud.

"I could not but regard him as the greatest leader of his people in modern times," McGillycuddy said. "In him everything was made secondary to patriotism and love of his people. Modest, fearless, a mystic, a believer in destiny, and much of a recluse, he was held in veneration and admiration by the younger warriors who would follow him anywhere. These qualities made him a danger to the government, and he became persona non grata to evolution and to the progress of the white man's civilization. Hence his early death was preordained."

Others saw the betrayal as the product of a sinister whispering campaign, a partnership of Indian and white that resulted in a perhaps unplanned but no less fatal conspiracy involving the white military and the two Indian agencies and their leaders. Culprits named included Crook, Bradley, Clark, James Irwin, and Frank Grouard, Red Cloud, Spotted Tail (both behind-the-scenes fomenters), American Horse, Little Big Man, Woman's Dress, No Water, and others.

The purpose of this quasi-conspiracy was to eliminate Crazy Horse and end the last resistance of the Lakota to the army's plans to move the tribe to the Missouri River reservation.

The wagon that waited at Fort Robinson, meant to take Crazy Horse to the nearest railhead for the journey to the Dry Tortugas, symbolized one solution to the problem the Strange Man posed. William Gentles's bayonet proved to be the final solution and to Crazy Horse it was a better one.

His body was conveyed by mule-drawn wagon to a point beyond the fort where his father took custody of it, taking it by travois east to the Beaver Creek area. There Crazy Horse was wrapped in deerskins, then in a buffalo robe snugged tightly with rawhide thongs. He was placed in a burial tree while the wake was held and later the body was removed and buried in a crevasse, a rock slide covering the grave. Some Lakota believe Crazy Horse's body was taken by his father and mother to the north, where they determined to escape into Canada and join Sitting Bull. En route, it is said, they buried their son somewhere in the southwest Dakotas near Chanke Opi Wakpala, a place where a final battle between the whites and Sioux would take place thirteen years later, the creek called Wounded Knee.

EPILOGUE

One final thing about these historical mysteries being connected, adjoined like patches on a quilt, parts of a bigger fabric—the saga of the West:

Billy the Kid is a patch adjoined to Custer and Boston Corbett because of General Lew Wallace, author of *Ben Hur*. Wallace served as judge advocate during the Lincoln conspiracy trial at which Corbett testified; he served on the board of inquiry during the trial of Major Marcus Reno, the officer whose detachment survived the Little Bighorn battle; and he served as governor of New Mexico Territory, and he knew the Kid.

Jesse James is connected to Crazy Horse because of Martha Jane Cannary. Known to history as "Calamity Jane," Cannary claimed to have met Frank Dalton in the 1880s and identified him as Jesse James, and she also served as sometime frontier nurse to Dr. Valentine McGillycuddy, the man who attended Crazy Horse as the great Oglala warrior lay dying at Fort Robinson.

And then there is the connection between no less than *four* of the subjects of this book with the little town of Granbury, Texas, southwest of Fort Worth. This is the place where a man named

John St. Helen first confessed that he was in reality John Wilkes Booth; it is the place where Frank Dalton, the Jesse James claimant, died and is buried; it is the place where Billy the Kid's tombstone, stolen from the Fort Sumner cemetery, was found; and it is the place where Elizabeth Crockett, Davy's second wife, is buried.

It is all coincidence, I'm sure, that four of my patches intersect in this tiny Texas town, but I mention it in case somebody thinks it is an adjoining I overlooked.

—Dale L. Walker

BIBLIOGRAPHY

1. The Day Davy Died

Baugh, Virgil E. *Rendezvous at the Alamo*. New York: Pageant Press, 1960; reprinted by University of Nebraska Press, 1985.

de la Peña, José Enrique. *With Santa Anna in Texas: Narrative of the Revolution*. Translated and edited by Carmen Perry. College Station: Texas A&M University Press, 1975.

Derr, Mark. *The Frontiersman: The Real Life and the Many Legends of Davy Crockett*. New York: William Morrow, 1993.

Groneman, Bill. *Defense of a Legend: Crockett and the de la Peña Diary*. Plano, Texas: Republic of Texas Press, 1994.

Hardin, Stephen L. *Texian Iliad: A Military History of the Texas Revolution*. Austin: University of Texas Press, 1994.

Long, Jeff. *Duel of Eagles: The Mexican and U.S. Fight for the Alamo*. New York: William Morrow, 1990.

Lord, Walter. *A Time to Stand: The Epic of the Alamo*. New York: Harper & Row, 1961. Reprinted by University of Nebraska Press, 1978.

Matovina, Timothy M. *The Alamo Remembered: Tejano Accounts and Perspectives*. Austin: University of Texas Press, 1995.

Nevin, David. *The Texans*. New York: Time-Life, 1971.

Nofi, Albert A. *The Alamo and the Texas War for Independence*. New York: Da Capo Press, 1994.

Shackford, James A. *David Crockett, The Man and the Legend*. Chapel Hill: University of North Carolina Press, 1956. Reprinted by University of Nebraska Press, 1994.

Tinkle, Lon. *13 Days to Glory: The Siege of the Alamo*. New York: McGraw-Hill, 1958. Reprinted by Texas A&M University Press, 1996.

2. Incident at Grinder's Stand

Ambrose, Stephen E. *Undaunted Courage: Meriwether Lewis, Thomas Jefferson, and the Opening of the American West*. New York: Simon & Schuster, 1996.

Chandler, David Leon. *The Jefferson Conspiracies: A President's Role in the Assassination of Meriwether Lewis*. New York: William Morrow, 1994.

Coues, Elliott. *A History of the Expedition Under the Command of Captains Lewis and Clark.* New York: Macmillan, 1965, 3 vols. (Originally published in 1893, 4 vols.)

Daniels, Jonathan. *The Devils' Backbone: The Story of the Natchez Trace.* New York: McGraw-Hill, 1962.

Dillon, Richard. *Meriwether Lewis.* New York: Coward-McCann, 1965.

Fisher, Vardis. *Suicide or Murder? The Strange Death of Governor Meriwether Lewis.* Athens: Ohio University/Swallow Press, 1993. (Originally published in 1962.)

Lavender, David. *The Way to the Western Sea: Lewis & Clark Across the Continent.* New York: Harper & Row, 1988.

3. The Life and Deaths of Sacajawea

Bakeless, John. *Lewis and Clark: Partners in Discovery.* New York: William Morrow, 1947.

Clark, Ella E., and Edmonds, Margot. *Sacagawea of the Lewis & Clark Expedition.* Berkeley: University of California Press, 1979.

Howard, Harold P. *Sacajawea.* Norman: University of Oklahoma Press, 1971.

Lavender, David. *The Way to the Western Sea: Lewis and Clark Across the Continent.* New York: Harper & Row, 1988.

Snyder, Gerald S. *In the Footsteps of Lewis and Clark.* Washington, D.C., National Geographic Society, 1970.

Speck, Gordon. *Breeds and Half-Breeds.* New York: Clarkson N. Potter, 1969.

4. The Man Who Would Be Jesse James

Breihan, Carl W. *The Complete and Authentic Life of Jesse James.* New York: Frederick Fell, 1953.

Croy, Homer. *Jesse James Was My Neighbor.* New York: Duell, Sloan & Pearce, 1949.

Love, Robertus. *The Rise and Fall of Jesse James.* New York: Putnam's, 1926.

Settle, William A. *Jesse James Was His Name.* Columbia: University of Missouri Press, 1966.

Steele, Phillip W., and Warfel, George. *The Many Faces of Jesse James.* Gretna, La.: Pelican Publishing Co., 1995.

Stevenson, Elizabeth. *Figures in a Western Landscape: Men and Women of the Northern Rockies.* Baltimore: Johns Hopkins University Press, 1994.

5. "I'm Billy the Kid"

Airy, Helen. *Whatever Happened to Billy the Kid?* Santa Fe, N.M.: Sunstone Press, 1993.

Cline, Donald. *Alias Billy the Kid: The Man Behind the Legend.* Santa Fe, N.M.: Sunstone Press, 1966.

Cunningham, Eugene. *Triggernometry: A Gallery of Gunfighters.* Norman: University of Oklahoma Press, 1996. (Originally published in 1962.)

Edwards, Harold L. *Goodbye Billy the Kid.* College Station, Tex.: Creative Publishing, 1995.

Fulton, Maurice G. *History of the Lincoln County War.* Tucson: University of Arizona Press, 1968.

Keleher, William A. *Violence in Lincoln County, 1869–1881.* Albuquerque: University of New Mexico Press, 1957.

Metz, Leon C. *Pat Garrett, The Story of a Western Lawman.* Norman: University of Oklahoma Press, 1973.

O'Neal, Bill. *Encyclopedia of Western Gunfighters.* Norman: University of Oklahoma Press, 1979.

Rasch, Philip J. *Trailing Billy the Kid.* Laramie, Wyo.: National Association for Outlaw and Lawman History, 1995.

Sonnichsen, C. L., and Morrison, William V. *Alias Billy the Kid.* Albuquerque: University of New Mexico Press, 1955.

Tatum, Stephen. *Inventing Billy the Kid: Visions of the Outlaw in America, 1881–1981.* Albuquerque: University of New Mexico Press, 1982.

Tunstill, William A. *Billy the Kid and Me Were the Same.* Roswell, N.M.: Western History Research Center, 1988.

Tuska, Jon. *Billy the Kid: A Handbook.* Lincoln: University of Nebraska Press, 1986. (Originally published in 1983.)

Utley, Robert. *Billy the Kid: A Short and Violent Life.* Lincoln: University of Nebraska Press, 1989.

Weddle, Jerry. *Antrim Is My Stepfather's Name: The Boyhood of Billy the Kid.* Albuquerque: University of New Mexico Press, 1996.

6. Bandit Laureate of the Mother Lode

Collins, William, and Levene, Bruce. *Black Bart*. Mendocino, Calif.: Pacific Transcriptions, 1992.

Dillon, Richard. *Humbugs and Heroes: A Gallery of California Pioneers*. New York: Doubleday, 1970.

———. *Wells Fargo Detective: The Biography of James B. Hume*. New York: Coward-McCann, 1969.

Hoeper, George. *Black Bart: Boulevardier Bandit*. Fresno, Calif.: Word Dancer Press, 1995.

Loomis, Noel. *Wells Fargo: An Illustrated History*. New York: Clarkson N. Potter, 1968.

Nevin, David. *The Expressmen*. Alexandria, Va.: Time-Life, 1974.

7. The Mad Hatter and the Assassin

Balsiger, David, and Sellers, Charles E., Jr. *The Lincoln Conspiracy*. Los Angeles: Schick Sunn Classic Books, 1977.

Bates, Finis L. *The Escape and Suicide of John Wilkes Booth*. Memphis, Tenn.: Pilcher Printing Co., 1907.

Clark, Champ. *The Assassination*. Alexandria, Va.: Time-Life, "The Civil War" series, 1987.

Dary, David. *True Tales of Old-Time Kansas*. Manhattan, Kans.: University of Kansas, 1984.

DeWitt, David M. *The Assassination of Lincoln and Its Expiation*. New York: Macmillan, 1903.

Forrester, Izola. *This One Mad Act: The Unknown Story of John Wilkes Booth and His Family*. Boston: Hale, Cushman & Flint, 1937.

Gainey, Paul, and Evans, Stewart. *The Lodger: The Arrest and Escape of Jack the Ripper*. London: Century, 1995.

Johnson, Byron Berkeley. *Abraham Lincoln and Boston Corbett*. Boston: Lincoln and Smith Press, 1914.

Lewis, Lloyd. *Myths After Lincoln*. New York: Harcourt, Brace, 1929.

Roscoe, Theodore. *The Web of Conspiracy*. Englewood Cliffs, N.J.: Prentice-Hall, 1959.

Sugden, Philip. *The Complete History of Jack the Ripper*. London: BCA Publishers, 1994.

8. The Old Gringo's Last Laugh

de Castro, Adolphe Danziger. *Portrait of Ambrose Bierce*. New York: The Century Co., 1929.

Fatout, Paul. *Ambrose Bierce: The Devil's Lexicographer*. Norman: University of Oklahoma Press, 1951.

Garvin, Richard. *The Crystal Skull*. New York: Doubleday, 1973.

Grattan, C. Hartley. *Bitter Bierce*. New York: Doubleday, Doran & Co., 1929.

McWilliams, Carey. *Ambrose Bierce: A Biography*. New York: A.C. Boni, 1929.

Mencken, H. L. *A Mencken Chrestomathy*. New York: Knopf, 1949.

Mitchell-Hedges, F. A. *Danger My Ally*. Boston: Little, Brown, 1955.

Morrill, Sibley S. *Ambrose Bierce, F. A. Mitchell-Hedges and the Crystal Skull*. San Francisco: Cadleon Press, 1972.

Morris, Roy, Jr. *Ambrose Bierce: Alone in Bad Company*. New York: Crown, 1996.

Neale, Walter. *Life of Ambrose Bierce*. Washington, D.C.: Walter Neale Publisher, 1929.

Nickell, Joe. *Ambrose Bierce Is Missing and Other Historical Mysteries*. Lexington: University Press of Kentucky, 1992.

O'Connor, Richard. *Ambrose Bierce: A Biography*. Boston: Little, Brown, 1967.

O'Reilly, Tex [Edward Synott], as told to Lowell Thomas. *Born to Raise Hell: The Life Story of Tex O'Reilly, Soldier of Fortune*. New York: Doubleday, Doran & Co., 1936.

Saunders, Richard. *Ambrose Bierce: The Making of a Misanthrope*. San Francisco: Chronicle Books, 1985.

Starrett, Vincent. *Ambrose Bierce*. Chicago: Walter M. Hill, 1920.

See also University of Nebraska Press for *The Complete Short Stories of Ambrose Bierce*, *The Civil War Short Stories of Ambrose Bierce*, and *The Poems of Ambrose Bierce*, all published in 1995.

9. "Do Your Duty!"

Brooks, Juanita. *The Mountain Meadows Massacre*. Norman: University of Oklahoma Press, 1991. (Originally published in 1950.)

Burton, Richard F. *The City of the Saints*. New York: Harper & Bros., 1862.

Gibbs, Josiah F. *The Mountain Meadows Massacre.* Salt Lake City: Salt Lake Tribune Publishing Co., 1910.

Myers, John. *Bravos of the West.* Lincoln: University of Nebraska Press, 1995. (Originally published in 1962.)

Stegner, Wallace. *Mormon Country.* New York: Bonanza Books, 1942.

Wise, William. *Massacre at Mountain Meadows.* New York: Thomas Y. Crowell, 1976.

10. An Afternoon on the Greasy Grass

Brininstool, E. A. *Troopers With Custer: Historic Incidents of the Battle of the Little Big Horn.* Lincoln: University of Nebraska Press, 1989. (Originally published in 1952.)

Connell, Evan S. *Son of the Morning Star.* San Francisco: North Point Press, 1984.

Frost, Lawrence A. *Custer Legends.* Bowling Green, Ohio: Popular Press, 1981.

Graham, W. A. *The Custer Myth.* Lincoln: University of Nebraska Press, 1986.

———. *The Story of the Little Bighorn.* Lincoln: University of Nebraska Press, 1988.

Gray, John S. *Centennial Campaign: The Sioux War of 1876.* Fort Collins, Colo.: Old Army Press, 1976.

Hardorff, Richard G. *The Custer Battle Casualties.* El Segundo, Calif.: Upton & Sons, 1989.

Hutton, Paul Andrew, ed. *The Custer Reader.* Lincoln: University of Nebraska Press, 1993.

Marshall, S.L.A., Brigadier General, U.S.A., ret. *Crimsoned Prairie: The Indian Wars on the Great Plains.* New York: Charles Scribner's, 1972.

Monaghan, Jay. *Custer.* Boston: Little, Brown, 1959.

Nightengale, Robert. *Little Big Horn.* Minneapolis: Blue Book Publications, Inc., 1996.

Sandoz, Mari. *The Battle of the Little Bighorn.* Lincoln: University of Nebraska Press, 1978. (Originally published in 1966.)

Stewart, Edgar I. *Custer's Luck.* Norman: University of Oklahoma Press, 1955.

Taylor, William O. *With Custer on the Little Bighorn.* Edited by Greg Martin. New York: Viking, 1996.

Utley, Robert N. *Cavalier in Buckskin*. Norman: University of Oklahoma Press, 1988.

———. *Custer Battlefield*. Washington, D.C.: National Park Service, 1987.

———. *The Lance and the Shield: The Life and Times of Sitting Bull;* New York: Henry Holt, 1993.

Van de Water, Frederic F. *Glory-Hunter: A Life of General Custer*. Indianapolis, Bobbs-Merrill, 1934.

11. A Waltz in the Superstitions

Arnold, Oren. *Ghost Gold*. San Antonio: Naylor Co., 1954.

Ely, Sims. *The Lost Dutchman Mine*. New York: William Morrow, 1953.

Jennings, Gary. *The Treasure of the Superstition Mountains*. New York: W.W. Norton, 1973.

Randle, Kevin D. *Lost Gold & Buried Treasure*. New York: M. Evans, 1995.

Thrapp, Dan L. *Encyclopedia of Frontier Biography*. Lincoln: University of Nebraska Press, 1995 (CD ROM version).

12. The Fall of Tashunke Witko

See the list of sources on the Custer chapter. Also, not surprisingly when the facts are so scarce, the finest work on Crazy Horse occurs in fiction: *Stone Song: A Novel of the Life of Crazy Horse* by Win Blevins (1995) is the best novel; Mari Sandoz's reconstruction (see below) is largely fiction but is treated as biography; and *No Survivors* (1950) by Will Henry and *Flashman and the Redskins* (1982) by George MacDonald Fraser contain well-researched portraits of Crazy Horse.

Axelrod, Alan. *Chronicle of the Indian Wars*. New York: Prentice Hall, 1993.

Ambrose, Stephen. *Crazy Horse and Custer: The Parallel Lives of Two American Warriors*. New York: Doubleday, 1975.

Hinman, Eleanor H. *Oglala Sources on the Life of Crazy Horse*. Lincoln: Nebraska State Historical Society, 1976.

Kadlecek, Edward and Mabell. *To Kill an Eagle: Indian Views on the Last Days of Crazy Horse*. Boulder, Colo.: Johnson Books, 1981.

Sandoz, Mari. *Crazy Horse, The Strange Man of the Oglalas*. Lincoln: University of Nebraska Press, 1992. (Originally published in 1942.)

Utley, Robert M. *The Lance and the Shield: The Life and Times of Sitting Bull.* New York: Henry Holt, 1993.

Periodicals

The Alamo Journal
American Heritage
American History Illustrated
American West
Frontier Times
Military History
Military History of the West
Natural History
Old West
Omni
Real West
Research Review: The Journal of the Little Big Horn Associates.
Southern Magazine
Southwestern Historical Quarterly
Studies in Battle Command
Texas Monthly
Tombstone Epitaph
True West
Wild West
William and Mary Quarterly

ACKNOWLEDGMENTS

I'm especially indebted to the late and much lamented *Louis L'Amour Western Magazine,* and its editor Elana Lore, for publishing my series of profiles of Western historical figures, out of which several of these chapters grew.

Each story in this book owes something to the generosity of writer friends who let me pick their brains and among their libraries. Most of these friends are fellow members of that most generous and inspiring of organizations, Western Writers of America, Inc., whose membership includes most of the best historians of the American West working today.

Frederic Bean of Austin, Texas, not only assisted me with research materials on the Corbett-Booth mystery but also on the Jesse James and Billy the Kid claimants, sharing valuable data with me.

I am indebted to many others as well:

Meriwether Lewis: Dee Brown, Little Rock, Ark., and David Lavender, Ojai, Calif.

Crazy Horse: Win Blevins, Bozeman, Mont.

Ambrose Bierce: Dr. Haldeen Braddy, University of Texas at

El Paso; Richard O'Connor, Ellsworth, Maine; Leon Day, Oakland, Calif.

Black Bart: Lewis Disbrow, Warrensburg, Ill.; Helen Mason of the Macon County Historical Society of Decatur, Ill.; Gordon R. Elliott and Joy Ann Elliott of Decatur, Ill.

Boston Corbett: Victor R.S. Tambling, Birmingham, England.

David Crockett: Bill Groneman, Malverne, New York; Paul Hutton, Albuquerque, N.M.

Jesse James: Richard C. House, Encinitas, Calif.; Lenore Carroll and Shirl Kasper, Kansas City, Mo.; Philip Steele, Springdale, Ark.; Suzann Ledbetter and Paul Johns, Nixa, Mo.

Billy the Kid: Leon C. Metz, El Paso, Texas; W. C. Jameson, Conway, Ark.

These generous friends are responsible only for making it easier for me to write the book. Any errors in it are mine, unassisted.

And for general assistance on many issues, thanks to George Skanse, Randy Eickhoff, and Karen Marasco, all of El Paso, Tex.; Richard C. Wheeler, Big Timber, Mont.; Jory Sherman, Branson, Mo.; James Carlos Blake, Deland, Fla., Ernest P. and Cheryl Munch of Brooksville, Fla., and the late Dan L. Thrapp, Tucson, Ariz., whose monumental four-volume *Encyclopedia of Frontier Biography* is indispensable to any writer working among the obscure (or celebrated, for that matter) figures of the Old West.

INDEX